Nuclear Papers

Nuclear Papers

DAVID OWEN

LIVERPOOL UNIVERSITY PRESS

First published 2009 by
Liverpool University Press
4 Cambridge Street
Liverpool
L69 7ZU

British Library Cataloguing-in-Publication data
A British Library CIP record is available

ISBN 978-184631-227-4 cased

Typeset by Koinonia, Manchester
Printed and bound by Bell and Bain Ltd, Glasgow

Contents

Dramatis Personae

Zbigniew Brzezinski, United States National Security Advisor to President Jimmy Carter, 1977–81.

Jimmy Carter, President of the USA 1977–81. Formerly Governor of Georgia.

Sir Bryan Cartledge, Private Secretary (Overseas Affairs) to Prime Minister, 1977–79.

Field Marshal Sir Michael Carver (later Lord Carver), Chief of the General Staff 1971–73; Field-Marshal 1973; Chief of Defence Staff 1973–76. Designated British Resident Commissioner in Rhodesia 1977–78.

Sir Anthony Duff, Deputy Under-Secretary of State, FCO, 1975–80; Deputy Governor, Southern Rhodesia, 1979–80; Deputy Secretary, Cabinet Office 1980–84, Director General, Security Service, 1985–87.

Sir Ewen Fergusson, Private Secretary to the Secretary of State for Foreign and Commonwealth Affairs 1975–78; Ambassador to South Africa 1982–84; Ambassador to France 1987–92.

Denis Healey, Chancellor of the Exchequer 1974–79, previously Secretary of State for Defence 1964–70.

Peter Jay, writer and broadcaster; economics editor, *The Times* 1967–77; presenter, *Weekend World* 1972–77; Ambassador to the US 1977–79.

Sir Paul Lever, Asst Private Secretary to Secretary of State for Foreign and Commonwealth Affairs, 1978–81; Deputy Secretary, Cabinet Office and Chairman, Joint Intelligence Committee 1994–96; Ambassador to Federal Republic of Germany 1997–2003.

Professor Sir Ronald Mason, Professor of Chemistry, University of Sussex, 1971–88; Chief Scientific Adviser, MOD, 1977–83; UK Member, UN Commission on Disarmament Studies, 1984–92; Chairman, Council for Arms Control, 1986–90.

Roy Mason, Secretary of State for Defence 1974–76; Secretary of State for Northern Ireland 1976–79.

Fred Mulley, Secretary of State for Defence 1976–79.

Sir Michael Quinlan, Permanent Under-Secretary at the Ministry of Defence 1988–92; Director, Ditchley Foundation, 1992–99.

David Stephen, political adviser to Dr David Owen, 1977–79.

Cy Vance, United States Secretary of State under President Jimmy Carter 1977–80. Resigned over opposition to the failed military action to free American hostages in US Embassy in Iran. UN peace negotiator in the former Yugoslavia 1991–93.

Lord Solly Zuckerman, Professor of Anatomy, University of Birmingham, 1943–68; Chief Scientific Adviser, Defence Secretary 1960–66; Adviser to HM Government on nuclear issues 1966–88.

Terminology and Acronyms

(as commonly used in the late 1970s)

Ballistic missile: one that is designed to be fired from the earth's atmosphere, then enter outer space and return into the earth's atmosphere, in contrast to other missiles which stay in the earth's atmosphere throughout their flight.

Borderline systems: these lie between the 'theatre nuclear' and the 'strategic nuclear' categories. For example, the SS-20 missile and the Backfire bomber are capable of inflicting a degree of damage on Western European countries which the Germans regarded as strategic – hence Germany resisted calling them theatre nuclear weapons, despite the fact that their range is limited so that they are not capable of hitting targets in the United States.

CASD (Continuous At Sea Deterrent): the concept of being in a position to deter a 'bolt from the blue'; letting one's enemy know that even if they hit us they will be hit as well from an inviolate submarine platform programmed to retaliate. Appropriate in the twentieth century for the Cold War. Highly questionable in the twenty-first century.

Chevaline: codename for a UK defence programme to enhance the Polaris submarine-launched ballistic missile system to enable it to defeat Soviet anti-ballistic missile defences around Moscow. The Chevaline project was conducted in great secrecy largely without scrutiny by the full Cabinet or Parliament. The project management of Chevaline left a lot to be desired. Initially, there was no formal staff requirement and the control of all the various UK and US contractors and the UK research establishment was very weak. There had been insufficient estimation of risk at the start of the project and what had been conceived as a relatively straightforward modification to the Polaris missile, through an improved front end, eventually necessitated major changes to missile, weapon system and submarine systems. The development work was accompanied by a major series of flight trials to test the penetration aids and also in 1974 a resumption of nuclear testing (after a nine-year self-imposed moratorium) in order to develop the new warheads. The Chevaline project was a financial disaster but claimed as a technical success. It entered service in 1982 and lasted until the mid-1990s when it was replaced by Trident.

Deterrent support infrastructure: comprises support and overhaul facilities at the HM Naval Base sites of Faslane and Coulport in Scotland and Devonport in Plymouth; in-service operational support; and the infrastructure associated with the command and control of the submarines.

Forward-based systems: a term used in the context of the SALT negotiations to describe the US's nuclear delivery systems deployed in Europe and in the Far East and at sea. Although it has never been precisely defined it has been tacitly assumed by both sides to refer only to systems capable of delivering strikes against Soviet territory, i.e. F111 aircraft based in Britain and F4 aircraft in the Far East and on aircraft carriers. There were no comparable forward-based Soviet systems capable of hitting the United States.

Grey area systems: a shorthand description of all those nuclear-capable delivery systems not so far included in the SALT talks. In practice, the term has a very similar application to the term 'theatre nuclear weapons' (as well as to the term 'non-central systems', which is sometimes used in the United States, i.e. systems not forming part of the American/Soviet central strategic balance). But 'grey area systems' is a more convenient formulation in that, while it is possible to argue about the mission of a system and hence about its proper categorisation as 'strategic nuclear' or 'theatre nuclear' or 'central', the designation 'grey area' simply reflects the fact of its exclusion from the then SALT negotiations.

INF (Intermediate Nuclear Forces) Treaty: the Intermediate-Range Nuclear Forces (INF) Treaty was a 1987 agreement between the United States and the Soviet Union. Signed in Washington, DC by US President Ronald Reagan and General Secretary Mikhail Gorbachev on 8 December 1987, it was ratified by the United States Senate on 27 May 1988 and came into force on 1 June of that year. The treaty is formally titled *The Treaty Between the United States of America and the Union of Soviet Socialist Republics on the Elimination of Their Intermediate-Range and Shorter-Range Missiles*. The treaty eliminated nuclear and conventional ground-launched missiles with intermediate ranges, defined as between 500 and 5,500 km (300–3,400 miles). By the treaty's deadline of 1 June 1991, a total of 2,692 such weapons had been destroyed, 846 by the US and 1,846 by the Soviet Union.

MIRVs: multiple re-entry vehicles, part of some nuclear warhead designs.

Neutron bomb/enhanced radiation weapon: designed for tank warfare and portrayed as being able to hold up a massive Soviet tank incursion into NATO's central front. Encouraged the mistaken concept of the feasibility of a limited battlefield nuclear exchange.

NPT (Non-Proliferation Treaty): The Treaty on the Non-Proliferation of Nuclear Weapons, also Nuclear Non-Proliferation Treaty (NPT or NNPT), is a treaty to limit the spread of nuclear weapons, opened for signature on 1 July 1968. There are currently 189 countries party to the treaty, five of which have nuclear weapons: the United States, the United Kingdom, France, Russia, and the People's Republic of China (the permanent members of the UN Security Council). Only four recognized sovereign states are not parties to the treaty: India, Israel, Pakistan and North Korea. India, Pakistan and North Korea have openly tested and possess nuclear weapons. Israel has had a policy of opacity regarding its own nuclear weapons programme. North Korea acceded to the treaty, violated it, and later withdrew.

Polaris: the UK Polaris A3T system entered service in 1968 following its procurement from the US. By that time the Soviet Union had deployed long-range nuclear-armed anti-ballistic missile (ABM) defences around Moscow with an expectation that similar defences might appear around other major Soviet cities. Polaris A3T carried three re-entry vehicles (RVs) which were vulnerable to the radiation from nuclear-armed ABMs and were only closely spaced in ballistic flight. The ability of UK Polaris to penetrate these ABM defences was therefore in some doubt from the outset. In great secrecy, technical studies were conducted at AWRE Aldermaston and RAE Farnborough to identify options for improving the Polaris effectiveness against the Soviet ABM defences. These were based on intelligence assessments derived both from open sources published by the Soviets for propaganda purposes and covert intelligence. Initially, these studies benefited from the US Antelope project, which had looked at the same problem, but the UK studies quite quickly diverged and identified innovative solutions for credible decoys (penetration aids) which could be deployed on Polaris to confuse and overwhelm Soviet defences. These were accompanied by RVs with an improved and radiation-hardened warhead.

Poseidon: the Royal Navy considered opting for the procurement of the Poseidon system as an alternative to Chevaline. During this time the US and the Soviet Union signed an ABM Treaty eventually limiting each country to the defence of a single site and 100 interceptors. This posed an upper limit for the threat that Chevaline had to face. Very late in 1973 or early in 1974, the Conservative Government, under Prime Minister Edward Heath, took the decision to proceed with Chevaline by a secret subset of the Cabinet.

SALT: the Strategic Arms Limitation Talks refers to bilateral talks and corresponding international treaties between the Soviet Union and the United States – the Cold War superpowers – on the issue of armament control. There were two rounds of talks and agreements: SALT I and SALT II. A subsequent treaty was START. Negotiations started in Helsinki, Finland, in 1969 and focused on limiting the two countries' stocks of nuclear weapons. These treaties have led to START (Strategic Arms Reduction Treaty). START I (a 1991 agreement between the United States and the Soviet Union) and START II (a 1993 agreement between the United States and Russia) placed specific caps on each side's number of nuclear weapons.

SLCM: Sea Launched Cruise Missile capable of carrying conventional or nuclear warheads.

SORT: Strategic Offensive Reduction Treaty. Treaty signed in May 2002 between the USA and the Russian Federation to reduce their deployed strategic nuclear wearheads. Expires December 2012.

SSN: Ship Submersible Nuclear. The Astute class of nuclear-powered, conventionally armed submarines is the replacement for the existing Swiftsure and Trafalgar classes. As well as fulfilling the traditional anti-submarine warfare role, the Astute class is designed to provide a wide range of support to joint operations, including land attack, intelligence-gathering and special forces operations. HMS *Astute* was launched on 8 June 2007 as the first of her class. She displaces 7,800 tonnes dived and is 97 metres long. The programme has suffered a number of problems, which have caused delays of 41 months and cost overruns of £1,220 million to date. The MOD expects to buy seven submarines in total.

SSBN: Ship Submersible Ballistic Nuclear. The Vanguard class of submarines, of which there are four. Each submarine has a 146-man crew and 16 missile tubes carrying up to 48 nuclear warheads. The first of the class began deterrent patrolling in 1994. Based on current assumptions about extending its planned service life, the Vanguard class is likely to start leaving service from the early 2020s.

Strategic nuclear weapons: designed to inflict massive and widespread destruction on an opposing country's civil, industrial and military facilities to an extent where that country's very survival would be in question.

Polaris submarines, although capable of being used for theatre nuclear purposes, are primarily designed as strategic systems and are hence justifiably referred to as such.

Theatre nuclear weapons: designed solely or primarily for use for some specific military purpose in a limited theatre of operations. On the Western side, theatre nuclear weapons include anything from short-range systems such as Lance, nuclear-capable artillery, and Nike Hercules air defence missiles through medium-range systems such as Jaguar, Buccaneer and Phantom aircraft and Pershing missiles up to longer-range systems such as European-based F111 aircraft capable of delivering limited military strikes against certain targets in the Soviet Union. On the Eastern side, theatre nuclear weapons would similarly include Scud, Frog and Scaleboard missiles, nuclear capable artillery and various types of aircraft.

TLAM-N: Tomahawk Land Attack Missile – Nuclear.

Trident D5 missile: each missile has a range of over 4,000 nautical miles. The UK does not have any sovereign missile production capacity and is reliant on the USA for supply. The nuclear warhead for the D5 is produced and supported in the UK by the Atomic Weapons Establishment with certain US-supplied non-nuclear components. The UK has a stockpile of fewer than 160 operationally available nuclear warheads.

Editorial Note

Papers referred to in the footnotes in the Introduction marked with **R** were released to the National Archives but have subsequently been withdrawn for review and have been redacted with the agreement of the Lord Chancellor following a public interest test under Section 26 (defence) or Section 27 (international relations). As a consequence some lack substance, reflecting the fact that large sections have disappeared. Letters from Sir Bill Jeffrey KCB, Permanent Under-Secretary of State, MOD, to Lord Owen dated 19 February, 29 May and 29 July 2009, shown in Annex C at the end of the Introduction, cover the main discussion over redacting – which is Whitehall's word for removing particular words in the text – and show how, facing resistance from Lord Owen to many of their suggestions, many more documents on nuclear questions are likely to be released. Redactions of documents in this book are shown by blacking out words and lines in the text. Many of the documents show their original security classification. They have, of course, since been declassified.

List of Documents

INTRODUCTION

Annex A: Explanation of Lord Owen's attempts to seek the release of the Duff–Mason Report

Annex B: Letter from Lord Owen to Mr Richard Thomas, Information Commissioner, 6 March 2007

Annex C: Letters from Sir Bill Jeffrey, Permanent Under Secretary of State, MOD, to Lord Owen, 19 February, 29 May and 29 July 2009

Annex D: Lord Owen's Speech in House of Lords Debate, 24 January 2007, on the Future of the UK's Nuclear Deterrence

THE NUCLEAR DETERRENT

1. Memo from Mr Wilberforce, 22 September 1977, on The Future of the British Strategic Nuclear Deterrent and accompanying paper

2. Summary Record of meeting, 17 October 1977, on Military Nuclear Issues in Foreign Secretary's office with covering note from Private Secretary, Ewen Fergusson, 25 October 1977

3. Memo from Foreign Secretary to Prime Minister on Chevaline, January 1978

4. Memo from Paul Lever to Mr Stephen, 16 March 1978, on Public Discussion of Nuclear Issues

5. Memo from Paul Lever to Private Secretary, 21 April 1978, on meeting with Mr Vance, 23 April: SALT

6. Memo from Paul Lever to Private Secretary, 9 May 1978, on NATO and Disarmament

7. Memo from Paul Lever to Private Secretary, 12 June 1978, on Views in the United States on Security Policy Issues

NUCLEAR WEAPONS POLICY

ENHANCED RADIATION WEAPONS

THE FUTURE

Introduction

The Need for an Open and Informed Debate on Britain's Nuclear Deterrent

As the world economic crisis continues and, within that global crisis, the UK's fiscal deficit deepens, the outlook from 2010 onwards for the UK defence budget is dire. It behoves everyone concerned about the state of our Armed Forces to rethink all large forward expenditure programmes with an open mind. Announcements have already been made on the deferred build of the two new aircraft carriers. It is no surprise that one of our most distinguished former Chiefs of Defence Staff, Field Marshal Lord Bramall, began 2009 by questioning the continuation of the Trident strategic nuclear deterrent replacement programme endorsed by Parliament in March 2007.

The UK government published in December 2006 a White Paper on 'The Future of the United Kingdom's Nuclear Deterrent'. It considered four possible generic delivery options for the future deterrent: a large aircraft equipped with cruise missiles; silo-based ballistic missiles; a surface ship equipped with ballistic missiles; and a submarine equipped with ballistic missiles.[1] The bias in favour of ballistic missiles was self-evident and confirmed by the strange omission of the one option that was considered carefully in 1978, namely a nuclear-powered submarine fleet capable of launching cruise missiles with nuclear warheads. This omission is even more bizarre in that the US Navy has deployed, since 1984, that very option as part of their overall deterrent posture. If the US Navy has successfully overcome all the logistical problems of having both nuclear and conventional warheads available on their SSN fleet, it is odd to say the least that this was not considered by the UK government (see Section 1: The Nuclear Deterrent, pp. 52–65).

At the time the White Paper did not appear to be based on serious study of the UK's strategic needs for the twenty-first century. It seemed to perpetuate a twentieth-century mindset based on the old Cold War and did not sufficiently reflect the world as it had become following the collapse of Soviet Communism. One cannot be sure that this perception of the government's

---

1 National Audit Office Report by the Comptroller and Auditor General, *Ministry of Defence: The UK's Future Nuclear Deterrent Capability*, London: The Stationery Office, 5 November 2008, p. 9.

White Paper is true because the facts surrounding its assessment will not be available for study until many years have elapsed. One fact, however, stands out: the decision announced in 2007 was more tentative than it may have appeared. Parliament has been specifically promised that there will be a formal reviewing of British nuclear weapons policy when contracts are due to be placed to build new SSBNs no later than 2014. This is called the 'main gate' decision.[2] Approval for the procurement of long-lead items had to be achieved in 2011. The 'initial gate' decision was due in September 2009, by which point decisions on the design and size of the missile compartment and the type of nuclear propulsion plant had to have been taken. This has now been postponed until at least May 2010, probably longer. The Prime Minister had already announced in March 2009 that the number of missile tubes would be reduced from 16 to 12, with further reductions left open. He then announced at the UN in New York in September 2009 that a Labour government would build only three SSBNs, not four.

Providing a Continuous At-Sea Deterrent (CASD) almost certainly needs four submarines. A more relaxed attitude to CASD might allow three. But the incident in early 2009 when an SSBN in the Royal Navy collided with a French SSBN, damaging both,[3] makes it a little harder to justify going down to three. It is also argued that to give up the concept of CASD and to move towards a 'surge' position would create serious operational problems for the Royal Navy personnel operating such extremely complex systems.

The last major across-the-board strategic nuclear study of the UK's needs appears to have been that undertaken in 1978. It was considered by both Labour and Conservative governments. In the summer of 1980 the Conservative government decided to replace the Polaris system with Trident. As Foreign Secretary from 1977 to 1979 my private papers on nuclear questions are now open for scrutiny under the 30-year rule. They have been added to my other private papers that are held by the Collections and Archives

---

2 Ibid., p. 12.
3 In early February 2009 two submarines carrying nuclear missiles, one French and the other British, collided while submerged on operational patrols in the Atlantic. Both vessels returned damaged but otherwise safe to their home ports. The episode raises troubling questions about the safety of ballistic missile submarines hiding their whereabouts even from NATO allies. Military experts in London and Paris described it as a one-in-a-million occurrence but more troubling was that the French Defence Ministry appeared not to have known in the immediate aftermath that its submarine, *Le Triomphant*, had struck the British submarine, HMS *Vanguard*. On 6 February, the Ministry released a statement in Paris saying that the French vessel had 'collided with an immersed object', which it described as probably a drifting cargo container, and that the submarine's sonar dome, located in its nose and crucial to its ability to track other vessels, had been seriously damaged. In 1992, an American nuclear submarine, the *Baton Rouge*, was struck by a surfacing Russian submarine in the Barents Sea. But that was at a time when each nation shadowed the other's submarines.

Department of the University of Liverpool, of which I was Chancellor from 1996 to 2009. Reading these nuclear papers, 30 years later, I thought they deserved to be published and made available to a wider audience. My hope is that they might be of assistance to anyone who is interested in redefining the nature of a minimum deterrent for the twenty-first century.

In January 2007, prior to the debate in the House of Lords on the UK's nuclear deterrent, I attempted to have released a number of papers dating from 1977–79 relating to the replacement of the Polaris strategic submarine deterrent system with Trident. In particular, I argued for the publication of the Duff–Mason Report, the report of two working parties chaired by the distinguished senior diplomat, Sir Anthony Duff – himself a wartime submariner – and the Chief Defence Scientist, Professor Ronald Mason, which I thought was relevant to the consideration in both Houses of Parliament of the government's White Paper 'The Future of the United Kingdom's Nuclear Deterrent' (Cmnd 6994), published in December 2006. Publication was refused. The full exchange of letters with Richard Thomas, the Information Commissioner, and Gus O'Donnell, the Cabinet Secretary, are available in my archives at the University of Liverpool. A short summary of the Freedom of Information issues raised is covered in Annexes A, B and C.

The Duff–Mason Report was prepared by the Cabinet Secretariat and was issued for ministerial discussion in December 1978 in the run-up to the meeting of heads of government (US/UK/France/Germany) in Guadeloupe in early January 1979. The papers were passed by the then Cabinet Secretary, Sir John Hunt, to the incoming Conservative government in May 1979 with the full support of the outgoing Prime Minister, James Callaghan. Throughout 1977–79, the accepted latest date in Whitehall for a smooth decision on a Polaris replacement was the autumn of 1979.

In August 1979 papers for the Chiefs of Staff discussed the 'general concept of deterrence, the strategy of flexible response imposed on the [NATO] Alliance by the establishment of strategic parity between the superpowers, and Soviet strategic philosophy with its emphasis on pre-emption, survival and war winning'.[4] The discussion then focused on the theory of deterrence by medium nuclear powers such as Britain and France, with emphasis upon Britain's contribution to NATO. This was defined partly as numerical, in providing a second-centre of decision on nuclear use within NATO, partly in terms of its capability to act independently, and lastly in terms of the political status and influence provided by nuclear possession. It was the second and third categories which drove the force levels and capabilities, such as those

---

4 TNA, DEFE 25/335, The Future of the UK Nuclear Deterrent, 13 August 1979. **R**

for Chevaline, along with the maintenance of the 'Moscow Criterion'.[5]

This criterion for unacceptable damage was set in the context of destroying the Soviet Union's capacity to compete with other superpowers in terms of industry and war-making potential. This criterion was defined in four scenarios:[6]

1. Disruption of the main governmental organs of the Soviet state.
2. Breakdown-level damage to a number of cities including Moscow.
3. Breakdown-level damage to significantly larger number of cities than under option 2, but without Moscow or any other city within anti-ballistic missile (ABM) coverage.
3b. Grave, but not necessarily breakdown-level, damage to 30 major targets outside ABM coverage.

The Duff–Mason Report had suggested that 'any one of the options would constitute an unacceptable level of damage'.

A ground-breaking paper by Kristan Stoddart entitled 'Maintaining the "Moscow Criterion", British Strategic Nuclear Targeting 1974–79',[7] which is in the public domain, has already used the paper 'Commentary on the Duff–Mason Report', put before the Chiefs of Staff in August 1980, it having been placed by the Ministry of Defence in the National Archive. This detailed paper makes it even more questionable that the Duff–Mason Report has still not been released by the government to inform public debate. The Chiefs of Staff Commentary was heavily redacted in 2008 when, in correspondence, I made the MOD aware of the fact that it was available to the public in the National Archives.

Stoddart, who has given me permission to quote extensively from his paper, writes that:

> by 1963/64 Britain had developed a nuclear strategy suitable for fulfilling national requirements through 'minimum' deterrence. This concept of 'minimum deterrence' was fulfilled first through targeting 40 Soviet cities, then 20 and finally 15 by 1962.[8] However, in October 1964 the Chief of the Naval Staff, Admiral Sir David Luce, again put forward a case for 20 cities. This

---

5 Ibid.
6 Ibid.
7 Kristan Stoddart, 'Maintaining the "Moscow Criterion": British Strategic Nuclear Targeting 1974–79', *Journal of Strategic Studies*, 31.6 (December 2008), pp. 897–924.
8 This revision was driven by the recommendations of the British Nuclear Deterrent Study Group in 1961. Still, as Clark and Baylis show, even these figures need interpretation and the fine detail of the targeting arrangements in this period is still obscure. Ian Clark, *Nuclear Diplomacy and the Special Relationship: Britain's Deterrent and America, 1957–1962* (Oxford: Clarendon Press, 1994), pp. 382–94 and John Baylis, *Ambiguity and Deterrence: British Nuclear Strategy 1945–1964* (Oxford: Clarendon Press, 1995), pp. 304–12.

would have required five Polaris submarines and was based on the operational requirements needed to maintain a 'comparable capability to the V-bomber force'.[9]

The UK independent plan was, according to Stoddart, 'targeted solely at Soviet cities and was centred, from at least 1962 onwards – the same year as the Cuban Missile Crisis – on the need to be able to destroy Moscow'.[10] Stoddart also corresponded with the former Permanent Under-Secretary in the Ministry of Defence, the late Sir Michael Quinlan, a thoughtful writer on nuclear questions, whose views were similar to that of the Chiefs of Staff in August 1978, who replied:

> the 'Moscow criterion' did not rest just on a narrow obsession with assailing the city itself, but reflected the fact that the characteristics of the Soviet ABM system meant that abandoning the attempt to be seen as capable of defeating it would have entailed conceding effective sanctuary to a very large area around the city – its exact size and configuration depending on the precise azimuth and elevation of the incoming attack [...] in the order of tens of thousands of square miles.[11]

The Labour Cabinet was informed by Harold Wilson in 1974 about the nuclear warhead modernization programme started by Edward Heath late in 1973, but in very guarded and low-key terms. But that the purport of what he said was understood is clear from the diaries published by (amongst others) Barbara Castle and Tony Benn, who referred to being told about 'a little bit of modernization'.

The existence of the Chevaline programme was not, therefore, kept secret from the Cabinet from 1974 to 1979, as is often alleged. What was kept within a small group of senior ministers was its technical charac- teristics and the cost escalation. This issue of what is legitimate secrecy based on the 'need to know' is a serious one for any democratic govern- ment. At that time the UK had an enemy in the Soviet Union. Secrecy was a legitimate part of defence policy. But the need for secrecy fades as the years pass. Openness is an essential part of democratic government learning from the past, and after the passage of 30 years, openness should prevail (See Annex C).

9 [Kew, United Kingdom, The National Archives] DEFE [Records of the Ministry of Defence] 13/350, PS to S of S, The Case for 5 SSBNs, 19 October 1964.
10 These two plans were encoded onto computer tapes on board Britain's four Polaris submarines as target packages (known by the Russian designation Teatre Voyenkh Destivii – TVD). There were hundreds of tapes, with the choice being made in London as to which to take on patrol. While on patrol the submarine captain also had his own target list (e.g. in case of missile failure). See Lawrence Freedman, *Britain and Nuclear Weapons* (Basingstoke: Macmillan, 1980), pp. xiii–xiv.
11 Private correspondence with Sir Michael Quinlan, 15 August 2006.

Stoddart writes that the Chief of Defence Staff, Field Marshal Sir Michael Carver, minuted Roy Mason, the Secretary of State for Defence, on 10 November 1975 that:

> until improvements can be introduced to counter Russian antiballistic missile (ABM) defences, there will be a period during which the British strategic nuclear force can have no assurance of penetrating the defences of the Moscow area and thus will not meet one of the criteria postulated for a credible national strategic deterrent [...] from the end of this year we can expect Russian ABM radar improvements to preclude us from penetrating the Moscow defences from the Atlantic.[12]

There was then a successful attempt from 1975 onwards to keep from the Chancellor of the Exchequer, Denis Healey, a former Secretary of Defence from 1964 to 1970, the views of the Chief of Defence Staff that we were precluded from penetrating Moscow's ABM defences. This was referred to in my correspondence with the Cabinet Secretary and the Commissioner for Information (Annexes A and B).

The reason for this exclusion was that the Chancellor of the Exchequer was trying, in 1975, to cancel the Chevaline modification to the front end of Britain's Polaris.[13] Indeed, that was felt by Whitehall civil servants to be Denis Healey's likely reaction as late as July 1978, though I believe he had become, by then, reconciled to the fact that the cost saving was not worth the political controversy. Healey regarded it as one of his mistakes as Chancellor not to get Chevaline cancelled.[14]

Stoddart writes that Field Marshal Carver evidently felt that the alternative deployment plans for UK SSBNs suggested to Roy Mason

> would leave Chevaline wide open to cancellation by the Chancellor. However, John Mayne, Mason's Private Under-Secretary counselled, that leaving the Chancellor out of the equation would be 'madness [...] inspite [sic] of the dangers'.[15] Mayne suggested that Mason simply restate to Healey the argument for retaining Chevaline that had been given back in September 1974. Cancellation would dilute the deterrent effect on the Soviet Union whilst concomitantly damaging relations with the United States who 'in past discussions stressed their wish to see Britain have a powerful deterrent capability'.[16] There does not appear to have been any overt political discussion by Mason regarding

12 DEFE 13/1039, MC to S of S, Meeting British National Criteria for Strategic Deterrence, 10 November 1975.
13 Ministry of Defence: Chevaline Improvement to the Polaris Missile System, Ninth Report from the Committee of Public Accounts, Session 1981–82, HC 269 (London: HMSO, 1982), pp. vi and 1 and confidential correspondence, October 2002.
14 Denis Healey, *The Time of My Life* (London: Penguin, 1990), p. 313.
15 DEFE 13/1039, J. F. Mayne to Secretary of State, 18 November 1975.
16 DEFE 13/1039, Prime Minister Polaris Improvements, 18 September 1975.

targeting policy; instead he chose to accept the military advice of his Chiefs of Staff to ensure the 'Moscow Criterion' through Chevaline.

On 18 November 1975, Mayne reminded Mason that until Chevaline was introduced into service Polaris could become ineffective in meeting the 'Moscow Criterion' from the end of the year. As well as restating the ten cities option, he also suggested that 16–32 cities east of the Urals could also be targeted. This too 'would probably be regarded by the Soviet Union as unacceptable damage at least up in the period to 1980'.[17] Mayne advised Mason to discuss these issues with both Carver and Sir Michael Cary, the Permanent Under Secretary of State in the MOD, before approaching the Prime Minister.[18]

These discussions regarding re-targeting continued to gather momentum. At a meeting between Sir John Hunt (the Cabinet Secretary), Secretary of State for Defence Mason, and CDS Sir Michael Carver, a little over a week later, it was agreed that the Chancellor should not be told about the minute circulated from the Chiefs of Staff (COS) to the Prime Minister revising their criteria for strategic nuclear deterrence. All three hoped that Healey could be kept away from the conclusions by the Chiefs that deterrence could also be demonstrated if Polaris were retargeted to ten cities excluding Moscow. It was decided that if the Prime Minister wished to inform the Chancellor they would issue a disclaimer that Healey did not 'need to know' about the retargeting debates.[19]

It appears that no immediate decision was forthcoming but by March 1976 Carver indicated to Mason that the Soviet 'Chekhov' Battle Management Radar was now operational.[20] As a result the CDS informed Mason that the independent nuclear targeting plan should now be altered to one of the two main options indicated above. This was either to fire from the Atlantic to attack ten cities other than Moscow, or to head into the Mediterranean to launch at Moscow. These plans were contingent upon 'prevailing circumstances'. These were not explicitly stated by Carver but would likely to have included the number of Polaris submarines available and the political climate during times of tension. As a result:

> we must now consider alternate attack plans for use until the Polaris Improvement Programme is completed … subject to your concurrence, the SSBN force will forthwith be instructed to be prepared to implement one of two targeting options in support of the National Retaliatory War Plan.[21]

17 DEFE 13/1039, J. F. Mayne to Secretary of State, 18 November 1975.
18 Ibid.
19 DEFE 13/1039, Meeting British National Criteria for Strategic Deterrence, 27 November 1975.
20 The Chekhov radar (known in the West as the Cat House) was declared operational on 29 October 1976. See Pavel Podvig, 'History and the Current Status of the Russian Early Warning System', *Science and Global Security*, 10/1 (2002), pp. 27–29. Podvig's work also reveals that British intelligence assessments of Soviet ABM developments were accurate.
21 DEFE 13/1039, MC to Secretary of State, 31 March 1976.

That same month Harold Wilson announced his intention to resign as Prime Minister. He was replaced by James Callaghan. As a result Mason delayed informing the Prime Minister.[22]

In light of these recommendations, a further high level MOD meeting on 1 June 1976 suggested that rather than targeting ten cities west of the Ural Mountains, five could be targeted. This could also fulfil the criteria of deterrence. Admiral Sir Edward Ashmore, the Chief of the Naval Staff, reminded the group that what 'constituted a credible development was political.'[23] It is unclear why five cities were now being suggested as an effective political deterrent. Targeting five cities whilst excluding Moscow from the target list would have led to further doubts placed against the case for Chevaline. As a result Mason again made the case for Chevaline in order to reinstate the 'Moscow Criterion'. In the climate of financial austerity brought about by the defence review he felt it would be necessary to remind the Prime Minister of this need.[24] Those present also noted that project costs had risen by £153 million and this 'could adversely affect our conventional capability.'[25]

Mason also expressed concerns that this review of the criteria for deterrence would be leaked.[26] A government leak threatened to bring out into the open the question of what constituted a politically acceptable minimum deterrent. This would cause further embarrassment to an administration battling industrial unrest and inflation in the domestic economy. Two weeks later Mason brought these issues before the new Prime Minister, James Callaghan. He was told that 'alternative target options are prepared.'[27] Mason wanted to discuss these issues with him before approaching the new Foreign Secretary, Anthony Crosland,[28] and Chancellor Healey.[29]

To question the basis of minimum deterrence, coupled with the risk of government leaks, could have proved extremely damaging to the confidence of those involved with the Chevaline programme and dented nuclear relations with the United States. It would also have given critics of the British nuclear programme, including those in the Labour Party with links to the Campaign

---

22 He was also waiting for a major report on the progress and costs of Chevaline to be issued. DEFE 13/1039, J. F. Mayne to Secretary of State, 1 April 1976. **R**
23 Present at the meeting were Roy Mason (Secretary of State for Defence), Bill Rodgers (Minister of State for Defence), Sir Michael Carver (CDS), Sir Frank Cooper (Permanent Under-Secretary of State at the MOD), Professor Hermann Bondi (Chief Scientific Advisor in the MOD), E. C. Cornford (Procurement Executive), Sir Edward Ashmore (Chief of the Naval Staff), A. P. Hockaday (Deputy Under-Secretary of State, Policy), Victor Macklen (Chief Adviser, Projects and Nuclear) and John Mayne (Private Secretary to Secretary of State for Defence). DEFE 13/1039, Record of a Meeting in the Defence Secretary's Office held on Thursday 27 May at 2.30 pm, 1 June 1976. **R**
24 Ibid.
25 Ibid.
26 Ibid.
27 DEFE 13/1039, RM to Prime Minister, 11 June 1976. **R**
28 Crosland was Foreign Secretary for a little over ten months. He died suddenly in February 1977.
29 DEFE 13/1039, Record of a Meeting in the Defence Secretary's Office held on Thursday 27 May at 2.30 pm, 1 June 1976. TNA, DEFE 13/1039, RM to Prime Minister, 11 June 1976. DEFE 13/1039, Frank Cooper to Secretary of State, 25 June 1976. **R**

for Nuclear Disarmament (CND), ammunition to attack the foundations of the nuclear deterrent.

Furthermore the arguments for Chevaline continuing to be granted the 'Super High Priority' status it had been accorded would have been diluted; leaving it vulnerable for cancellation. David Owen (Crosland's successor as Foreign Secretary in 1977) had no knowledge of these discussions when he became Foreign Secretary.[30] Moreover, no evidence exists that Healey was told of these re-targeting recommendations.[31]

Related debates were also ensuing during that June meeting. It was put forward that if Chevaline was cancelled then resources would be freed up and could be reallocated to a successor system.[32] Under these circumstances Mason suggested any talk of successor systems 'should cease forthwith, at least for two years. Such talk would undermine Chevaline; and the possibility was politically out of the question.'[33] Mason subsequently agreed to approach Crosland armed with a full presentation team prior to recommending to the Prime Minister that Chevaline should be allowed to continue at 'full speed.'[34]

The cost of Chevaline was still rising noticeably during this period leading to a dramatic note from the Ministry of Defence on 7 June 1976 that these rising costs should be concealed to minimise the risk of cancellation. The MOD stated, '"Concealment" covers both the normal security aspects and the information available externally.'[35] It was agreed to hide it among the Navy Votes in the Defence budget. This concealment was later to be severely criticised by the Public Accounts Committee following the public announcement of the programme in 1980.[36]

This policy by the Ministry of Defence demonstrates the lengths to which the British government felt it necessary [to go] to protect its national security. It also illustrates Britain's so-called Culture of Secrecy, in what Peter Hennessy characterises as 'the Secret State.'[37] Even for senior members of the civil service this secrecy meant personnel were being '"bounced" on occasion into decisions.'[38] The omission of the Treasury from these discussions also meant cost controls were inadequate and oversight of the project at a political level was becoming more limited.[39]

30 Transcript of 'The Chevaline Experience and the First Trident Decision, 1967–1980', Witness Seminar held at Charterhouse, Surrey, UK, 13 April 2007 conducted by the Mountbatten Centre for International Studies, University of Southampton, UK.
31 Private correspondence with Lord Owen, March 2006. See also Chevaline Witness Seminar, Charterhouse, 13 April 2007.
32 DEFE 13/1039, Record of a Meeting in the Defence Secretary's Office held on Thursday 27 May at 2.30 pm, 1 June 1976. **R**
33 Ibid.
34 Ibid.
35 DEFE 24/895, F. W. Armstrong, Chevaline: Vote Arrangements, 7 June 1976.
36 Ninth Report from the Committee of Public Accounts, pp. v, 15, 20.
37 This was the title of Hennessy's 2002 book.
38 DEFE 24/895, Frank Cooper to DUS(FB), Nuclear Weapons Research, 8 November 1976.
39 These were some of the findings of the Public Accounts Committee inquiry on Chevaline in 1982.

From 1977 to 1979 I was, as Foreign and Commonwealth Secretary, challenging the Moscow Criterion, and putting forward detailed written arguments (see Section 1: The Nuclear Deterrent) over a UK minimum deterrent. I was never informed that the UK was throughout that time *precluded* from penetrating ABM defences around Moscow, though I knew there were doubts about our capacity to penetrate. The detailed way in which Carver had proposed to deal with the Soviet ABM defences around Moscow is well described by Stoddart and forms an essential background for the current debate over Trident replacement.

In order to maintain the 'Moscow Criterion' Carver suggested that the Polaris submarines could be moved from their patrol areas in the Atlantic into the Mediterranean.[40] They would then be able to outflank the Soviet ABM radars.[41] This revision did not necessarily affect NATO operations, which could be conducted with the full weight of American strategic forces. This did affect the targeting options of the relatively small UK force in an independent action where only a maximum of two submarines were available for patrol at any given time.[42]

However, the shallower waters and the narrower patrol lanes of the Mediterranean meant that the large Polaris nuclear-propelled ballistic missile-firing submarine (SSBNs) would be more vulnerable to Soviet anti-submarine warfare capabilities (ASW). Moreover, Carver anticipated that by 1977 the Soviets were expected to deploy a further early-warning radar system which would cover missile approaches from the Mediterranean. This could be overcome by two boatloads of missiles; one firing from the Atlantic 'to take out the early warning radar', and one firing from the Mediterranean to 'outflank the full battle-management radar systems protecting Moscow from the Atlantic.'[43] However a further expansion of Soviet battle-management radar batteries 'would preclude even this option' but it was felt by CDS that this would not be achieved before 1979.[44]

I informed the House of Lords about Field Marshall Carver, the Chief of Defence Staff's view in 1975 in the debate on the future of the UK's nuclear deterrence on 24 January 2007, in the following terms (Hansard Col: 1129–1130):

40 Patrolling in the Mediterranean was not an easy option due to the distances involved, with the low optimum speed of the SSBNs a significant operational impediment. Confidential correspondence, 14 May 2008.

41 Ibid.

42 For targeting arrangements prior to 1975 see John Baylis, 'British Nuclear Doctrine: The "Moscow Criterion" and the Polaris Improvement Programme', *Contemporary British History* 19.1 (2005), pp. 53–65.

43 DEFE 13/1039, MC to S of S, Meeting British National Criteria for Strategic Deterrence, 10 November 1975. **R**

44 Ibid. This was the reason why the in-service date for Chevaline had originally been 1978. PREM 15/1359, MO 18/1/1 Appendix 1 to Annex B Future Super Antelope Background, 11 April 1972. **R**

The Polaris was not able to penetrate Soviet ABM defences in the view of the then-chief of defence staff from November 1975 as relayed to Ministers and as revealed in documents that are in the public domain until Chevaline was deployed for the first time in the summer of 1982. There was a seven-year period during which time, first, the Ministry of Defence tried – in fact I believe that it succeeded – to stop the then Chancellor of the Exchequer knowing that there was this gap; and secondly, there was no overt debate about the question. Of course we had to keep it private. One was not in those days able to let the Soviet Union know that one had doubts about one's own deterrent capacity, so there are limits, but now it is a completely different situation. Some of the language is as though the Cold War is still continuing. [See Annex D for full speech.]

The following is the text of the letter sent by the Cabinet Office to me on 3 July 2007:

I am writing further to my letters of 30 March and 27 June concerning your request for information on any communication made to James Callaghan when Foreign Secretary, or Tony Crosland or yourself, his successors in the Labour administration, on the Chief of the Defence Staff's advice that Polaris missiles could not penetrate Moscow's ABM defences; also any communication with the Chancellor on this subject at some time later than the summer of 1976.

We have searched our records and can find no communication with the Chancellor on this subject at some time later than the summer of 1976. Regarding the first part of your request, we have located a brief prepared for new Labour ministers in late February 1974 that suggests that from mid-1970s Polaris may not be able to penetrate Moscow's radar cover. There is no source given for this and the Chief of the Defence Staff is not mentioned. This is the only information that we have identified relevant to your request.

Open debate on a future minimum nuclear deterrent will be very difficult if the government's attitudes to releasing documents from over 30 years ago persist. The review of the 30-year rule commissioned by the Prime Minister on 25 October 2007 and chaired by Sir Paul Dacre was published in January 2009. The report concluded that the government should replace the current 30-year rule with a 15-year rule retrospectively. In the event the government did not accept this recommendation but have chosen 20 years instead. Redactions insisted on by the government are signified by blacked-out lines in this book. Initially some of the suggested redactions were underpinned by neither logic or rationality. I have argued that over 30 years later I should be allowed to publish all the words specifically ascribed to myself at the time in these documents but I have not felt it worthwhile to resist redactions where they affect civil servants, even if unnamed. Eventually, after writing to Sir Bill Jeffrey specifically about the Moscow Criterion redactions, I am glad to record that an agreement has been reached and the remaining redactions are ones which I have accepted.

30 YEARS ON

The world in relation to nuclear weapons is very different in 2009 from that of 1978 when the Duff–Mason Report was written. It is a very different world even from that when President Reagan and President Gorbachev, in their 1986 Reykjavik meeting, discussed, for the first time, the concept of a nuclear-free world. At that time the concept was derided by the then British Prime Minister, Margaret Thatcher, who believed that the genie was out of the bottle and that with nuclear weapons having been invented it was too dangerous to even contemplate their elimination. Although some want to depict today's Russian Federation as a threat and are busy reviving images of the Cold War, there is a very substantial difference in power terms between the Soviet Union at the time of the fall of the Berlin Wall in 1989 and the Russian Federation twenty years later. In 2009, in an article in the *Wall Street Journal*, four prominent US political figures, including Henry Kissinger, endorsed 'setting the goal of a world free of nuclear weapons and working energetically on the actions required to achieve that goal'.[45] This was followed by a somewhat similar initiative in the UK in an article written by Douglas Hurd, Malcolm Rifkind, George Robertson and myself.[46] President Barack Obama has spoken of his determination to 'show the world that America believes in its existing commitment under the Nuclear Non-Proliferation Treaty to work ultimately to eliminate all nuclear arms'. This concept of a negotiated elimination of nuclear weapons in steps over a period is also endorsed by the Russian, British and French governments. President Obama's speech in Prague on 5 April 2009 showed that he had learnt the lessons of the past and will build on the pending limited agreement this year with Russia on reducing nuclear warheads and seek step-like further cuts in the future. Meanwhile he will ask the US Congress to proceed towards ratifying the Comprehensive Test Ban Treaty. This progression will be easier because Obama has removed the more complex issue of defence missile deployment in Poland and the Czech Republic from the negotiating table.

The Duff–Mason Report in 1978 considered the options of a nuclear deterrent system designed to destroy the Soviet government both within Moscow

---

45 'A World Free of Nuclear Weapons', by George P. Shultz, William J. Perry, Henry A. Kissinger and Sam Nunn, *Wall Street Journal*, 4 January 2007, p. A15.
46 Douglas Hurd, Malcolm Rifkind, David Owen and George Robertson, 'Start Worrying and Learn to Ditch the Bomb', *The Times*, 30 June 2008, p. 26.

and ███████████████████ Such a sophisticated, high deterrent threshold
for the UK is considered by many in 2009 to be excessive. People who believe
in such a high threshold invoke a 'bolt from the blue', a possible threat from
North Korea and Iran, countries that will not have ABM defence systems
in the foreseeable future, against which they want a nuclear deterrent that
provides 100 per cent assurance that a retaliatory blow can be delivered via
an invulnerable delivery platform. They argue that anything that does not
fulfil these criteria provides an incentive for coercion or attack.[47] Apart from
the question of whether such a provocative strategy is even contemplated by
North Korea or Iran against the UK, if these countries were to plan such a
strike they would have to gamble that the US, which will maintain for some
years to come a sophisticated all-purpose deterrent, would not respond.
However, during a phase in which nuclear states are progressively eliminating nuclear weapons, it is likely that the US will be particularly vigilant to
provide retaliatory cover for such states as they reduce their stockpiles. It is
also essential during this period of progressive elimination that we recognise
that, as long ago as 15 February 1994, in a joint declaration in Moscow by
the President of the Russian Federation, Boris Yeltsin, and the British Prime
Minister, John Major, it was stated that the chance of a surprise Russian first
strike nuclear attack was so low as to be near zero. Further, in 1997 the former
CIA director, Admiral Stansfield Turner, was advocating a 'de-alerting' of
the US and Russian nuclear deterrents with their warheads stored in secure
facilities some distance away, reducing their capacity for instant firing. The
'bolt from the blue' threat should therefore not be given the credibility that
was claimed for it in 2006 by the then British government.

The US defence cuts announced in April 2009 envisage cutbacks in
the American ABM defence systems. Neither the Russian Federation nor
China is likely to build new sophisticated ABM defences around Moscow
or Beijing, but even if they did it is not realistic to believe that a future UK
minimum deterrent has to be designed for such a possibility. Some even
invoke a terrorist threat as needing to be deterred by nuclear weapons, but
nuclear retaliation is hard to conceive even for a radioactive 'dirty bomb'.

While there may be new threats to the UK, which need to be deterred
by nuclear weapons, any such threat is very considerably less than the
threat the UK faced from the Soviet Union 30 years ago. The Duff–Mason
Report considered then that both a significant extension in ABM missile
range and the possibility of a wider distribution of ABMs beyond Moscow

47 See Des Browne, *The Future of the UK's Strategic Nuclear Deterrent: The White Paper. Volume II:
Oral and Written Evidence*, House of Commons Defence Committee report HC 225-II (London:
HMSO, March 2007), p. Ev 68.

were technically feasible. Thirty years on, neither of those developments has happened. Indeed it is very probable that President Obama will negotiate an agreed deal with President Medvedev and Prime Minister Putin involving nuclear warheads by December 2009. The capability to shoot down inter-continental missiles launched from Iran, if thought desirable at some time in the future, is something that could and should be developed in concert with the Russian Federation and needs a far less sophisticated system than an ABM defence against MIRVs, hardened warheads and penetration aids.

CRUISE MISSILES

Over the last 30 years the size of the Royal Navy has been slashed. There are many senior military figures within the Royal Navy who have increasingly begun to question whether we can afford a dedicated strategic nuclear submarine force carrying expensive ballistic missiles. Instead of replacing our four SSBNs we should be even readier to consider the cheaper SSN alternative that I advocated in 1978–79: deploying nuclear warheads on the cruise missiles that are already deployed on our too-small SSN fleet. Some of the money saved could increase the number of SSNs to a minimum of eight to ten. It should be technically feasible for the UK to develop such simple warheads without nuclear testing (see p. 43).

It is surprising how often cruise missiles with conventional warheads fired from submarines have been used over the last 18 years. Cruise missiles have been fired by UK SSNs against Iraq in 1991, 1998 and 2003 and in Afghanistan in 2003. They were also used by NATO, with pinpoint accuracy, to take out government ministries on the main street of Belgrade during the 1999 Kosovo war. It has long been suspected that the three Tomahawk cruise missiles which hit the Chinese embassy in Belgrade on 7 May 1999, 'mistakenly' as it was claimed at the time, were in fact deliberately targeting the embassy. The line taken at the time was that they had been aimed at the Yugoslav Federal Directorate for Supply and Procurement (FDSP) which was located some 500 metres down the street. Immediately after the Chinese embassy was hit the Clinton administration stated that the strike was accidental, due to faulty maps and intelligence. However, far from being accidental, the attack appears to have been based on intelligence that the Serbian leader, Slobodan Milošević, was in the embassy at the time. The *Observer*'s report of 19 October 1999 was the first in the UK to suggest that the attack had been deliberate, stating:

> Politiken newspaper in Denmark and Ed Vulliamy cites senior military and intelligence sources in Europe and the US stating that the embassy was bombed

after its NATO electronic intelligence (ELINT) discovered it was being used to transmit Yugoslav army communications. Supportive evidence is provided by three other NATO officers – a flight controller operating in Naples, an intelligence officer monitoring Yugoslav radio traffic from Macedonia and a senior headquarters officer in Brussels [...] All three say they knew in April that the Chinese embassy was acting as a 'rebro' (rebroadcast) station for the Yugoslav army. The embassy was also suspected of monitoring NATO's cruise missile attacks on Belgrade, with a view to developing effective countermeasures.[48]

The intelligence officer, based in Macedonia during the strike, claimed that 'Nato had been hunting the radio transmitters in Belgrade. When the President's [Milošević's] residence was bombed on 23 April, the signals disappeared for 24 hours. When they came on the air again, we discovered they came from the embassy compound.'[49] It has been put forward that the success of earlier strikes had compelled the Yugoslav Army to use Milošević's residence as a rebroadcast station. When that was struck it was relocated to the Chinese embassy. The air controller claimed that '[the] Chinese embassy had an electronic profile, which Nato located and pinpointed.'[50] The NATO flight control officer in Naples stated to the *Guardian* that a map of 'non-targets' such as churches, hospitals and embassies (including the Chinese embassy) existed. On this map the Chinese embassy was properly located at its current site, and not where it had been until 1996, which both the United States and NATO claimed.[51]

The 'outdated' intelligence information had been provided by the Central Intelligence Agency (CIA). US Defence Secretary William Cohen claimed that '[one] of our planes attacked the wrong target because the bombing instructions were based on an outdated map.'[52] However, sources within the US National Imagery and Mapping Agency did not take kindly to the allegation that their mapping was to blame, with one official calling it 'a damned lie.'[53] It is alleged that George Tenet, the Director of the CIA at the time, also provided further disinformation regarding the attack. In July 1999, Tenet testified to Congress that out of the 900 targets hit by NATO during the three-month Kosovo campaign, just one was tasked by the CIA.[54] It

48 http://www.globalresearch.ca/index.php?context=viewArticle&code=20051229&artic leId=1665, retrieved 5 May 2009.
49 http://www.guardian.co.uk/world/1999/oct/17/balkans, retrieved 5 May 2009.
50 http://www.guardian.co.uk/world/1999/oct/17/balkans, retrieved 5 May 2009.
51 http://www.guardian.co.uk/world/1999/oct/17/balkans, retrieved 5 May 2009.
52 http://www.globalresearch.ca/index.php?context=viewArticle&code=20051229&artic leId=1665, retrieved 5 May 2009.
53 http://www.guardian.co.uk/world/1999/oct/17/balkans, retrieved 5 May 2009.
54 http://www.globalresearch.ca/index.php?context=viewArticle&code=20051229&artic leId=1665, retrieved 5 May 2009.

has been put forward by *Defense & Foreign Affairs Strategic Policy* that the attack was based on intelligence that the Serbian leader Slobodan Milošević was suspected to be in the embassy at the time of the attack. This would mean that the strike was deliberately orchestrated as a 'decapitation' strike to assassinate Milošević.[55]

Cruise missiles with nuclear warheads as an option for a minimum nuclear deterrent are dealt with in detail in Section I: The Nuclear Deterrent, where it is explained that the US Navy already maintains that nuclear option in addition to its ballistic missile deterrent and is looking at developing a supersonic cruise missile.

The Duff–Mason Report in 1978 discussed as one option four or five purpose-built cruise missile carriers instead of building four or five ballistic missile-carrying submarines (SSBNs). This was no cheaper and much less effective. It stemmed from a Whitehall option first proposed in a paper from the IISS by Ian Smart.[56] It never had any serious adherents in the late 1970s. However, in 2002, the US Navy started to convert four of its 18 Ohio-class Trident submarines for conventional war-fighting, putting seven TLAM cruise missiles in each of their 24 tubes, together with an advanced SEAL Delivery System in two converted missile tubes, deploying up to 66 special operation forces personnel. Nick Ritchie, in his paper 'Replacing Trident Two Years On: What has Happened?', writes, 'It is possible to envisage a future UK successor submarine with 4–8 launch tubes dedicated to the delivery of Trident missiles if required with the rest of the missile compartment designed for delivering TLAMs'.[57] He also suggests the possibility of giving up some missile compartments to the delivery of special forces. If a government decides that it wants to retain some ballistic missiles this might be an option worth considering. It is at least a multi-purpose use for an extremely expensive platform combining nuclear and conventional warheads. Duff–Mason did also consider putting a smaller number of missiles on the planned SSN fleet and wrote that there might, in addition to four SSBNs, be a case for SSNs in a theatre nuclear role. This was when nuclear weapons were still contemplated for theatre use. Fortunately they are now only contemplated for use in dire circumstances and as a strategic weapon.

Duff–Mason, importantly, took for granted a UK nuclear-powered

---

55 http://www.globalresearch.ca/index.php?context=viewArticle&code=20051229&articleId=1665, retrieved 5 May 2009.

56 Ian Smart, 'Study on the Future of the British Nuclear Deterrent: Technical, Economic and Strategic Issues'. Extracts reprinted by permission of RIIA in IISS journal *Survival*, Jan/Feb 1978.

57 Nick Ritchie, 'Stepping Down the Nuclear Ladder: Options for Trident on a Path to Zero', Bradford Disarmament Research Centre, Department of Peace Studies, University of Bradford, May 2009, p. 10.

conventionally armed submarine fleet (SSNs), then planned to comprise 16 vessels. In 2009–2010, we have a situation in which, because of financial constraints, and justified by a much reduced Russian naval threat, we will be lucky to carry forward a conventional nuclear-powered submarine force of seven SSN vessels. At present there is only money for four Astute class SSNs. The cost of the two proposed carriers (CVF), already postponed, will also significantly impact upon the defence budget over the next 10–15 years.

NON-PROLIFERATION TREATY REVIEW CONFERENCE 2010

The UK government will go into the NPT Conference in 2010 able to say that it has over the past few years substantially reduced the number of nuclear warheads on Trident submarines from 200 to below 160 operationally deployable warheads. Prime Minister Gordon Brown made it clear that these may be further reduced as the UK contribution to what is now widely accepted for the UK is only a minimum nuclear deterrent. **A minimum nuclear deterrent is not, however, a static concept. If we are to start, in 2010, the process of genuinely contributing to the elimination of nuclear weapons, it will not be credible if the British government commits to a new UK ballistic missile deterrent similar to Trident into the years 2050–60.**

Substantial reductions in missile numbers and warheads from the US and the Russian Federation are rightly the first priority in the push towards global elimination. Russia currently operates 14 SSBNs of four different classes. The US currently operates 14 SSBNs of the Ohio class. Both China and France have what they term a 'minimum deterrent'. China is somewhat opaque but appears not to have engaged in ballistic missile defence projects. It is building a new Jin class of SSBNs and has a lower operational nuclear stockpile than the UK. President Sarkozy's speech at Cherbourg in 2008 covered France's nuclear strategy in much more detail than previously. This speech can be found in the 2008–2009 NPT Briefing Book.[58]

Many complex issues are likely to come to the fore at the Non-Proliferation Treaty Review Conference in 2010. The previous session in 2005 was held in an atmosphere of rancour and disillusionment among non-nuclear weapon states, frustrated by the failure of the nuclear powers to live up to their commitment to Article VI of the Treaty. Already the Nuclear Suppliers Group's readiness to restrain trade in materials and items that could be used to manufacture nuclear weapons is under question. For example, the

58 http://www.mcis.soton.ac.uk/publications/briefingbook2008.html.

US–India bilateral agreement on cooperation on civilian nuclear power will require considerable exceptions to rules that have so far been accepted by the Nuclear Suppliers Group. It is quite likely that the Russian Federation will request somewhat similar exceptions for Iran, whom they are supplying with nuclear power stations. Perhaps China will request exceptions for Pakistan. No one can take NPT renewal for granted. The greater the cooperation beforehand between the US and Russia in particular, the better.

What is needed is momentum to be established before the 2010 NPT Review Conference gets underway towards the elimination of nuclear weapons by all five of the existing declared nuclear weapon states. It is becoming clear that all political parties in the UK are reconsidering the 2006 White Paper over Trident. Embracing a non-ballistic missile system would be, in NPT terms, highly significant.

For the UK to build only three SSBNs and stop attempting to keep one submarine with nuclear weapons at instant readiness would be a contribution to establishing momentum, but it would still be a very expensive option for the UK to pursue. Even the all-party readiness to reopen the debate about a Trident successor will make a modest contribution to developing the necessary momentum before the NPT Conference. It may be that France and the UK will decide to run their nuclear deterrence in harness, still remaining the decision-makers as two sovereign nations but serving the general interest of the European Union – a concept easier to contemplate now that France has again become a full member of NATO.

What I most fear is that the recent commitment to the elimination of nuclear weapons by NWSs can easily become just another aspiration similar to the commitment already within the NPT. Yet the fact that a 'Global Zero' campaign[59] has been launched in 2009 with so much support is a sign of hope. Some argue that the fact that the nuclear threat has receded allows the UK to give up its nuclear deterrent in its entirety. That is not my view in 2009. I believe that the retention of a UK minimum nuclear deterrent is still necessary – for how long I cannot predict. Complex questions about abolishing nuclear weapons still have to be answered.[60] The UN Security Council debate at heads of government level in September 2009 was just a start.

The task for the UK is to plan for a minimum level of nuclear deterrence for the next decade at least, which can be eliminated as the next step perhaps as early as 2020–25. The US, China and Russia, and probably France, will

---

59 www.globalzero.org
60 George Perkovitch and James M. Acton, 'Abolishing Nuclear Weapons', Adelphi Paper 396, IISS, 2008.

still keep nuclear arsenals. I am not convinced that the successful projection of UK political and military power in the twenty-first century depends on being a nuclear weapons state. Nor does retaining our veto power as a permanent member of the Security Council depend on remaining a nuclear weapons state. The UK's power depends on having agile, well-equipped, rapid reaction military forces capable of being deployed worldwide either through NATO, the UN or, in very rare instances, as in the Falkland Islands, nationally.

Unless we learn to focus our defence budget far better than in the last decade Britain will look increasingly like a toothless lion. That will diminish our influence and power in the UN Security Council far more than moving to a non-ballistic cruise missile minimum nuclear deterrent (see Document 8, paras 38–40).

ANNEX A

In asking the Cabinet Secretary to release the Duff–Mason Report on 24 January 2007 I wrote that in this 'consideration I am sure you will take account of the fact a digest of its main points was produced by the defence policy staff for the Chiefs of Staff as a background for discussions with the Secretary of State for Defence and this has been placed in the public domain (DEFE 25/335, dated 13 August 1979 entitled "The Future of the UK's nuclear deterrent")'.

In replying, on 2 March 2007, the Cabinet Secretary replied, 'The Duff–Mason papers were the subject of a Freedom of Information (FOI) request in late 2005. After careful consideration, the papers were withheld under a number of exemptions provided by the FOI Act, as they contain sensitive information relating to the operation of our current deterrent system. Given that the FOI request was so recent, and that we expect the current deterrent to last into the 2020s, we will not be able to release the papers for the House of Commons debate.'

I appealed this decision not to release the Duff–Mason Report to the Information Commissioner on 6 March (see Annex B). This letter referred to the fact that the Chiefs of Staff Commentary on the Duff–Mason Report was already available to the public in the National Archives. My letter said:

> I wish to appeal the Government decision reported in the Cabinet Secretary's letter to me of 2 March, to recall the file which the Government claims they released in error and are now looking to withdraw from the National Archives. It seems to me there are very serious issues raised in recalling documents which are already in the public domain. One of the documents in that file is called 'The Future of the Nuclear Deterrent: A Commentary'. This is described as being in 'the form of a commentary on the so-called Duff–Mason Report, which was first submitted to Ministers of the previous Government in December 1978 and resubmitted to Ministers of the present Government in June 1979'.

The Information Commissioner replied on 19 March 2007:

> There is an exemption from disclosure under the Freedom of Information Act 2000 (FOIA), section 21, when information is reasonably accessible to the applicant by other means. However, it is not possible to ascertain from the correspondence whether the Cabinet Office is relying upon this or any other exemptions.

The Cabinet Office replied on 30 March:

> Please accept my apologies that the Cabinet Office did not pay regard to all requirements of the Act when considering this request. We have now regis-

tered the request as falling under the terms of the Act and it has been given the Cabinet Office reference FO1248670. We consider that this information is exempt under the provisions of s.21 of the Act relating to information accessible to the applicant by other means. As Sir Gus O'Donnell stated in his letter of 23 January, this information can be made available to you under the convention governing the access by former ministers to their ministerial papers.

As a result the Duff–Mason Report is still not available to the public. Two years later, after some prompting, and with apologies, I received an answer to my other queries to the Cabinet Secretary from Sir Bill Jeffrey, Permanent Under-Secretary of State at the Ministry of Defence (see Annex C). The file called *The Future of the Nuclear Deterrent: A Commentary* for the Chiefs of Staff Committee was available in the National Archive, Kew (DEFE 25/335) for some years. It has now had large sections redacted, following the MOD's being alerted to its existence in the public domain by my correspondence with the Cabinet Secretary. The grounds for this are that the information should never have been released in the first place. A copy is, however, in my possession, as it is in that of others who researched the original document. Three extracts which cannot conceivably be considered classified information are discussed below.

The document was headed:

TOP SECRET UK EYES A
Chiefs of Staff Committee Meeting
Tuesday, 21 August 1980
Nuclear Matters
The Future of the UK Nuclear Deterrent
Commentary on the Duff–Mason Report

and began with a 'Background' section. Page 1 of 5 refers to the fact that the Terms of Reference had been 'approved by the previous Administration in February 1978. The Study by the NWWP was completed towards the end of 1978 and the Report (the Duff–Mason Report) (Flag 1) was seen by the Cabinet in late December 1978. I understand that Sir John Hunt personally authorised that the Report should be made available to the incoming Government.'

The Duff–Mason Report was, in fact, not seen by the then Labour Cabinet and the paper contains therefore an important error which may have led the incoming Conservative government to feel that a decision had been delayed on Polaris replacement. This was not the case, since it had always been accepted that consideration of the matter was premature at that time and did not need to be considered by Cabinet until

the autumn of 1979, which is exactly what happened. This belief that decisions had been delayed may have led the incoming government to conclude that Chevaline's cost escalation had also been hidden to avoid political embarrassment. In fact at the time the MOD view was that the Soviet Union should believe that our modernisation of the Polaris warhead had been achieved much earlier and for that reason all discussions on Chevaline were very highly classified. Discussion on the Duff–Mason Report was brought forward as the background for briefing the Prime Minister, James Callaghan, on his January 1979 visit to Guadeloupe to meet President Carter, President Giscard d'Estaing and Chancellor Schmidt.

Another aspect of the Background paper worth commenting on is paragraph 10 on page 3: 'Should the point arise, you may wish to remind colleagues that Option 7(b) (30 bangs in 30 places) is a surviving fragment of the so-called "Owen Criteria" of a "million dead" which was to support the case for a cruise missile option'.

I was unaware that my arguments against the Moscow Criterion had been labelled the 'Owen Criteria', but at least this demonstrates that the Conservative government was aware of that part of the Duff–Mason Report that discussed options other than the Moscow Criterion. In fact, in a memo to the Prime Minister in December 1978 (Document 11), I said, 'I am not convinced by the contention in the earlier parts of the official's paper that the ability to destroy ten major cities or inflict damage on 30 major targets, including Leningrad, is the minimum criterion for a British deterrent'.

This issue is also covered in another part of the file. On page 3, in the Introduction, where the text refers to paragraph 7(b), the document reads:

> We thus regard the second and third purposes, as stated in Part I, to be interdependent. The key quality they demand is credibility, and this is particularly critical to the ultimate deterrent threat of retaliation against a Soviet nuclear assault against the United Kingdom. Part of the Report rightly in our view, says that credibility resides partly in the material and organisational ability to count on unacceptably damaging strikes whatever the conditions, and partly on the will to do so. These two factors support each other; the realisation of Owen must sufficiently impact the Soviet Union to ensure deterrence. We would add only that Soviet leaders now, and probably in the future, are realists: while they will take due allowance for the uncertainties that surround nuclear matters, they will not be impressed – or deterred – by strategic systems that have a very low chance of inflicting unacceptable damage against the defensive measures of the day.

This double reference to my view that an SLCM with a nuclear warhead would have provided a sufficient deterrent to replace the Polaris missile system targeted on a number of large Soviet cities is very relevant to the new government's 1980 Open Government Discussion Document, which was drafted by Michael Quinlan around the time the Chiefs of Staff were considering the Duff–Mason Report (see Section 1: The Nuclear Deterrent, pp. 47–50). It is clear that in Quinlan's view the summer of 1980 was the time when a significant change was made in UK targeting strategy, away even from that which was in the Duff–Mason Report about targeting Soviet cities. It is not clear how much the Chiefs of Staff or senior Cabinet ministers were aware of the implications of this Open Government Discussion Document.

Speaking notes are also included in the file, on page 1 of 7, for the Chief of Defence Staff: 'I envisaged the Commentary would highlight those areas of the Duff–Mason Report which in our view required a particular military emphasis. I believe this has been admirably achieved.'

What it did not achieve was accuracy in describing what actually happened under the previous Labour government. **There is no doubt in my mind that the Duff–Mason Report and the Commentary on it presented to the Chiefs of Staff Committee should now be published in full before the end of 2009, and with the minimum of redactions.**

ANNEX B

House of Lords,
Westminster,
London SW1A OPW

Mr Richard Thomas
The Information Commissioner's Office
Wycliffe House
Water Lane
Wilmslow
Cheshire SK9 5AF

6 March 2007

Dear Commissioner

I wrote to you on 12 January, 2007 and it was explained to me that on procedural grounds I had to first approach the relevant Department and allow 20 working days for their response.

I wrote to the Cabinet Secretary on 19 January and received their initial response on 23 January, to which I replied on 24 January. I have now received a full reply from the Cabinet Secretary dated 2 March. I enclose copies of this correspondence for your information.

Sadly, I recognise that these papers will not now be released before the House of Commons debate on Trident scheduled for next week. Nevertheless, the issue of whether or not we can maintain a submarine based nuclear deterrent, by Cruise missiles, at less cost than Trident, is an issue unlikely to disappear, particularly in view of the budgetary constraints building up on defence budgets. I wish, therefore, to pursue my belief that these should be opened up for public debate and that while it is very necessary to retain a nuclear deterrent into the future, it is no longer necessary for such a deterrent to be able to penetrate anti-ballistic missile (ABM) defences.

In view of the Government's decision not to release the Duff–Mason report, arising out of two Working Parties, I would now like to appeal that decision and would ask that you make a ruling in favour of disclosure.

I would also wish to appeal the Government's decision reported in the Cabinet Secretary's letter to me of 2 March, to recall the file that Government claims they released in error and are now looking to withdraw from the National Archives. It seems to me there are very serious issues raised in recalling documents which are already in the public domain. One of the documents in that file is called 'The Future of the Nuclear Deterrent: A Commentary'. This is described as being in 'the form of a commentary on the so-called Duff–Mason Report, which was first submitted to Ministers of the previous Government in December 1978 and resubmitted to Ministers of the present Government in June 1979'. I would ask that you rule that this particular document should remain in the public domain. It might help you form a judgement on these requests if I indicate to you why I believe it to be in the national interest that these documents should, in the case of the Duff–Mason Report, be brought into the public domain, and, in the case of 'The Future of the Nuclear Deterrent: A Commentary' should remain in the public domain.

Ever since the Berlin Wall fell in 1989 it seems to me that the arguments for the British nuclear deterrent have to be adjusted to the reality that the Cold War was ending. Subsequent developments with the collapse of the Soviet Empire and the emergence of the Russian Federation, the abandonment of nuclear weapons on the territory of Kazakhstan, Belarus and the Ukraine, present a very different picture of the threat that had previously existed in the UK. These changes were compounded by the readiness of the South African government to give up the pursuit of nuclear weapons. There have also been other developments, like the failure of the US, UK and France to stop Pakistan becoming a nuclear weapon state and the spreading of Pakistan know-how. Also the clear evidence of a nuclear weapon aspiration in North Korea and in Iran and the end of Iraq's nuclear weapons programme, and that of Libya. Many arguments can be adduced about the British nuclear deterrent but I think it is important before we make final decisions in the UK that there is the fullest understanding of why successive governments, for many decades, have considered it necessary to be able to threaten Moscow with nuclear annihilation. I strongly believe that this element in the UK nuclear deterrent is no longer necessary and that in specific terms UK nuclear deterrence does not require the capacity to penetrate ABM defences. The Duff–Mason Report represents an interesting in-depth study of nuclear deterrence strategy, which covered a both Labour and Conservative government's review of what was necessary replace Polaris. Though the circumstances are very different today it seems to me very important that these issues should be opened up for Parliamentary and public debate over the next few years when the cost of a deterrent will need to be weighed against other defence priorities and expenditure. Realistically, there is no the way that the debate in the House of Commons this month, any more than the debate in the House of Lords last month, can be definitive particularly since we do not yet know the outcome of the current public expenditure review and its impact on the Defence Budget.

There are other alternatives to a ballistic missile defence system, in particular the deployment of Cruise missiles. I believed in 1978, as Foreign Secretary, and argued the case in a detailed written submission to Ministerial colleagues in relation to the Duff–Mason Report, that it was necessary to maintain the UK's nuclear deterrent but that the then Government should not be bound, in choosing which weapons system to adopt for such a deterrent, that it had to be able to penetrate the anti-ballistic (ABM) defences surrounding Moscow. This was looked at in July 1980 by the then Conservative Government and discussed in the Defence Open Government document 80/23 'The Future United Kingdom Strategic Nuclear Deterrent Force' in a section on Cruise missiles, para 35–43.

It is argued by the present Labour Government that these papers, both the Duff–Mason Report and what I will call hereafter the 'Commentary', already made public, 'contain sensitive information relating to the operation of our current deterrent system.' I hope that you will, in making your own determination, take the view of some independent experts, military and diplomatic, no longer employed within the government. Also take into account the fact that various academics have already published material which draws on the 'Commentary'.

I await your judgement. Meanwhile I will abide by the request of the Cabinet Secretary and 'refrain from referring publicly to the contents of one specific document, the 'Commentary'.

I cannot, however, accept that I refrain from referring publicly to the contents of some of the other documents in the public domain. You will see from my letter to the Cabinet Secretary and his reply that the Government may be considering withdrawing the public status of some documents which relate to a matter which I have already referred to in the House of Lords (Hansard, 24 January 2007 Col 1129–1130). I said it in that debate, 'Polaris was not able to penetrate Soviet ABM defences in the view of the then-Chief of Defences Staff from November 1975 as relayed to Ministers and as revealed in documents that are in the public domain until Chevaline was deployed for the first time in the summer of 1982. There was a seven year period during which time, first, the Ministry of Defence tried – in fact I believe it succeeded – to stop the then Chancellor of the Exchequer knowing that there was this gap.'

The Official Secrets Act does not exist to protect former Ministers, military figures and civil servants from embarrassment. There are a number of documents in the public domain which the government are now reviewing, with a view to possibly recalling, which make clear the circumstances surrounding a meeting involving the then Chief of Defence Staff, Field Marshall Sir Michael Carver, the then Permanent Under Secretary at the Ministry of Defence and the then Secretary of State for Defence, on 24 November, 1975. A period which it is important to note is outside the 30 years which normally restrict the publication of Ministerial documents. At that meeting a decision was taken to withhold from the then Chancellor of the Exchequer the advice of the Chief of Defence Staff that 'without Chevaline and without Variant A the Polaris force did not constitute an adequate national deterrent' and that 'while we ought to retain Moscow as the criterion for unacceptable damage, this could not necessarily be guaranteed in the interim period until Chevaline was introduced'. The Chief of Defence Staff had earlier suggested a repositioning of Polaris submarines and re-targeting of the missiles. It appears from later documents that the Chancellor of Exchequer was not informed – at least until the summer of 1976. Nor was the then Prime Minister, Harold Wilson, although the new Prime Minister, James Callaghan, was eventually informed that summer. At the meeting an attempt was made to justify the exclusion of the Chancellor of Exchequer on the basis that he did not 'need to know'. This appears to be a judgement based on targeting strategy being the preserve of the Prime Minister and the Secretary of State for Defence, usually with one other Minister nominated by the Prime Minister. The issue, however, of the effectiveness of the Polaris missile was crucial to the Chancellor's concern about whether to proceed with the programme to enhance the capability of the warheads penetrating ABM defences. On 18 November, 1975 in a personal memo to Secretary of State for Defences, Roy Mason, one of his Private Secretaries, J F Mayne, wrote 'can you afford not to copy your minute to the Chancellor of the Exchequer? I think it would be madness to exclude him from the correspondence, in spite of the dangers of copying the minute to him'. Agreement to exclude the Chancellor was taken in the light of the reported view of Sir John Hunt, the then Cabinet Secretary, who 'was concerned about the possibility of the cancellation of CHEVALINE in the forthcoming PESC exercise. The European allies might not be too worried by such a cancellation, but the United States might be concerned. If CHEVALINE were cancelled and VARIANT A substituted, savings would be negligible; but if VARIANT A was not proceeded with, then the savings would be £30m a year over the PESC period, and £178m in total. Such savings might be very attractive to the Chancellor.'

A number of documents also in the public domain relate to what was told to the new Prime Minister, James Callaghan. There are notes for an oral presentation by the Secretary of State for Defence to the Prime Minister and then a letter sent by him, dated 11 June, 1976 about being 'unable to guarantee the destruction of Moscow'. That wording appears more opaque than those used previously by the Chief of Defence Staff where he makes it quite clear that Soviet ABM defences had made the Polaris missile ineffective and unable to penetrate.

In view of all this, I request that you do not agree that any documents relating to this matter, already in the public domain, should be withdrawn from the National Archives. For your information, I will be requesting of the Cabinet Secretary the release of all documents, if they exist, relating to this matter which informed other key Ministers in the Government of the fact that the Chief of Defence Staff considered Polaris could not penetrate Moscow's ABM defences. In particular, any communications on this subject to James Callaghan, when he was Foreign Secretary. Also any communications, if they exist, on this subject to his successor, Tony Crosland and then to myself, as Foreign Secretary. It is possible, though very unlikely, that I received any such communication. Because if I had I would have certainly discussed it with Field Marshal Lord Carver informally in a number of discussions which I had with him on the nuclear deterrent in 1978. I am certain that I never did discuss this with Lord Carver. Nor have others in my Private Office at the time any recall of seeing any document relating to Carver's views in 1975. All we knew was of the concerns that it was getting harder to guarantee penetration of ABM defences; that we could not penetrate was never revealed to us. Also I will request any communication which told the Chancellor of the Exchequer at some later date than the summer of 1976, if they exist, of the then Chief of Defence Staff's view.

I would be grateful also if you would authorise the release of other papers specified in my letter to the Cabinet Secretary. It should be noted that some of these letters and documents relate to my own period in office as Foreign Secretary and which have already been released into the public domain. For example, Fred Mulley's memo to the Prime Minister on the British Nuclear Test programme, copied to me, dated 3 November 1978. I have no objection to this but I do not see how it is possible to justify partial release and then invoke the 30 year limitation on allowing me to release my own response to the Duff–Mason Report a month later in December of that year. There seems no logical pattern to the disclosure policy adopted by the Government. Even more cause for concern is that they now seem to believe they are entitled to arbitrarily, and retrospectively, withdraw documents they themselves have released.

I am not sure whether your terms of reference, on which I have focused my requests, allow you to go any further than whether or not to release classified documents. But if there is any lee-way I hope you will consider enquiring further into all of this in a way which will establish exactly what did happen on this very important matter.

These are, I accept, very complicated questions and I would be ready to come and talk to you personally about these issues if you considered this would be helpful.

Finally, I would much appreciate being given some idea of how long you think it would take for you to reach a decision on the requests I have made.

Yours sincerely

DAVID OWEN

ANNEX C

SIR BILL JEFFREY KGB
PERMANENT UNDER-SECRETARY OF STATE

MINISTRY OF DEFENCE
FLOOR 5, ZONE D, MAIN BUILDING
WHITEHALL
LONDON SW1A 2HB

D/PUS/17/1 (075)

19 February 2009

Dear Lord Owen

I know that Gus O'Donnell wrote to you on 5 February to relay my sincere apologies for my Department's failure to write to you with further details of the public status of a number of the documents you referred to in your letter of 19 January 2007. I am now in a position to do so.

In that letter you referred to several MOD documents:

a. A letter relating to the British Nuclear Test Programme sent to the Prime Minister by Fred Mulley on 3 November 1978;

b. A Note for the Record [MO18/1/1] relating to a meeting between the Secretary of State, CDS and PUS on 24 November 1975; a note to the Secretary of State from JF Mayne dated 27 November 1975 (these papers are one and the same);

c. A minute to the Secretary of State from JF Mayne dated 18 November 1975;

d. A minute from the CDS [1141/5] of 10 November 1975.

As you know, before 2007 these papers were available in full in the National Archives (in files DEFE25/335 and DEFE13/1039), but they were recalled for re-review because we believed they might contain sensitive material which had been released in error. This has since been confirmed and both files have had papers redacted with the agreement of the Lord Chancellor. Redactions were undertaken following a public interest test on the basis of section 26 (defence) and section 27 (international relations) of the Freedom of Information Act. You are of course now free to examine these papers in The National Archives, but for ease of reference I enclose with this letter copies of the versions of these papers which now appear on the files there. You will see that these documents identify the redactions as having been withheld under section 3(4) of the Public Records Act; this means they are retained in MOD under Public Records Act retention criterion six, which is essentially that Act's equivalent of the Freedom of Information Act section 26. You will also see that papers (c) and (d) lack much substance, reflecting the fact that large sections have been redacted and retained.

You also asked for a number of papers which are the responsibility of the Cabinet Office and the Foreign and Commonwealth Office, but which MOD might hold:

e. The Terms of Reference of the Sub-Committee of the Ministerial Committee on Nuclear Policy
f. Terms of Reference for the 1978 study of factors relating to further consideration of the future of the UK Nuclear Deterrent and the Committee meeting discussion held on 21 December 1978 with the papers submitted by Lord Owen to the Committee when he was Foreign Secretary and the discussion on 2 January 1979
g. The 'Duff-Mason' Report
h. Minutes of meetings of the sub-committee relating to Chevaline and Polaris replacement and the CTB negotiations
i. Your own letter dated 31 October 1978.

Formally speaking, this part of your request has already been dealt with by the Cabinet Office's Histories, Openness and Records Unit's letter to you of 30 March 2007 citing a FOI Art section 21 exemption, and I understand from Foreign Office officials that you may have seen a number of these papers recently when you exercise your right of access as a former Minister. At the time you made your request we reviewed our files and confirmed that the MOD does hold a copy of the Duff–Mason report and may well hold some or all of these other papers in around 70 files that officials have identified. We have also identified about forty files which are relevant to the final part of your request:

Papers relating to the Internal Ministry of Defence options Paper regarding successor systems commenced at the beginning of 1978 with particular reference to Cruise missiles.

Searching, identifying, extracting and redacting all of these papers would be a substantial task, whose cost would certainly exceed the normal cost limit of £600 under the FOI arrangements. This is partly because these files, some of which run to over 600 pages, have had to be reconstituted as digital images as a result of asbestos contamination, and the time taken to examine the electronic scans is much greater than would have been the case had the files remained as paper. If, however, you were able to identify any of these papers which are likely to be held by the MOD and which you did not see when you visited the Foreign Office, we will do our best to find them. I have, in any event, asked that the relevant files be put into the MOD's record review process so that the ones which can be released are transferred to the National Archives later this year. I will write to you again to let you know when this has happened.

May I again apologise for our failure to respond to your earlier request in a timely fashion. If you would like to discuss any of this with me, either by phone or in person, I would of course be happy to do so.

Yours sincerely

BILL JEFFREY

SIR BILL JEFFREY KGB
PERMANENT UNDER-SECRETARY OF STATE

MINISTRY OF DEFENCE
FLOOR 5, ZONE D, MAIN BUILDING
WHITEHALL
LONDON SW1A 2HB

D/PUS/17/1 (328)

29 May 2009

Dear Lord Owen

PUBLICATION OF PAPERS ON THE NUCLEAR DETERRENT

Thank you for your letter of 30 April.

As you will appreciate, the Government's main concern is to protect the capability and operational effectiveness of the current deterrent, and the longevity of these systems is such that some of the issues which were sensitive in the late 1970s remain so today. Even so, having looked at the papers myself, I agree with you that the material you were sent is much more heavily redacted than is necessary, given the passage of time and the extent of earlier disclosures. I have asked staff here and in the FCO to go through the papers again, and to identify only those redactions which are strictly necessary, of which we judge there will still be a few. You should receive a revised set of papers during the week of 8 June. If you still feel we are going too far, I would be grateful if you could get in touch with my office, and I would be glad to discuss the matter. I am sorry you found it necessary to write to me on this.

You may be interested to know that we are making good progress in reviewing the files relating to your earlier request and anticipate transferring them to the National Archives in July.

Yours ever

BILL JEFFREY

SIR BILL JEFFREY KGB
PERMANENT UNDER-SECRETARY OF STATE

MINISTRY OF DEFENCE
FLOOR 5, ZONE D, MAIN BUILDING
WHITEHALL
LONDON SW1A 2HB

D/PUS/17/1 (483)

29 July 2009

Dear Lord Owen

PUBLICATION OF DETERRENT PAPERS

When I wrote to you on 29 May about the policy papers on the deterrent which you intended to place with Liverpool University I mentioned that I hoped that other relevant papers that we were reviewing following your letter to the Cabinet Secretary would be available at The National Archives in July.

Unfortunately our work on guidance in this area for Whitehall record reviewers is taking longer than first envisaged and I now expect the files to be available in The National Archives in the early Autumn.

I am sorry that this has slipped. I remain keen that we release as much information as possible while protecting our current nuclear capability. It is, I think, better that we ensure that this is done correctly now rather than have to deal retrospectively with problems as we have had to in the past.

Yours ever

BILL JEFFREY

ANNEX D

5 pm

Lord Owen: My Lords, my noble friend has made a very dignified and serious speech, which deserves close attention.

The issue before us is summed up in the words of the White Paper:

> 'The investment required to maintain'

our deterrent,

> 'will not come at the expense of the conventional capabilities that our armed forces need'.

Were that to be true, I would find it much easier to be enthusiastic in support of the White Paper, but all experience shows that that is not true.

I remember that in 1968, when I had a small responsibility for the Royal Navy, it was genuinely believed by the admirals that the Polaris programme was outwith the rest of the defence budget and that the naval budget and capabilities would be judged quite separately. That was wrong then and it has been wrong ever since. Let us be clear: that statement is historically incorrect and it is very unlikely to be true in future.

I then looked at what is the Royal Navy at present. In 1968, we had our first Polaris boat going out on patrol. We could claim, broadly, 200 naval ships; we had a substantial Navy. In 1980, Royal Navy personnel numbered 75,000. There were 8,000 to 10,000 Marines and a hundred capital ships. What is it today? There are roughly 33,000 Royal Navy personnel, 6,000 Royal Marines and 35 major ships. The Royal Navy is very close to lacking all-round capability and capacity.

We have to face that. If we are really to make this decision as early as it is being asked for, it must coincide with the public expenditure review for 2007, not come before it. It needs to be taken into account in what we are going to do about, for example, the two carriers that have been consistently promised. It needs to be taken into account against the other service budgets. The Navy cannot be considered in isolation. Many naval personnel are involved in Afghanistan at the moment, if we consider the Royal Marines and others.

All of us are in a way responsible for the fact that we have not kept the covenant with the Armed Forces. I must say that I object to the business of using naval ships as a background for political speeches. We have not done that in this country before; we have always kept that sort of thing to when we are actually operational abroad. It appears that the Prime Minister, after 10 years, accepts that he has not lived up to that covenant. If so, that is a very welcome change, but let actions speak louder than words and let us now look at the budget.

Do we really accept in this House that we do not have enough Chinooks in Afghanistan and that, as a consequence, some of our soldiers die? Do we really accept the story about armaments, body armour, and so on? We can all agree about the aim – there is no question that anyone intended the situation – but it worked out so that many people believe that we were not putting basic resources into that fairly minor item of expenditure.

We also need to look at many other aspects. I start with the belief that the defence budget at the moment is seriously inadequate. We are therefore being asked to take on a new commitment. I make absolutely no secret of my belief, and never have, that a ballistic weapons system is the best form of deterrent, provided that the warheads are sophisticated enough to be able to penetrate ABM defences. At least I have a track record on this. I argued in 1977, 1978 and 1979 that we had to be very careful before we committed ourselves to a belief that a deterrent was credible only if it could penetrate ABM defences, because I believed then, and events have subsequently borne this out in spades, that we in this country did not have the capability to keep ahead of the complicated and sophisticated changes in ABM defences.

Just look what happened to the Chevaline programme, which started in effect under Harold Wilson's Labour Government in 1967–68 as the Antelope programme. It became the Super Antelope programme, and then became the Chevaline programme. In 1972, which was probably the first time you could reasonably estimate its costs, it was going to cost £175 million. It ended up costing more than £1 billion – the cost escalated year by year; I could read the figures to the House – which is also a staggering increase in real terms.

The House of Commons Select Committee report of 2006–07 on the provisions for nuclear submarines quite sensibly looked at all aspects, including asking whether there was sufficient capacity to build and maintain them and whether Rolls Royce had the nuclear capacity. It was an extremely good report. I came across this little statement on the Select Committee's visit to Aldermaston and seeing the A91 building – the integrated radioactive liquid effluent treatment plant – which was completed but the plant was never used – a loss of expenditure of £147 million. I simply thought to myself that that was another sign that the programme, which is now a different Chevaline programme or whatever equivalent, demonstrates yet again our incapacity to contain our costs.

On the basis of the argument as we currently see it, I reluctantly understand why the Government have taken the decision that they have. Certainly, the decision to participate in the Trident D5 life-extension programme, at a cost of some £250 million, is prudent, and keeps the options open. However, the section on dual use in the White Paper is extremely depressing. I believe that, in our economic situation, we must consider dual use for almost everything. The section on cruise missiles is one paragraph, with an absurd statement that,

'Any programme to develop and manufacture a new cruise missile would cost far more than retaining the Trident D5 missile'.

What does that mean? Does it mean that Britain will develop a cruise missile by itself? We have never yet done so; we have very sensibly bought from the Americans. Are we then saying that the Americans will not make any changes to their cruise missiles? Why are they spending as much money as they are on hypersonic technology? It is perfectly possible that we may see a cruise missile of greater sophistication and perhaps particularly of greater speed.

I happened to be in Belgrade a few years ago. I drove down the street and saw the Ministry of Defence, in which, for my sins, I had to spend some time in 1992–93 talking to the then Serbian military. The whole place had been completely destroyed. The buildings on either side were completely intact. I went further down the same street and saw the same thing with the Ministry of the Interior. I remember our Ministry of Defence telling me in 1978 that cruise missiles were inaccurate and unproven technology, and that was why the MoD could not make any commitment to it. Let us at least admit when we have made a mistake. The arguments have not been truthfully used under successive Governments, in part because of far too much secrecy. The present Government deserve some credit for coming up with an early proposal and giving us the potential – after all, we are only taking note of this White Paper – to explore it much more fully.

As I understand it, the Government looked at dual use of Trident – whether one could put a battery of cruise missiles on those large boats, which one has to have if one is going to use Trident missiles, so one could have a cruise missile battery and also the possibility of being able to deploy Royal Marines in it – and they came out against it. I can understand that, with a dedicated programme and the possibility of only three submarines, but I am told by people who should know that at no stage has there been a serious look at dual use of cruise missiles and at no stage has there been a serious look at where new cruise missile technology could take us. That is not good enough. It means that we are not looking at all the options. The only justification for that would be if one had decided that any nuclear deterrent has to penetrate ABM defences.

First, let us remember the Polaris situation. The Polaris was not able to penetrate Soviet ABM defences in the view of the then-chief of defence staff from November 1975 as relayed to Ministers and as revealed in documents that are in the public domain until Chevaline was deployed for the first time in the summer of 1982. There was a seven-year period during which time, first, the Ministry of Defence tried – in fact I believe that it succeeded – to stop the then Chancellor of the Exchequer knowing that there was this gap; and secondly, there was no overt debate about the question. Of course we had to keep it private. One was not in those days able to let the Soviet Union know that one had doubts about one's own deterrent capacity, so there are limits, but now it is a completely different situation. Some of the language is as though the Cold War is still continuing.

What was needed to penetrate Soviet ABM defences and the argument about the Moscow criterion was the linchpin of the debates in 1978–79, yet they had to be kept private. Now we can openly discuss the question and it is not yet apparent for me whether that is the Prime Minister's criterion: that he wants a missile to be able to land on any country anywhere from any naval space. If we had all the money of the United States of course we would sign up to it tomorrow: that is a reasonable deterrent force. The Government can claim – they deserve some credit for it – that they have substantially reduced all the so-called tactical strategic nuclear weapons; taken them right out. They are wise and sensible for doing so. This is the start, not the end of a debate. This is the start of a discussion. If we replace the present Vanguard class I hope very much that the type of submarine is different from the one that we are currently imagining.

It is not an appropriate response to mirror the situation of the government decision, which I broadly supported, to replace Trident in the early 1980s. We would be much wiser to start to think afresh on all those different questions. I do not mind taking a decision in principle that at the moment that looks the best option, which are much the same words as the previous speaker used, but I would not want to close down a cheaper option, particularly if I find out, as is highly likely, that we have insufficient money for the defence budget and for the maintenance of a credible Royal Navy.

1

The Nuclear Deterrent

In response to my request at a meeting on 18 July, I received on 22 September 1977 a paper by Foreign Office officials on the Future of the British Strategic Nuclear Deterrent. The minutes of a meeting on 17 October describe my personal views as Foreign Secretary very frankly on the Moscow Criterion, the Chevaline programme, Polaris successor systems, cruise missiles and theatre nuclear weapons.

At a meeting called by the Prime Minister on 28 October 1977, with three ministers, the Chancellor of the Exchequer, the Secretary of State for Defence and myself, we agreed to continue to fund Chevaline despite its considerable cost overrun. I deployed arguments similar to those I had outlined within the Foreign Office on 17 October when I had said that the time to cancel Chevaline was when Labour initially came back into government, saying that it 'was conceptually misguided and ought to have been abandoned in 1974'. Other arguments were that any decision to cancel would become public and it would be damaging for the Soviet Union to know. We would save a relatively small part of the overall cost. But as part of my prior understanding with the Secretary of State for Defence, Fred Mulley, it was agreed that our going ahead with Chevaline was not a decision to endorse the Moscow Criterion and to underline this a study was commissioned on the continuing validity of the Moscow Criterion. The aim was to submit that study to the Ministers by May 1978.

At a further meeting with the Prime Minister on 1 December 1977 it was agreed to set in hand a study, without any commitment, to consider the future of the UK's nuclear deterrent. This was to be separate from the study on the Moscow Criterion, but its terms of reference circulated to ministers in a minute from the Prime Minister's Private Secretary, Ken Stowe, recognized a need for it to draw upon the Criterion study.

On 17 July 1978, Paul Lever had minuted me on the possibility that the Strategic Arms Limitation Talks (SALT) might put limits on the range and number of cruise missiles. By then, with the Moscow Criterion paper not yet available, I grew suspicious that with a general election possible in the autumn, the Criterion paper was being deliberately delayed and the issue kicked into touch by Whitehall.

My private office began to make enquiries of the Cabinet Office. It became evident that the Criterion paper was available and could have been circulated before the summer recess of 1978, and that one of the options envisaged targets other than Moscow. The possibility of moving away from the Moscow Criterion was, therefore, still being left open. I discovered the three reasons given to the Prime Minister to delay a ministerial meeting on the Criterion report. The first was the approaching parliamentary recess and some difficulties with fixing meetings. The second was that ministers might find it easier to come to a view on the Criterion when the study on the future of the UK deterrent had been completed, envisaged for the early part of 1979. So Whitehall (by which I mean the formal meetings of Permanent Secretaries chaired by the Cabinet Secretary, or sometimes informal meetings in smaller numbers to mirror our meetings of ministers) was now arguing against itself. Previously it had been pushing for a decision in principle on the Moscow Criterion as necessary for the rest of the study to proceed. There was also a third, and embarrassing, reason put to the Prime Minister for delaying a ministerial meeting. Whitehall suspected that if the decision was taken to set aside the Moscow Criterion, the Chancellor of the Exchequer, Denis Healey, would argue for the cancellation of the Chevaline programme. Officials drew a distinction between my position as Foreign Secretary and that of Denis Healey in that I was reluctantly ready to proceed with Chevaline. So Whitehall had squared the relevant departments, in particular the Treasury and the MOD, and officials were ready to support interim funding arrangements for Chevaline for a further year. A year, although this was not stated in the paper to the Prime Minister, would virtually cover the latest period when there could be a general election. This, it was argued, would allow room for manoeuvre for a new Labour government to take decisions in due course on the report of the study on the UK deterrent. It would also, of course, have left the decision open for a new Conservative government. These arguments to the Prime Minister reminded me of *Yes, Minister* in terms of their techniques, tactics and smooth presentation.

In part sensing what was happening in Whitehall, in part realizing we needed a position over SALT, on 31 July I sent over to No. 10, for the Prime Minister's personal attention only, a four-page memo and a much longer detailed paper on Nuclear Weapons Policy (Document 8). On 8 August, the Prime Minister threaded his way, with considerable skill, through the carefully worded Whitehall proposition. He decided not to postpone for a year but to have ministers discuss the Moscow Criterion paper in the autumn, and he informed the three ministers concerned that, in the meantime, he had approved the continuing funding of Chevaline with no timescale mentioned.

My paper was read by the Prime Minister during the August holiday period when he was starting to weigh up when to call an election. He and I discussed it at some length, privately, travelling in a plane to Nigeria in September, particularly the aspect of extending submarine hull life and targeting half a dozen cities in the USSR with cruise missiles, the option which interested him if there was to prove to be insufficient money for a ballistic system, which he preferred.

Whether my paper to the Prime Minister went to the Cabinet Secretary I do not know but I suspect it went through him to the Duff–Mason committee for their consideration. This grouping of civil servants and military advisers had been deliberately established to be independent of any ministerial input. But I hoped they would be alerted to some of my arguments so that they could deal, in their paper, with some of my points. I suspected that Sir John Hunt, the Cabinet Secretary, was in favour of continuing with a ballistic system, and on nuclear matters he had a key coordinating role, which the Cabinet Secretary had acquired after Prime Minister Harold Macmillan's meeting with President Kennedy in Nassau in the Bahamas in 1962. It appears that that role is no longer the preserve of the Cabinet Secretary, part of the ill-judged reforms introduced by Prime Minister Tony Blair in 2001.[1]

It will be seen from the various other papers in this section that I assembled an independent capacity inside my private office to advise me on defence and particularly nuclear matters, liaising with our ambassador in Washington, Peter Jay, to keep abreast of US nuclear thinking, and this continued until I left office in May 1979.

I asked Paul Lever, who virtually ran this personal 'think tank', to prepare my views so as to be able to react rapidly to the tabling of any papers by officials. Sure enough, on 7 December, a minute was sent out on the first of two parts of the Duff–Mason Report and we were told that part three would follow soon thereafter. Fortunately we were ready with an alternative view, and I sent an immediate holding reply on 11 December; a nine-page paper followed on 12 December with a further minute on 19 December (Documents 9–11). The ministerial meeting was held on 20 December 1978. Subsequently, further briefing took place with the Prime Minister prior to his flying to Guadeloupe.

---

1 Lord Owen, 'The Ever-growing Dominance of No 10 in British Diplomacy since 5 April 1982', in Graham Ziegner (ed.), *British Diplomacy: Foreign Secretaries Reflect* (London: Politico's, 2007), pp. 21–43.

There is no evidence that the option of using SSNs with nuclear warheads on cruise missiles for the UK deterrent I favoured in December 1978 has as yet ever been seriously considered by any subsequent British government. The decision by the incoming Conservative government to try to procure the Trident C-4 system from the US was made by a Cabinet Committee (MISC 7) on 6 December 1979. The Cabinet was informed later. John Nott, who was then Secretary of State for Trade and Industry, wrote in his memoirs that he was 'shocked that the Cabinet had neither been given any facts nor consulted on the issue'.[2]

I have often pondered why Chevaline was made public in 1980 by the incoming Conservative government. The most respectable argument would be that 'the time was right' in relation to the Soviet Union. Yet it appeared at the time to be more like a party political decision taken against the previous Labour government and a most unfortunate lapse in the broadly bipartisan approach to nuclear deterrence. Another charitable explanation, to which I drew attention in the Introduction (pp. 20–21), may be that they thought, wrongly, that the previous Labour government had considered the issues in Cabinet in late December 1978, as the Chiefs of Staff paper mentioned, and concluded that the Labour government had put the replacement of Polaris at risk by sitting on the report and keeping the cost escalation of Chevaline secret to avoid political embarrassment at the general election.

As I mentioned at the beginning of the Introduction, using SSNs was not one of the four options considered in the December 2006 White Paper on 'The Future of the United Kingdom's Nuclear Deterrent'. If this option is to be considered in 2010 it is, therefore, necessary to consider the American experience with their nuclear-armed sea-launched cruise missile (SLCM) programme. Few people in the UK seem to be aware that the US has maintained the nuclear warheads for some of its cruise missiles ashore for over 15 years with a capability for redeployment within 30 days of a decision to do so. They have integrated this additional nuclear option into their national nuclear war game on an annual basis.

---

2 John Nott, *Here Today, Gone Tomorrow: Recollections of an Errant Politician* (London: Politico's, 2002), p. 206.

TOMAHAWK MISSILES[3]

Development and deployment

The United States Navy began developing a nuclear-armed sea-launched cruise missile (SLCM) in 1971. The first underwater test launch took place in 1976. The first launch of a production Tomahawk Land Attack Missile (TLAM-N) equipped for a nuclear warhead took place from the submarine USS *Guitarro* in 1980 and it entered into service in 1984. It is defined as a 'sea-based nuclear system with less than intercontinental range that is used to strike targets ashore.'[4] Its range is 2,500 km compared to approximately 11,000 km for the Trident II D5 missiles.

Versions of the missile were developed with conventional warheads for deployment on surface ships for anti-ship warfare (labelled the Tomahawk Anti-Ship Missile, or TASM), for land attack (labelled the Tomahawk Land Attack Missile – Conventional [TLAM-C, also known as Tomahawk Block II], and as the nuclear-armed Ground-Launched Cruise Missile (GLCM) deployed in Europe from 1983 to 1991.

The original programme of 758 SLCMs for 200 ships and submarines was reduced to 367.[5] Around 100 were deployed at sea at a time.[6] They were able to deliver a W80-Mod 0 nuclear warhead that had a variable yield of between 5 and 150 kt. The first W80-Mod 0 was manufactured in 1983 and first deployed on a TLAM-N missile in 1984.

In September 1991 President George H. W. Bush announced what became known as the first Presidential Nuclear Initiative (PNI) to authorize the withdrawal of most of the United States' forward-deployed non-strategic nuclear forces and the de-alerting or cancellation of some strategic nuclear systems. This included the withdrawal of all tactical nuclear weapons from surface ships, submarines and land-based naval aircraft, including the TLAM-N.[7]

---

3 I am indebted to Dr Nick Ritchie, Research Fellow, Bradford Disarmament Research Centre, University of Bradford, who has kindly allowed me to use the factual information that he has researched in this section. He has now published two important monographs in May 2009. One is detailed on p. 16, n. 57. The other is a paper entitled 'Replacing Trident Two Years On: What Has Happened?', similarly published by the Department of Peace Studies, University of Bradford.

4 'Nuclear Supplement to the Joint Strategic Capabilities Plan for FY1996', Joint Chiefs of Staff, 12 February 1996, p. GL-15 (heavily redacted). Obtained under the Freedom of Information Act by Hans Kristensen. Available at http://www.nukestrat.com/us/jcs/98-53h_AnnexC96.pdf.

5 Robert Norris and William Arkin, 'U.S. Nuclear Weapons Stockpile, July 1996', *Bulletin of the Atomic Scientists*, July–August 1996, p. 63.

6 Joshua Handler, 'PNIs and TNW Elimination, Storage and Security', in Brian Alexander and Alistair Millar (eds.), *Tactical Nuclear Weapons* (Dulles, VA: Brassey's, 2003), p. 22.

7 Full details of the September 1991 and January 1992 PNIs are set out in R. B. Cheney (1992), *Prepared Statement by Richard B. Cheney, Secretary of Defense*, Hearing before the Senate

Bush said that 'under normal circumstances, our ships [including submarines] will not carry tactical nuclear weapons. Many of these land- and sea-based warheads will be dismantled and destroyed. Those remaining will be secured in central areas where they would be available if necessary in a future crisis'.[8] All TLAM-Ns were withdrawn from operational service by the end of 1992.

In 1994 the Department of Defense undertook a Nuclear Posture Review, the first comprehensive review of US nuclear weapons policy, force structure and arms control in 15 years. The review recommended that the US Navy and Air Force eliminate the ability of carriers and other surface ships to deploy the nuclear weapons that were withdrawn under the first PNI in 1991 but maintain the ability to redeploy TLAM-N missiles on nuclear attack submarines (SSNs).[9]

A 1997 Congressional Research Service report stated that 'around 350 nuclear-armed sea-launched cruise missiles are held in storage areas in the United States'.[10] On the Atlantic side the SLCMs were stored at the Naval Weapons Station in Yorktown, Virginia until 1997 when they were transferred to the Strategic Weapons Facility Atlantic at King's Bay, Georgia, to be stored with Trident nuclear warheads for the Atlantic SSBN fleet. On the Pacific side they were stored at Naval Air Station North Island, San Diego, until they too were transferred to the Strategic Weapons Facility Pacific at Bangor, Maine, to be stored with Trident nuclear warheads for the Pacific SSBN fleet.[11]

The 1997 Department of Defense report on 'Nuclear Weapons Systems Sustainment Programs' states that '[twice] a year, Navy selects an attack submarine and conducts a regeneration exercise that demonstrates and appraises the capability to redeploy nuclear-armed cruise missiles on such submarines. This exercise tests the ability of the submarine and crew to re-establish nuclear weapons capability in a relatively short time'.[12]

In addition to the certification inspection process, a few SSNs are occasionally ordered to conduct a live test firing of an unarmed TLAM-N. The US Navy's website, for example, states that

---

Committee on Armed Services 'Military Implications of START I and START II', 28 July 1992, United States Senate, Washington, DC, pp. 11–18.

8 Cited in Alexander and Millar (eds.), *Tactical Nuclear Weapons*, p. 169.

9 'Overview of Nuclear Posture Review (NPR) Results', U.S. Strategic Command, September 22, 1994'. Obtained under the Freedom of Information Act by Hans Kristensen. Available at http://www.nukestrat.com/us/reviews/usstratcom0994.pdf.

10 Amy Woolf, 'Nuclear Weapons in U.S. Defense Policy: Issues for Congress', 1 July 1997, Congressional Research Service, Library of Congress, p. 8.

11 Handler, 'PNIs and TNW Elimination, Storage and Security', p. 23.

12 'Nuclear Weapons Systems Sustainment Programs', Office of the Secretary of Defense, Department of Defense, May 1997.

[two] submarines participated in unusual Tomahawk exercise launches in 1998. USS Atlanta (SSN-712) conducted a dual launch consisting of a TLAM-C and a TLAM-N Quality Assurance Test (QAST). This was the first combined conventional and unarmed nuclear test launch from the same platform. USS Minneapolis-St. Paul (SSN-708) also fired a successful TLAM-N QAST during Exercise GLOBAL GUARDIAN '99, marking the first time that the European Command exercised unarmed nuclear command and control authority over a LANTFLT SSN.[13]

The command history for the USS *Bremerton*, a Los Angeles-class SNN operating out of US Naval Submarine Base San Diego, for the period 18 March 2000–5 March 2002 states that 'BREMERTON successfully completed a Nuclear Weapons Acceptance Inspection, and proceeded to Bangor, Washington to load an exercise TLAM-N and conduct a successful QAST-TLAM-N launch in March'.[14]

Global Guardian is an annual exercise to test the nuclear Operational Plan (OPLAN) for all US nuclear forces. It is run by US Strategic Command (STRATCOM) to 'test and validate nuclear command and control and execution procedures. Exercise objectives include live communications and the participation of all elements potentially assigned to USSTRATCOM in wartime'.[15] It includes all three legs of the strategic nuclear triad (ICBMs, SLBMs and long-range nuclear-armed bombers), as well as Dual Capable Aircraft tasked to carry non-strategic nuclear bombs and SSNs certified to deploy TLAM-Ns.[16]

The 1998 report of the Defense Science Board Task Force on Nuclear Deterrence stated that 'the Navy is not tasked for day-to-day tactical nuclear forces. TLAM/N can be regenerated within 30 days on attack submarines'.[17]

In 2001 Robert Norris *et al.* stated that in the Pacific Fleet less than half of the attack submarines undergo regular nuclear certification.[18] They also stated in 2002 that 'the reduced nuclear requirement is also illustrated by the fact that after passing inspections, SSNs are subsequently de-certified to save resources for more urgent, non-nuclear responsibilities. If necessary, however, Tomahawks can be redeployed in only 30 days. To ensure training

13 See http://www.navy.mil/navydata/cno/n87/usw/Issue_3/Pullout/submarine_strike.htm.
14 Command history available at http://www.history.navy.mil/shiphist/b/ssn-698/2000.pdf.
15 'Nuclear Weapons Systems Sustainment Programs', Office of the Secretary of Defense, Department of Defense, May 1997.
16 'Report of the Defense Science Board Task Force on Nuclear Deterrence', Department of Defense, October 1998, p. 30.
17 'Report of the Task Force on Nuclear Deterrence', Defense Science Board, Department of Defense, October 1998, p. 28.
18 Robert Norris, William Arkin, Hans Kristensen and Joshua Handler, 'U.S. Nuclear Forces, 2001', *Bulletin of the Atomic Scientists*, March–April 2001.

and force integration, Tomahawk operations are included in STRATCOM's annual Global Guardian nuclear exercises'.[19]

According to Joshua Handler, writing in 2003, 'Every unit that has a nuclear-weapons mission of transporting, storing, or firing nuclear weapons must be certified to do so by its service and by the Department of Defense'.[20] A number of SSNs in the Pacific and Atlantic fleets are therefore required to undergo periodic certification to ensure they can deploy and fire TLAM-Ns if called upon to do so in a crisis.

Robert Norris and Hans Kristensen wrote in 2007: 'We estimate that no more than 12 SSNs have a nuclear capability. TLAM/Ns are earmarked for deployment on selected Los Angeles-class, improved Los Angeles-class, and Virginia-class SSNs'.[21] There are currently 24 SSN boats in the Pacific Fleet.[22]

The future of the TLAM-N arsenal

A second Nuclear Posture Review was conducted in 2001, this time by the George W. Bush administration. It is estimated that 100–120 TLAM-Ns and their W80-Mod 0 warheads were moved to reserve or inactive status, leaving an operational pool of 200.[23] By 2007 it was estimated that only 100 remained in the operational stockpile, with the remaining 220 in reserve or inactive status.

Two years after the 2002 NPR the Department of Defense took another look at the rationale for retaining the TLAM-N force and opted to keep them. As Robert Norris and Hans Kristensen wrote in 2004, 'The Pentagon decided in late 2003 to retain the Tomahawk because of its ability to secretly deploy anywhere on the globe, according to *Inside the Navy*. The TLAM/N is earmarked for deployment on selected Los Angeles-class, Improved Los Angeles-class, and Virginia-class attack submarines. The missiles and their W80-Mod 0 warheads are expected to undergo refurbishment to extend their service life to around 2040'.[24]

Nevertheless, a 2008 Report of the Secretary of Defense Task Force on DoD Nuclear Weapons Management expressed real concern over the long-term viability of the TLAM-N mission. It stated: 'Although the Navy has

19 Robert Norris, William Arkin, Hans Kristensen and Joshua Handler, 'U.S. Nuclear Forces, 2002 (NRDC Nuclear Notebook)', *Bulletin of the Atomic Scientists*, May–June 2002, p. 74.

20 Handler, 'PNIs and TNW Elimination, Storage and Security', p. 25.

21 Robert Norris and Hans Kristensen, 'U.S. Nuclear Forces, 2007 (NRDC Nuclear Notebook)', *Bulletin of the Atomic Scientists*, January–February 2007, p. 82.

22 See 'Submarine Force U.S. Pacific Fleet' at http://www.csp.navy.mil/content/comsubpac_subsquadrons.shtml.

23 Norris et al., 'U.S. Nuclear Forces, 2002', p. 74.

24 Robert Norris and Hans Kristensen, 'U.S. Nuclear Forces, 2004 (NRDC Nuclear Notebook)' *Bulletin of the Atomic Scientists*, May–June 2004, p. 70.

several times been directed by the Secretary of Defense to maintain the TLAM-N program until a follow-on capability is developed, the Navy has failed to take the actions necessary to implement this decision. The matter was considered by the Deputy's Advisory Working Group (DAWG), with a decision deferred to the next administration. The situation requires Secretary of Defense involvement to monitor implementation of the decision.'[25] It went on: 'Policy documents and a memo by the Secretary of Defense directed that the Navy should maintain the system until a follow-on program is developed. However, as viewed by the Navy, USSTRATCOM, and the Joint Staff, there is no specific military capability or gap identified that the TLAM-N would satisfy. To date, no follow on program of record has been established and no funding has been programmed for long-term sustainment of this system.'[26]

The report estimates that the missile's service life will end in 2013 and said that a decision on developing a replacement was deferred to the next administration. A third Nuclear Posture Review will take place at the end of 2009. It is likely that the 2009 NPR will recommend the TLAM-N be removed from service as President Obama seeks to reduce the US nuclear stockpile.

RELEVANCE FOR THE UK

There are important differences between the use of the TLAM-N in the US, which has a large sophisticated ballistic nuclear missile defence, and the UK deploying a TLAM-N equivalent as its sole deterrent. It would mean reconceptualizing the UK's prevailing understanding of deterrence and its core concepts of survivability and assured retaliation at short notice. Nevertheless, the TLAM-N operation in the United States demonstrates the practicability of such an operational posture were the UK minded to deploy a minimum nuclear deterrent of this type.

In early 2009 Michael Quinlan published *Thinking about Nuclear Weapons*.[27] He argues that 'the most explicit conceptual account of what it was thought during the cold war that the UK nuclear strategic nuclear force should be able to do is to be found in Defence Open Government Document 80/23 of July 1980'.[28] For ease of reference, I include the relevant quotation below from the Open Government Document:

25 'Report of the Secretary of Defense Task Force on DoD Nuclear Weapons Management', Phase II: Review of the DOD Nuclear Mission, December 2008, p. viii.

26 Ibid., p. 25.

27 Michael Quinlan, *Thinking about Nuclear Weapons: Principles, Problems, Prospects* (Oxford: Oxford University Press, 2009).

28 Ibid., p. 124.

The 'Second-Centre' Role

9. If Britain is to meet effectively the deterrent purpose of providing a second centre of decision-making within the Alliance, our force has to be visibly capable of posing a massive threat on its own. A force which could strike tellingly only if the United States also did so – which plainly relied, for example, on US assent to its use, or on attenuation or distraction of Soviet defences by United States forces – would not achieve the purpose. We need to convince Soviet leaders that even if they thought that at some critical point as a conflict developed the US would hold back, the British force could still inflict a blow so destructive that the penalty for aggression would have proved too high.

10. There is no way of calculating exactly how much destruction in prospect would suffice to deter. Clearly Britain need not have as much power as the United States. Overwhelming Britain would be a much smaller prize than overwhelming the United States, and a smaller prospective penalty could therefore suffice to tilt this assessment against starting aggression that would risk incurring the penalty. Indeed, one practical approach to judging how much deterrent power Britain needs is to consider what type and scale of carnage Soviet leaders might think likely to leave them critically handicapped afterwards in continuing confrontation with a relatively unscathed United States.

11. The Soviet Union is a very large and powerful state, which has in the past demonstrated great national resilience and resolve. Its history, outlook, political doctrines, and planning all suggest that its view of how much destruction would constitute intolerable disaster might differ widely from that of most NATO countries. Appalling though any nuclear strike would be, the Government does not believe that our deterrent aim would be adequately met by a capability which offered only a low likelihood of striking home to key targets: or which posed the prospect of only a very small number of strikes, or which Soviet leaders could expect to ward off successfully from large areas of key importance to them. They might even be tempted to judge that if an opponent equipped himself with a force which had only a modest chance of inflicting intolerable damage there might be only a modest chance that he would have the resolve to use it at all.

12. Successive United Kingdom Governments have always declined to make public their nuclear targeting policy and plans, or to define precisely what minimum level of destructive capability they judged necessary for deterrence. The Government however thinks it right now to make clear that its concept of deterrence is concerned essentially with posing a potential threat to key aspects of Soviet state power. There ought with changing conditions to be more than one way of doing this and some flexibility or contingency planning is appropriate. It would not be helpful to deterrence to define particular actions further. The Government however regards the considerations noted in paragraphs 10 and 11 above as important factors in deciding the scale or capability we need.

Quinlan goes on to emphasize that in paragraph 12 the phrase 'threat to key aspects of Soviet state power' was of particular significance, though public commentary mostly did not pick this up. It was designed to emphasize a shift in British targeting priorities away from counter-value targeting (cities) to counter-force targeting (military). He was the key writer of this document so he writes with authority when he asserts that 'the language was deliberately chosen – partly with ethical concerns in mind – to convey that while cities would not be guaranteed immunity, the UK approach to deterrent threat and operational planning in the Trident era would not rest on crude counter-city or counter-population concepts.'[29]

COUNTER-FORCE/COUNTER-VALUE

The questions that arise 20 years after the fall of the Berlin Wall and the end of the Soviet Empire, along with the ideological collapse of Soviet communism, is whether these concepts from 1980 still apply. Quinlan argues that this language sought to avoid the false exclusivity of a targeting strategy whereby a head of government authorizing a nuclear attack had to choose simply between the destruction of cities and the neutralization of the adversary's power to retaliate. But it is clear that Quinlan, from an earlier comment in his book on targeting, was not just arguing to keep open targeting options, but had convinced not only himself but British governments after 1979 that not to go with the trend 'in the West during the later years of the cold war away from counter-population targeting would be of low credibility, of little political acceptability, either internationally or domestically, and ethically intolerable.'[30] This is not the language of someone who wants to keep open the options on targeting, but the language of someone using emotive words such as 'ethical', 'brutal' and 'crude' to disparage any targeting strategy other than that which reduces the adversary's power to retaliate. It comes too close for my liking to a nuclear war fighting strategy. Some argue that this strategy is appropriate for a large country and the most powerful nation in the world, the USA. It is a strategy which launches, on first detection of incoming missiles, outgoing missiles with nuclear warheads aimed at the missile launcher sites and radars of the country that has made the first strike. For a small country like the UK, which cannot survive, in any true sense of the word, even one nuclear hit, the vital need in deterring a first strike is to let any adversary know from the outset that they will pay a massive retaliatory price following any first strike. The UK, therefore, wanted for some years to have the ability to hit Moscow – not just its ABM defences, but also its population. Quinlan is telling us that UK strategy shifted in July 1980

29 Ibid., p. 126.
30 Ibid., p. 107.

to 'counter force targets', in effect military targets. That is a fundamental change in strategy and one which was not even contemplated a year before under James Callaghan's government. Nor was it recommended in the Duff–Mason Report.

Sadly, Michael Quinlan died in February 2009 and so cannot personally continue the debate on targeting strategy which his book was written in part to provoke. But that debate must now be held in the context of defining a minimum nuclear deterrent for the UK in the twenty-first century. This is a very different question from that of what would constitute a minimum nuclear deterrent strategy for the USA in the twenty-first century and also a very different question, I would suggest, from that of what was required 30 years ago by the UK facing the Soviet Union.

Those who knew and worked with Michael Quinlan do not question that over the years he became increasingly uncomfortable with the notion of a deterrence posture based on the ability to hit population centres. He questioned both the moral justifiability and the domestic political acceptability of such a strategy and hankered therefore after an alternative targeting policy. The problem, however, is that his preferred targeting policy is also, surely, of doubtful moral superiority. It amounts to the proposition that it is wrong to threaten to kill large numbers of civilians by attacking cities; but acceptable to threaten to kill slightly less large, but still massive, numbers as the by-product of attacks on military targets. For a small country it also demands a very sophisticated and expensive deterrent, in order to avoid population centres and target military installations. Such a strategy of nuclear war-fighting, I believe, is wholly inappropriate for a small deterrent force like that of the United Kingdom.

But there is perhaps another moral dimension to the issue of targeting criteria. The phrase 'key aspects of Soviet state power' used in the 1980 document was shorthand for the ability to hit Moscow and thus to put at risk the capacity of the Soviet state to function, including – depending on the thickness of the concrete of their underground bunkers or their dispersal arrangements – the chances of survival of its leadership. If one is to use the word 'moral' in relation to targeting policy (a usage about which I have considerable reservations), it can perhaps be argued that those who made the decision to attack should be targeted; but that, almost by definition, requires more than a minimum deterrent.

PAST UK TARGETING POLICY

In a paper titled 'Minimum Deterrence: A Force Posture for the Twenty-First Century',[31] Kristan Stoddart writes:

> British V-bomber targets under NATO's General Strike Programme were counter-force targets. These included major city ports on Russia's Arctic coast such as Murmansk and Archangel. For operations from Cyprus 'Targets were Batumi, Tbilisi, Baku and Yerevan. These were probably UK counter-value targets. Less to our liking were targets like Mary, Bukhara, Samarqand and Dushanbe'.[32] Despite clear strategic distinctions made publicly by British and American governments, and by NATO, regarding the delineations between counter-force and counter-value targets it would have made little practical difference to the outcome. This is clear from plans for a V-force attack on Kiev. The target in Kiev was its military headquarters under SACEUR's counter-force Nuclear Strike Plan. Those headquarters lay in the city centre. This would have left large-scale, indiscriminate civilian casualties. The UK National Retaliatory War Plan sent crews to very similar targets on very similar routes and although the NATO/Single Integrated Operational Plan (SIOP) target set was perhaps more counter-force-based, the targets set were often in or around counter-value areas. They were the targets deemed essential in prosecuting a military victory or at least averting military defeat. However, as one British official suggested:

> > In trying to decide what size of stockpile is necessary, we are in an area where there are few possibilities for quantification, and where almost every decision must rest on judgement exercised against a background of zero experience. The numbers now deployed in NATO stem from a form of quantification which has its basis in the 'military use' theory which should have been modified in the light of NPG studies. It fusses me a good deal that the NPG has been cracking on for many years, that it has published the latest available authorised version of the creed of nuclear theology, that these tablets have been blessed at the highest levels and received the DPC seal of approval, and yet everything goes on exactly as before. If the NPG studies mean anything, they mean that much of the conventional wisdom which has led to existing stockpiles should be discarded.[33]

This argument still has modern relevance. Military targets remain close to urban areas. The vast majority of military bases are served by nearby urban centres. Examples of this include U.S. Strategic Command (Omaha),

31 Published for the Project on Nuclear Issues (PONI), Center of Strategic and International Studies, Washington, DC, 2009.
32 Quoted in Kristan Stoddart, *Losing an Empire and Finding a Role* (Palgrave, forthcoming), chapter 4.
33 The National Archives, Kew, UK. Henceforward TNA. TNA, FCO 41/1649, Dr I. J. Shaw ACSA(S) to AD of DP(B), Group Captain Ashford, 6 January 1975.

Fort Carson (Colorado Springs), Point Loma (San Diego), Severomorsk (Murmansk), Rybachiy (Petropavlovsk) and Kuntsevo (Moscow). ICBM bases tend to be in more geographically remote areas but civilian population centres remain vulnerable to fall-out.

The numbers [of missiles] possessed by both the US and Russia would suggest that contingency plans are still available to also exclusively target high value military sites such as nuclear forces and C^3 assets (centres of command, control and communications).

However, even precision attacks on such targets cannot be discriminatory and prevent major collateral damage upon (often very large) urban centres. This is particularly the case with strategic thermonuclear weapons. Whether explicitly counter-force or counter-value these are nuclear war-fighting options. Even with significantly lower numbers of warheads and delivery systems mutual vulnerability will not change and these notions should be open to much greater political scrutiny.

For the UK, I argue that a targeting strategy should combine counter-force and counter-value, as we did in targeting Moscow, but it should not drop counter-value, as it appears to have done. The UK has to deter any first strike and that means making the leader of any country that might threaten the UK with nuclear weapons question whether Britain as a target is worth taking out if there is a high price to be paid in terms of its own population. Capital cities might be well safeguarded, but even the most ruthless politicians want to stay in power and this is difficult if large numbers of the people they rule have been killed. Given the relatively small gains from hitting the UK with nuclear weapons, in terms of strategic balance they have to believe that it is not worth even contemplating since there is a very high chance of millions of their people in large cities, not necessarily their capital, being killed after launching an attack. Of course such a counter-value strategy is best supported by a sophisticated ballistic nuclear-tipped missile fired from dedicated submarines. For the US that system is both necessary and can be sustained without losing other defence capabilities. The UK cannot afford to do the same.

A UK counter-value strategy can, however, be credibly threatened by nuclear warheads deployed on SLCMs if the UK decides to step back from replacing the Trident submarines. Watching on TV the initial bombardment of Iraq in 1991 and seeing cruise missiles follow the street map of Baghdad and deliver their conventional warheads onto military buildings in streets with civilian houses, leaving the latter intact, gave no indication that this was a crude delivery system. Cruise missiles are undoubtedly more vulnerable to interception than ballistic missiles and carry a smaller payload, but their precision, proven at subsonic speeds, enables them to hit many cities within range for decades ahead. If the US develops a supersonic/hypersonic cruise missile capability these missiles will have a much improved chance of not being shot down. No existing defence against cruise missiles could be trusted to stop all, or even many, incoming missiles.

FUTURE UK TARGETING POLICY

The White Paper of December 2006 judges that 'no state currently has both the intent and the capability to pose a direct nuclear threat to the United Kingdom or its vital interests'. But it offers three generic future scenarios in which the possession by Britain of a nuclear deterrent force would be relevant. These are the risk that 'a major direct nuclear threat to the UK's vital interests will re-emerge'; the risk that 'new states will emerge that possess a more limited nuclear capability'; and the risk that 'some countries might in future seek to sponsor terrorism from their soil'.

The word 're-emergence' can probably be interpreted as pointing towards the Russian Federation. But this is not explicitly acknowledged; and there is no attempt to analyse in relation to specific targets the level of capability which would be needed for a British national deterrent to be credible. All that is said is that the force needs to be invulnerable to pre-emption; that its range should be 'anywhere in the world'; and that the judgement of the minimum destructive capability necessary requires 'an assessment of the decision-making processes of future potential aggressors and an analysis of the effectiveness of the defensive measures that they might employ'.

The White Paper does not address the question of what sort of targets the deterrent force needs to be able to hit and where. This may be the explanation as to why the present government has refused to abide by the normal practice of releasing after 30 years documents like the Duff–Mason Report, and why it has so heavily redacted the commentary on that paper for the Chiefs of Staff Committee that had already been published. To publish those papers would raise fundamental questions which the present government appears to want to exclude from public debate and may never have debated collectively.

The 2006 White Paper lists 'five enduring principles', of which the third is '[a] continuing policy of strategic ambiguity regarding potential employment including the potential for first use'. In a speech the then Defence Secretary said that the British government 'would only consider using nuclear weapons in the most extreme situations of self defence'.[34] This is legal wording covering the United Kingdom in terms of international law. Part of

34 Des Browne MP, King's College London, 25 January 2007.

the deterrent is committed to NATO through SACEUR. Interestingly, in the late 1970s the UK contribution to NATO's nuclear strategy did not require a specific UK capability for major strikes against cities or reinforced missile silos, so in NATO terms there was then no need to be able to penetrate ABM defences. I doubt, but have no specific knowledge, if that has changed. The present Labour government has, to its credit, had a more open debate on the deterrent than its Labour predecessors. It is doubtful, however, to say the least that many Labour MPs in 2006 had any idea that they were endorsing first use. Indeed it is a very difficult concept to justify, particularly now that the Russian Federation no longer has a conventional army of the size or power that it had in the 1970s and would not be able to punch a hole in NATO defences in the way that was feared possible right up until the fall of the Berlin Wall in 1989.

CRUISE MISSILE TARGETING: PAST AND FUTURE[35]

Cruise missile operations

The current generation of Tomahawk US cruise missiles (Tomahawk Land Attack Missile – TLAM) have a maximum range of between 1,250 and 2,500 km from a sea-based platform (see Table 1) and have been used in a wide range of conflicts for the past fifteen years (see Table 2). They are subsonic with a maximum speed of 550mph (0.98 mach), which means that at their maximum range they can take between two and three hours to reach their target. Vessels carrying cruise missiles need to be within range of potential targets in order to conduct operations. As a result of these limitations the US Navy (and other states[36]) have looked to examine the possibility of extending the range and speed of next-generation cruise missiles. This would reduce the time-to-target as well as increasing the operating range of the platform, which decreases its vulnerability by providing greater sea-room in which to operate, thereby reducing the risk of interdiction of the vessel.

US cruise missile use

The Block III version, which entered service in 1993, added a capability for more precise satellite navigation than through the TERCOM (TErrain COntour Matching) guidance system alone by use of the US Global

---

35 I am indebted to Kristan Stoddart, whom I commissioned to provide me with the factual information in this section.

36 Information on cruise missiles from other states can be found in Andrew Feickert, 'Cruise Missile Proliferation', *CRS Report for Congress*, 28 July 2005. Available from http://fas.org/sgp/crs/nuke/RS21252.pdf, retrieved 27 April 2009.

Table 1: Current US Cruise missiles

	Range	Guidance system
Block II TLAM-A	1,350 nautical miles (1,500 statute miles, 2,500 km)	INS, TERCOM
Block III TLAM-C	900 nautical miles (1,000 statute miles, 1,600 km)	INS, TERCOM, DSMAC, and GPS
Block III TLAM-D	700 nautical miles (800 statute miles, 1,250 km)	INS, TERCOM, DSMAC, and GPS
Block IV TLAM-E	900 nautical miles (1,000 statute miles, 1,600 km)	INS, TERCOM, DSMAC, and GPS

Source: http://www.navy.mil/navydata/fact_display.asp?cid=2200&tid= 1300&ct=2

Positioning System (GPS). It also had an improved time-to-target and contained an improved warhead, but, according to the US Navy's Fact Sheet, had a reduced range of 1,600 km (1,000 statute miles). Although reduced range would have been a negative side effect, US theatre commanders preferred the Block III version to the older and less accurate Block II. For example, the new version resolved problems occurring from poor TERCOM fixes in flat or unremarkable terrain, characteristic of major Middle Eastern, shore and seaborne environments. As a consequence the Navy testified to the Senate Armed Services Committee in March 1999 that of TLAMs used in recent military operations, about 90 per cent had been the Block III variant.[37]

Operations against Iraq, 1991–2003

During the 1991 Gulf War cruise missiles were used extensively to attack Iraqi air defence facilities, their command, control and communications infrastructure and electrical power grid in Operation Desert Storm. Tomahawks and Conventional Air-Launched Cruise Missiles (CALCMs) fired from submarines and surface ships were targeted against heavily defended targets deep in Iraq without putting aircraft and pilots in danger. Most were fired early on in Desert Storm. According to their own figures the United States Navy launched a total of 297 Tomahawks with 288 reaching their target, demonstrating a 95 per cent success rate.[38] As Anthony H. Cordesman of the Center for Strategic and International Studies indicates, 'Many of our strategic cruise missile strikes and air sorties had considerable tactical success, particularly in striking major fixed command and control facilities,

---

37 Ronald O'Rourke, 'Cruise Missile Inventories and NATO Attacks on Yugoslavia: Background Information', *Congressional Research Service*, 20 April 1999.

38 http://www.fas.org/man/dod-101/sys/smart/bgm-109.htm, retrieved 27 April 2009.

Table 2: Numbers of CALCMs and TLAMs fired in combat, 1991–present

Date	Operation name	Location of targets	Number of missiles fired	
			CALCM	TLAM
Jan.–Feb. 1991	Desert Storm	Iraq	35	288
17 Jan. 1993	Southern Watch	Iraq	0	45
26 June 1993	Bushwhacker	Iraq	0	23
10 Sep. 1995	Deliberate Force	Bosnia	0	13
3–4 Sept. 1996	Desert Strike	Iraq	13	31
20 Aug. 1998	Resolute Response	Afghanistan, Sudan	0	79
17–20 Dec. 1998	Desert Fox	Iraq	~90	~325
24 Mar.–16 Apr. 1999*	Allied Force	Yugoslavia	~60?	~150?
7 Mar. 2002	Enduring Freedom	Afghanistan	0	50
20 Mar.–1 May 2003	Iraqi Freedom	Iraq		1,600 (800 from sea)**

Original source: Ronald O'Rourke, Cruise Missile Inventories and NATO Attacks on Yugoslavia: Background Information, *Congressional Research Service* (20 April 1999). Amendments made to take into account operations after 1999.

Sources:
Operations prior to Resolute Response. For CALCM: Information supplied to CRS by US Air Force Office of Legislative Affairs, 2 April 1999. For TLAM: US Congress House Committee on National Security. Hearings on National Defense Authorization Act for Fiscal Year 1999 ‹ H.R. 3616, and Oversight of Previously Authorized Programs. 105 Cong., the 2 Sess., Title I ‹ Procurement [and] Title II ‹ Research, Development, Test and Evaluation, and Hearings held February 26, March 4, 5, 10, April 1, and June 11, 1998, Washington, 1999, p. 263. *Resolute Response and subsequent operations*: newspaper and trade press reports.
* Operation Allied Force was still ongoing as of 16 April 1999 at the time the report was written; data presented are estimated numbers fired up to 16 April 1999.
** Estimated by Kristan Stoddart from http://www.airforce-magazine.com/Magazine-Archive/Pages/2003/October%202003/1003strategic.aspx, retrieved 27 April 2009, and http://findarticles.com/p/articles/mi_m0IBQ/is_1041/ai_115694518/, retrieved 27 April 2009.

bridges and major road facilities, and POL facilities'.[39] They were navigated en route by their TERCOM guidance system, switching to optical DSMAC (Digital Scene Matching Area Correlator) to produce a high Circular Error Probability (CEP) in their terminal phase to target, which could be as little as three metres.

39 http://www.csis.org/media/csis/pubs/dflessons21599.pdf, p. 9, retrieved 26 April 2009.

MAPS SHOWING DIFFERENT FIRING ZONES

The generation of cruise missiles used in the Gulf War and in subsequent operations through to 1993 still had deficiencies when it came to targeting. They could only be used against fixed targets with the data uploaded to the missile prior to launch. As a result targets of opportunity could not be engaged. Fortunately, in the current (and future) strategic environment, these key factors for politico-military engagement have been largely resolved (see Kosovo campaign, p. 62).

However, determining the effectiveness of both Tomahawk and CALCMs is complicated by a number of factors. The aim points used by the United States Department of Defense (DOD) combined with a lack of timely battle damage evaluations during Desert Storm make it extremely difficult to determine their effectiveness. Target analysts were not able to obtain damage assessments for each aim point post-attack. This is because many targets were attacked more than once by both aircraft and cruise missiles, making it an arduous task to determine which attack originated the damage observed. Moreover, since numerous aim points were also targeted by multiple missiles, it complicated the task of determining how many weapons caused the consequent damage.[40]

The scientific community, particularly those involved in the nuclear effects industry, understood from the 1960s that '[pulsed] X-rays can produce such violent reactions within materials that they could turn out to be the most hazardous nuclear threat for missiles and satellites in space', effects such as a violent '"boiling" within a material' exploding 'from the inside, throwing off high-velocity fragments'.[41] Over 75 per cent of a nuclear explosion comes in the form of thermal radiation, with a large proportion in the form of X-rays:

> the range at which a nuclear weapon can produce these destructive thermal effects within a missile varies according to the altitude at which it is exploded. At lower altitudes the soft X-rays [...] are absorbed by the surrounding atmosphere [...] at altitudes above 90 mi. there is no longer enough atmosphere to absorb the X-rays. They spread their energy over thousands of miles [...] reducing the severity of the anti-missile guidance problem. [However, the exact] range at which the X-ray effect is damaging depends on the yield of the device and how energy is partitioned.[42]

---

40 http://www.tpub.com/content/cg1995/ns95116/ns951160026.htm, retrieved 20 April 2009.
41 Rex Pay, 'New Effort Aimed at X-Ray Protection', *Technology Week*, 2 January 1967. The issue of ABMs is discussed at length in many of the industry journals such as this, as well as in the newspapers of the time.
42 Ibid.

Map 1: Approximate firing areas of Block II TLAM-A cruise missiles fired at Baghdad during the 1991 Gulf War and 2003 invasion from the Red Sea and Persian Gulf

The arc demonstrated in Map 1 falls within the range of the Block II TLAM-A (2,500 km or 1,350 nm), with the furthest point of the arc at 1,136 nm. Most were fired from ,the Red Sea or the Persian Gulf. As Map 1 illustrates, the maximum spread of the arc falls within the range of the older version of the Tomahawk cruise missile. The firing arc of the newer, more accurate, Block III TLAM-C (Map 2) is much more limited.

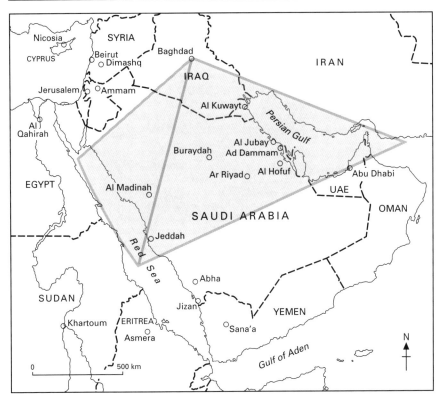

Map 2: Firing arc of TLAM-C Block III cruise missiles fired at Iraq during the 1991 Gulf War and 2003 invasion

Cruise missiles were also fired from the Mediterranean Sea during Desert Storm, while it appears that attacks in 2003 were from air-launched cruise missiles flying from aircraft carriers stationed in the Mediterranean (Maps 3 and 4).[1] However, there is very little public information (or none that is easily accessible despite extensive searches in the public and academic literature) regarding either the precise firing position of the naval vessels that launched cruise missiles or the exact targets they were aimed at in Iraq for the period 1991–2003.

1 http://www.sci.fi/~fta/cruise.htm, retrieved 30 April 2009, and http://www.pbs.org/newshour/updates/baghdad_03-20-03.html, retrieved 30 April 2009.

Map 3: Block II TLAM-A 2,500 km Baghdad target fired from the Mediterranean Sea

Map 4: Block III TLAM-C, 1,600 km Baghdad target fired from the Mediterranean Sea

Although this is more applicable to inter-continental ballistic missiles (ICBMs), the X-ray problem could potentially apply even to hypersonic cruise missiles, which could need to enter and exit the upper atmosphere to arrive at their target. Depending on their attack profile they could be vulnerable to a pre-emptive detonation, but given their speed and range the warning time would be so short that even an advanced nuclear weapons state such as Russia would have virtually no time to respond. Less mature nuclear weapons states, or non-nuclear weapons states, would have no defence.

On 17 January 1993, during Operation Southern Watch, US forces hit eight buildings at the Zafraniyah Nuclear Fabrication Facility, just outside Baghdad. Tomahawks were chosen for the strike because there was a need to avoid any potential loss of pilots or aircraft and collateral damage to non-military targets. US forces fired 46 Block II TLAM-C missiles, of which 42 (91 per cent) were launched successfully and transitioned to cruise flight. Although the vast majority of the missiles hit the target complex, one was allegedly hit by Iraqi anti-aircraft fire, leading it to crash into the Al Rasheed Hotel, where it killed two civilians with seven unaccounted for.[43]

In response to the Iraqi-sponsored assassination attempt on former President Bush during a visit to Kuwait in March 1993, the United States launched Operation Bushwacker on 27 June 1993. The US destroyer USS *Peterson* and the cruiser USS *Chancellorsville* launched a total of 23 Tomahawks at Mukhabarat, General Directorate of Iraqi Intelligence, again in Baghdad. Sixteen successfully hit their targets, with four landing elsewhere in the complex. Three went off-target and landed in urban areas, leading to the deaths of eight civilians.[44]

In Operation Desert Strike on 3 September 1996, the Iraqi air defence infrastructure was targeted through a coordinated attack with cruise missiles to enforce the no-fly zone over Southern Iraq. These included surface-to-air missile sites and command and control nodes. There were around 15 targets in the initial strike; however, doubts regarding the effectiveness of this attack led the United States to order a re-strike on four targets. In total, 44 cruise missiles, 13 CALCMs and 31 TLAMs were fired. Of the TLAMs, some were fired from the *Laboon* and *Shiloh* while Air Force B-52s, escorted by F-14s, fired the remainder. The following day, a second strike of Tomahawks from the destroyers *Russell*, *Hewitt*, *Laboon* and the SSN *Jefferson City* was launched. However, the precise targets do not appear

---

43 http://www.globalsecurity.org/military/ops/strike_930117.htm, retrieved 24 April 2009.
44 Reuben E. Brigety, *Ethics, Technology and the American Way of War* (London: Routledge, 2007), p. 92. This book contains much valuable information on cruise missile history.

to be accessible in the public domain, making it difficult to assess the ranges from which they were launched. Assessments of their effectiveness are also very difficult to make.[45]

In Operation Desert Fox, conducted between 17 and 20 December 1998, 325 TLAMs were fired (and 90 CALCMs), with the TLAMs scoring an 85 per cent success rate.[46] Targets included the headquarters of the Ba'ath Party in Baghdad and targets in Basra as well as a large number of the regime's secret police and Republican Guard forces, airfields and air defence sites across Southern Iraq (Maps 1–4).[47] The ranges of the Block II and III versions of the TLAM can be contrasted by means of these maps.

The 2003 invasion, codenamed Operation Iraqi Freedom, saw a total of 35 ships, both surface vessels and submarines, of the US Navy fire Tomahawks into Iraq against high-value military targets.[48] According to official figures released by the US Navy there were more than 800 cruise missiles fired from ships and around 700 aircraft strikes across Iraq, which targeted command and control, communications, and Republican Guard headquarters and facilities.[49]

Former Yugoslavia

During 1995 13 Tomahawk cruise missiles were launched from the USS *Normandy* against surface-to-air missile systems around Banja Luka in Bosnia-Herzegovina as part of NATO's Operation Deliberate Force against Bosnian Serbs.[50] Whether Block II or III versions were fired is unknown, but as they were fired from the Adriatic Sea (Map 5) this fell well within the range of both versions. The *New York Times* reported that the launch from the *Normandy* was only 220 miles from Banja Luka.[51]

In total 238 Block III Tomahawks were fired during the NATO campaign Operation Allied Force in Kosovo in 1999, with 198 successful hits according to official published US and British reports. Surface ships and submarines

45 http://www.defenselink.mil/transcripts/transcript.aspx?transcriptid=678, retrieved 24 April 2009, and http://www.globalsecurity.org/military/ops/desert_strike.htm, retrieved 24 April 2009.
46 http://www.csis.org/media/csis/pubs/dfairdefwar.pdf, retrieved 26 April 2009.
47 http://news.bbc.co.uk/1/shared/spl/hi/middle_east/02/iraq_events/html/desert_fox.stm, retrieved 26 April 2009.
48 Nicholas D. Evans, *Military Gadgets: How Advanced Technology is Transforming Today's Battlefield and Tomorrow's* (New Jersey: FT Press, 2003), p. 108.
49 http://www.airforce-magazine.com/MagazineArchive/Pages/2003/October%20 2003/1003strategic.aspx, retrieved 27 April 2009, and http://findarticles.com/p/articles/mi_m0IBQ/is_1041/ai_115694518/, retrieved 27 April 2009.
50 http://edition.cnn.com/WORLD/Bosnia/updates/sep95/9-10/pm/index.html, retrieved 24 April 2009.
51 http://www.nytimes.com/1995/09/11/world/nato-shifts-focus-of-its-air-attacks-on-bosnian-serbs.html, retrieved 24 April 2009.

from the United States Navy launched 218 TLAMs at 66 targets. One hundred and eighty-one of these hit their intended targets. The Royal Navy's submarine HMS *Splendid*, the first British submarine to be equipped with TLAMs, launched 20 missiles with 17 hitting their aim points – a strike rate of 85 per cent.[52]

The accuracy of the attacks in the 1999 Kosovo campaign is worthy of note. Eight TLAMs were targeted on the multiple-floor headquarters of the Socialist Party and state-run television headquarters in Belgrade. Targeting staff were able to assess the probable location in the building of systems which controlled the sprinklers and alarms in order to maximize the damage. The missiles were then programmed to hit exact aim points – with missiles fired into the sixth floor and through the roof – so that any fire would spread. The attack upon the Yugoslav Interior Ministry Police (MUP) headquarters in Pristina used aim points on the same floor because intelligence sources believed it was the location of senior MUP officials and police intelligence offices.[53] The targeting of the Chinese embassy in Belgrade is discussed in the Introduction (pp. 14–15).

The firing areas are known to have been in the Adriatic Sea but their precise location is classified. However, these were well within the maximum range of both the Block II TLAM-A and the Block III Tomahawks, both available at the time, used by both the US Navy and the Royal Navy during the campaign.

By the time of the Kosovo conflict in 1999 TLAMS were also able to be targeted against mobile targets, such as equipment and forces that can be moved quickly, but not targets on the move. By utilizing high-speed communications links to broadcast timely intelligence from 'sensors to shooters', 26 TLAMs were launched at 18 mobile targets, including 16 unitary and 10 sub-munition variants. US Navy accounts suggest that 10 ground-based aircraft and 14 radars were damaged or destroyed, with TLAMs accounting for almost 50 per cent of the total number of strikes on mobile air defence radars. This near real-time precision targeting was made possible by utilizing satellites from the US GPS through its ability to process and relay longitude and latitude coordinates as well as elevation and time.[54]

---

52 http://www.janes.com/defence/naval_forces/news/jdw/jdw000718_1_n.shtml, retrieved 20 April 2009.

53 http://www.janes.com/defence/naval_forces/news/jdw/jdw000718_1_n.shtml, retrieved 20 April 2009.

54 http://www.janes.com/defence/naval_forces/news/jdw/jdw000718_1_n.shtml, retrieved 20 April 2009.

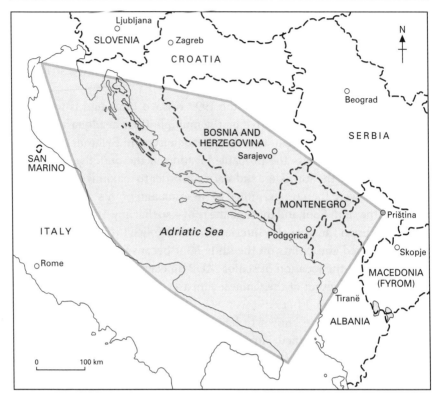

Map 5: Location of missile targets in Kosovo during the 1999 campaign and Bosnia during 1995

Resolute Response

Operation Resolute Response in 1998 was a direct result of the terrorist bombings of American embassies on 7 August 1998, led by al-Qaeda, in Nairobi, Kenya, and Dar es Salaam, Tanzania, which killed more than 250 people and injured 5,000. Terrorist training camps in eastern Afghanistan and a suspected chemical weapons factory in Khartoum, Sudan, were targeted by TLAMs on 20 August. As President Clinton put it, 'Our goals were to disrupt bin Laden's terrorist network and destroy elements of its infrastructure in Afghanistan and Sudan. And our goal was to destroy in Sudan the factory with which bin Laden's network is associated, which was producing an ingredient essential for nerve gas.'[55]

The arc in Map 9 represents the maximum range of the cruise missiles fired into eastern Afghanistan during the 2001 invasion. This covers a wide sea-area in which the submarines or surface vessels could operate. Targets

55 http://www.freerepublic.com/focus/f-news/930723/posts, retrieved 30 April 2009.

were struck in the cities of Kandahar, Kabul, Jalalabad and Herat, while other locations such as targets in Mazar-e-Sharif could also have been hit. The strikes involved 50 TLAMs launched from US and Royal Navy surface ships and submarines stationed in the Arabian Sea, plus 15 B-1 and B-2 stealth bombers flying out of the continental United States, B-52H bombers launched from Diego Garcia in the Indian Ocean and 25 US strike aircraft based on aircraft carriers. It is difficult to assess from the declassified literature precisely what forces were used for what targets.[56]

The United States currently operates four submarines designated as SSGNs (Ship Submersible Guided [Missile] Nuclear). These were previously SSBNs (Ship Submersible Ballistic Nuclear) converted to cruise missile use, primarily the Tomahawk, and for the covert deployment of Special Operations Forces (SOF), following the Strategic Arms Reduction Treaties (START I and II) of 1992–93.[57] SSNs (Ship Submersible Nuclear) can also carry cruise missiles and SOF but their mission profile is of a more general character.

HYPERSONIC TECHNOLOGY

The term 'hypersonic' refers to speeds exceeding Mach 5, which can be achieved by two types of jet engine. The first is the ramjet, which works by utilizing the forward movement of the engine to help produce thrust. As speed increases the atmosphere in front of the platform (be it an aircraft or missile) is compressed, while the air behind is at lower pressure. The high pressure is used by the ramjet to force oxygen through its chambers where it is ignited with fuel, such as hydrocarbon, which is then passed through a nozzle to produce thrust from the exhaust. Drag is (by its nature) a limiting factor but at speeds above Mach 2–3 the ramjet is self-sustaining. Ramjets can be either liquid- or solid-fuelled, with the choice being dictated by the platform requirements. The platform, and the requirements of the ramjet, are optimized by designing them for a specific altitude and speed. However, at speeds above Mach 6 current ramjets suffer a degradation of performance as the airflow is decelerated to subsonic speeds to allow for combustion which in turn produces heating which needs to be dissipated. This sets an upper performance limit.

The second type is a scramjet. Scramjets (supersonic combustion ramjets) work in a similar way to conventional ramjets but use supersonic combustion to fully exploit the efficiency of the combustion process. In common

---

56 http://www.janes.com/security/international_security/news/jdw/jdw011007_1_n.shtml, retrieved 27 April 2009.

57 START I is due for renewal or replacement by December 2009. Russia withdrew from START II in 2002, a day after the United States withdrew from the 1972 ABM Treaty.

with conventional ramjets they have either no moving parts or only a small number, with no fast-moving turbine. This reduces the internal heating problem of conventional ramjets. The oxygen required by the engine to combust flows from the atmosphere passing through the vehicle, instead of from internal fuel supplies. This reduces weight and as a result the craft can be made smaller, lighter and faster and can be defined as an 'air-breathing' engine. Air-breathing vehicles rely on aerodynamic forces rather than on pure rocket thrust and as a result have greater manoeuvrability.

There have already been several demonstrations of scramjet technology providing a 'proof of concept'. On 16 August 2002, the University of Queensland completed the first successful flight of a scramjet vehicle. Meanwhile between March and November 2004 NASA's Hyper-X programme produced a 12-foot-long scramjet-powered research vehicle, X-43A[58] – flown aboard modified Pegasus rockets dropped by a B-52 aircraft. It was launched to an altitude of over 90,000 feet, where the X-43A was released and where it flew under its own power to Mach 9.6. NASA believes this technology could be developed for speeds of up to Mach 15. As the fact sheet for the Hyper-X programme states:

> The eight-year, approximately $230 million NASA Hyper-X program was a high-risk, high-payoff research program. It undertook challenges never before attempted. No vehicle powered by an air-breathing engine had ever flown at hypersonic speeds before the successful March 2004 flight. In addition, the rocket boost and subsequent separation from the rocket to get to the scramjet test condition had complex elements that had to work properly for mission success. Careful analyses and design were applied to reduce risks to acceptable levels; even so, some level of residual risk was inherent to the program.
>
> Hyper-X research began with conceptual design and wind tunnel work in 1996. Three unpiloted X-43A research aircraft were built. Each of the 12-foot-long, 5-foot-wide lifting body vehicles was designed to fly once and not be recovered. They are identical in appearance, but engineered with slight differences that simulate variable engine geometry, generally a function of Mach number. The first and second vehicles were designed to fly at Mach 7 and the third at Mach 10. At these speeds, the shape of the vehicle forebody served the same purpose as pistons in a car, compressing the air as fuel is injected for combustion. Gaseous hydrogen fueled the X-43A.[59]

Scramjet technology has applications beyond NASA's space programmes. It has military applications in terms of aircraft development as well as next-

---

58 Detailed information on the X-43A can be found at http://www.globalsecurity.org/space/systems/x-43.htm, retrieved 22 April 2009.
59 http://www.nasa.gov/centers/dryden/news/FactSheets/FS-040-DFRC.html, retrieved 21 April 2009.

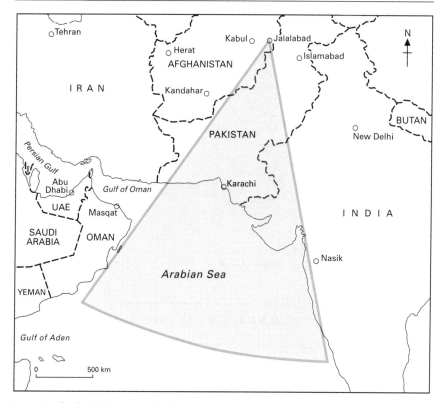

Map 6: Block II TLAM-A (2,500 km) 1998 attacks against Afghanistan

generation cruise missiles. One such programme is the X-51A WaveRider, developed by Boeing. This can fly five times faster than the Tomahawk on current specifications. If launched from the Arabian Sea it would take only twenty minutes to reach eastern Afghanistan. It is currently being designed only to carry out conventional missions and it is not known whether the vehicle can be engineered to house a nuclear warhead. However, given that the current generation of cruise missiles are dual-capable (i.e. capable of both a conventional and a nuclear role) it is reasonable to suggest that it will be possible to modify the X-51A to carry a nuclear warhead. The customers are the US Air Force Research Laboratory (AFRL) and the Defense Advanced Research Projects Agency (DARPA), with support from NASA and Pratt & Whitney Rocketdyne.

A press release by Boeing in June 2007 stated:

> During the successful firing of the Pratt & Whitney X-1 demonstrator engine, test engineers used a Full Authority Digital Engine Controller to simulate flight conditions at Mach 5 air speed. Test of the hydrocarbon-fueled scramjet engine also demonstrated a closed-loop thermal management system that

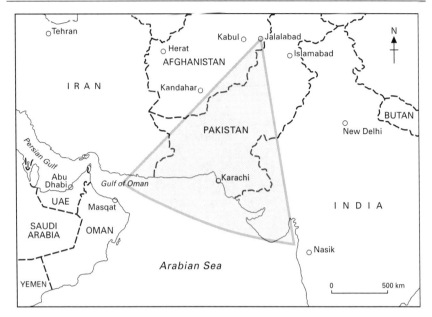

Map 7: Block III TLAM-C (1,600 km) 1998 attacks in Afghanistan

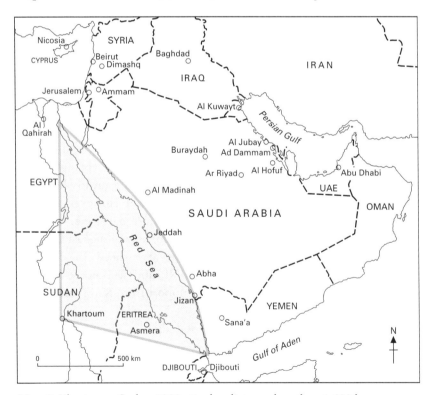

Map 8: Khartoum, Sudan 1998 attacks, distance less than 1,600 km

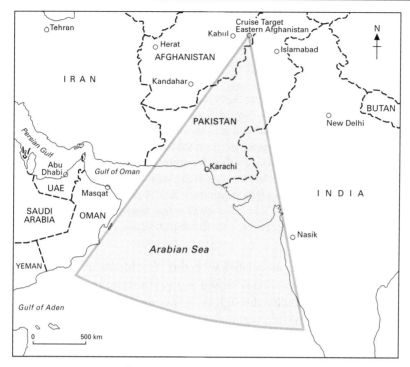

Map 9: Approximate firing areas of TLAM-A Block II cruise missiles fired at Afghanistan during the 2001 invasion

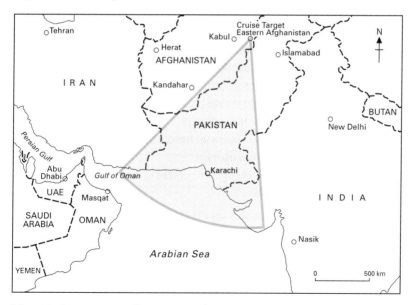

Map 10: Approximate firing areas of TLAM-C Block III cruise missiles fired at Afghanistan during the 2001 invasion

cools engine hardware and regulates fuel for the engine's combustor. The X-1 is the first of two ground test engines proposed for the program.

The successful completion of the CDR and X-1 ground demonstration indicates that the X-51A program is on track to proceed with its first flight tests in 2009.

'The CDR and engine test are key validation points for the X-51A program,' said George Muellner, president of Boeing Advanced Systems. 'The X-51A is a remarkable system that will answer many questions necessary for the development of future hypersonic propulsion vehicles that can be used for delivering payloads to space as well as for atmospheric flight applications.'

'These successes are critical for the development of the X-51A,' said Charlie Brink, U.S. Air Force Research Laboratory X-51A program manager. 'It also marks the first time that a scramjet engine was tested in its simulated "full flight" propulsion configuration – the Boeing-designed full vehicle fore-body inlet and nozzle.'[60]

There are problems associated with this should the nuclear option be considered. The X-51 is being designed to meet the requirements for Prompt Global Strike – the ability through real-time intelligence to be able to hit anywhere on the globe. It is estimated it might take ten years to develop the WaveRider into a deployable system.[61] In the altered security environment following 9/11, and given the increasing requirement to strike hard and sure against fleeting terrorist targets, the need for a range of options beyond the current range of systems is clear. However, fitting a nuclear warhead to the X-51 would raise a series of political and strategic questions should Britain seek to examine this particular option as a nuclear delivery system.

Would the United States be prepared to sanction the sale of such a system or allow Britain to participate in the development programme? I cannot imagine circumstances in which the US would say no, particularly since the initiative to purchase would be seen in the context of a significant step towards a nuclear-free world and the abandonment of plans to build a follow-on submarine-launched ballistic missile system to replace Trident in the middle of the twenty-first century.

In May 2002 Jane's, the respected defence and security information company, reported as follows:

> The USA, joined it hopes shortly by the UK, plans to begin a research and development programme to look at a new land-attack supersonic cruise missile that could help strike time-critical targets and ones buried underground. The programme, an advanced concept technology demonstration being sponsored by the US Defense Threat Reduction Agency and the US Navy, will explore

---

60 http://www.boeing.com/news/releases/2007/q2/070601a_nr.html, retrieved 22 April 2009.
61 http://www.popularmechanics.com/technology/military_law/4203874.html?page=3, retrieved 19 April 2009.

development of a cruise missile capable of carrying a 200 lb (90.7kg) payload at least 400nm and preferably 600nm. The missile would have a speed of M3.5 with a goal of M4.5 and a circular error of probability accuracy of 3m.[62]

Given that this report dates from 2002 it is possible, perhaps likely, that this research and development programme has evolved into the hypersonic programme already described.

In February 2007 Jane's reported that:

Lockheed Martin Missiles and Fire Control has broken cover on studies for a next generation very long range cruise missile for the USAF and US Navy. Lockheed Martin's concept is known as Cruise Missile Extended Range (Cruise Missile XR) and gives an indication where the thinking of US rivals – Raytheon and Boeing – may also be headed. The weapon will be a 5,000 lb (2,268 kg) class missile (incorporating a 2,000 lb warhead) with a range in excess of 1,000 n miles (1,852 km). It will be fully datalinked and capable of 'seekerless precision' (potentially combining enhanced GPS navigation with networked third-party targeting data). The warhead (ideally a multi-mode unit) will be effective against hardened buried targets with the potential to fit precision-guided submunitions if ever required.

What the US is seeking is a new cruise missile system with more or less the same reach as today's Tomahawk weapons, but with much increased accuracy and a significantly larger payload. The Cruise Missile XR has been designed for carriage by tactical fighters, large bombers or even submarines. Other similar designs will emerge from the shadows sooner or later as the US considers its long-range strike options for the 2015–2020 timeframe.[63]

Additional information from the journal *Aviation Week* from March 2009 makes this more explicit:

Unlike NASA's pioneering X-43A Hyper-X, which flew on gaseous hydrogen for a 10-sec. flight at Mach 9.6 in 2004, the X-51A is aimed at proving the longer-endurance, weapon-like capability of a hydrocarbon-fueled scramjet. Carrying around 270 lb. (45 gal.) of JP7 fuel, the 168-in.-long cruiser is expected to fly for approximately 300 sec. at full power until the fuel runs out. Optimized for a missile application, a modular version of the existing X-51A would travel around '600 mi. in 10 min. – well in excess of any conventional cruise missile,' says Charles Brink, AFRL X-51A program manager.[64]

AFRL, US Air Combat Command and Pacific Command are evaluating long-range strike weapon options through a project codenamed Trespass/

---

62 http://www.janes.com/defence/air_forces/news/jdw/jdw020507_1_n.shtml, retrieved 20 April 2009.

63 http://www.janes.com/defence/air_forces/news/jalw/jalw070219_1_n.shtml, retrieved 20 April 2009.

64 http://www.aviationweek.com/aw/generic/story_channel.jsp?channel=defense&id=news/ SCRAM033109.xml, retrieved 22 April 2009.

Trespals. The former is aimed explicitly at air-strike weapons, with the latter focused on a broader combination of air-, land- and sea-strike operations. Phase I of these studies, including other hypersonic projects such as the US Navy's HyFly and RATTLRS (Revolutionary Approach To Time-critical Long-Range Strike), is expected to be completed by the late summer of 2009. However, a decision on whether to pursue a scramjet-based joint concept technology demonstrator is likely be deferred until late 2010.[65]

Moreover, a March 2009 report in *Flight International* stated that the USAF has set a deadline of 27 October 2009 for the first flight test of the WaveRider, 'but there is already talk of expanding the rigidly controlled hypersonic test programme'.[66] There are already plans to increase the flight trials from four to six, partly to allow for a margin of error but also possibly to explore the use of the X-51A's GPS antenna for a demonstration of waypoint guidance in the terminal phase. This appears to have firm military implications but there are well-known risks in expanding the operational requirements of leading-edge technologies such as the WaveRider. Furthermore, at the moment the use of GPS is limited to speeds below Mach 10, at which point plasma formation around the platform makes communications difficult.[67] Follow-on flight tests are scheduled for 15 January 2010, mid-February and again in mid-March. There are also plans to fund an X-51B prototype.

There is evidence that the Russian Navy is exploring the options related to hypersonic cruise missiles.[68]

Highly relevant to any UK decision on future cruise missiles in a submarine platform is timing, a factor borne out by a Congressional Research Service Report from April 2008 which stated:

> Navy and industry officials, Members of Congress, and other observers are concerned that unless a major submarine-design project is begun soon, the submarine design and engineering base will begin to atrophy through the departure of experienced personnel. Rebuilding an atrophied submarine design and engineering base, Navy and industry officials believe, could be time-consuming, adding time and cost to the task of the next submarine-design effort, whenever it might begin. Concern about this possibility among some Navy and industry officials was strengthened by the UK's difficulties a few years ago in designing its new Astute class SSN. The UK submarine

65 http://www.aviationweek.com/aw/generic/story_channel.jsp?channel=defense&id=news/ SCRAM033109.xml, 22 April 2009.
66 http://www.flightglobal.com/articles/2009/03/26/324373/afrl-mulls-adding-scope-to-x-51a- waverider-hypersonic.html, retrieved 22 April 2009.
67 http://www.aviationweek.com/aw/generic/story_channel.jsp?channel=defense&id=news/ SCRAM033109.xml, retrieved 22 April 2009.
68 http://www.aviationweek.com/aw/generic/story_channel.jsp?channel=defense&id=news/ NUKETAC033009.xml, retrieved 22 April 2009.

design and engineering base atrophied for lack of work, and the subsequent Astute-class design effort experienced considerable delays and cost overruns. Submarine designers and engineers from GD/EB were assigned to the Astute-class project to help the UK overcome these problems.[69]

By choosing the SSN-launched cruise missiles as the UK's future minimum deterrent we will keep our nuclear design and building expertise by building more SSNs at Barrow than planned, initially the Astute class. Depending on the size of the enlarged SSN fleet, at least eight to ten submarines would be built instead of SSBNs, with conventional and nuclear warheads.

One of the great advantages of basing a UK minimum nuclear deterrent on existing cruise missiles for the next 20 years is that they are a proven weapon system with known capabilities and costs. Further, as is clear from this study, these missiles have been used in widely different parts of the globe. There are no sovereign countries that might threaten the UK, or countries from which terrorist organizations might operate, that we could not target. Cruise missiles fired from UK submarines would be able to reach important military installations and headquarters, even if not capital cities in all cases. I judge that there would be sufficient targets for such a system to meet the UK requirements of a minimum deterrent, in most cases a deterrent operating in conjunction with friends and allies.

CONCLUSION

One of the attractions of the UK's choosing a dual-use SSN-based nuclear deterrent for the future, rather than a dedicated SSBN-based force, is that it can operate without the need for CASD or permanent deterrence patrols. Its dual-use aspect obviates the problems that, in order to maintain the effectiveness of a dedicated SSBN force, one of the vessels must always, or virtually always, be at sea and that SSBN crews need to be regularly deployed. By contrast, SSN crews can operate with only occasional refresher training in nuclear material handling. For the rest of the time they can be deployed on 'conventional' patrol duty. Furthermore, the UK would be able to afford to deploy a larger SSN force if we were to decide not to replace our existing SSBN fleet. The dual-use option is attractive when financial constraints are considerable. An SSN-based deterrent, therefore, offers an important element of flexibility for an international environment in which a government judges that it does not need a deterrent force at instant readiness to fire. It could also be a potential asset in nuclear arms elimination negotiations

---

69 Ronald O'Rourke, 'Navy Attack Submarine Procurement', *Congressional Research Service*, 8 April 2008. This is available from http://assets.opencrs.com/rpts/RL32418_20080408.pdf.

when Britain decides to become involved. An SSN force would offer the British government a range of options for scaling down its nuclear capability gradually. By contrast, besides its expense, a new SSBN force of three or four boats quickly reaches a tipping point beyond which it cannot be reduced any further while still remaining operational.

It is interesting that Michael Quinlan, though having developed over the years most of the key intellectual arguments in favour of the present UK deterrent, was not dismissive of the need for Parliament to reconsider the SSBN choice. He wrote that it should be done 'not later than about 2013. The central decision of principle might at that stage be significantly influenced by whether the cost estimates remained of the same order as those assessed in 2006–7'.[70] He also argued that this revisiting should be approached 'seriously'. Such a revisiting could also fit in with the findings of the International Institute for Strategic Studies on the systematic and independent study of what would be required, politically and technically, to achieve a nuclear-weapon-free world – a study to which the British government is making a financial contribution.

70 Ibid, p.129.

DOCUMENT 1

TOP SECRET
Mr Moberly
PS/PUS
Private Secretary

cc:
Sir A Duff o.r.
Mr Crowe, Planning Staff

FUTURE OF THE BRITISH STRATEGIC NUCLEAR DETERRENT

1. In response to Dr Owen's request (at a meeting on 18 July), I submit a paper on the various possible options for replacing our Polaris force. The work on the paper has been kept within Defence Department (and is principally that of Mr Lever, with my guidance), drawing on such knowledge as we have. We have deliberately avoided discussion of the subject with the Ministry of Defence at this stage, because of the obvious delicacy of our working on it in this way. This means, however, that the paper necessarily lacks the authority which a fuller study, with military and scientific participation, would carry.

2. Dr Owen will also wish to see Mr Mulley's Top Secret minute of 19 September to the Prime Minister which, after answering some questions the latter had put, discusses briefly (in paragraphs 6 and 7) the need to "face up to" the question of a successor generation. I understand that the Prime Minister's meeting to discuss this has been fixed for 24 October, and that the Ministry of Defence are preparing for Mr Mulley suggestions which he might put forward then on the best method of starting a proper study of a Polaris replacement. I believe that FCO participation is envisaged for whatever group would be commissioned.

3. Returning to our own paper, I would like especially to emphasize the very tentative character of what we have said about the possible cruise missile options. The background to this is a shifting one, because of the uncertainty over the exact character of such limitations as may be incorporated in a SALT II agreement, and (just as importantly) because the Americans themselves are still in mid-stream in developing advanced cruise missiles and reaching judgements on their potentialities. As an example of this, I only heard after completing our paper that a well-placed Pentagon official had said the other day that the Americans had had to increase from 15–20% to 50% the allowance for evasive routing (to circumvent Soviet defences) in the designed range of cruise missiles, and that this meant that a SALT 2,500 km range limit for the B-52 ALCMs might not be enough.

4. Despite the uncertainty whether in the end cruise missiles could present a valid option for us, the final conclusion in our paper remains important. In considering cruise missiles in the SALT context, the Americans have had to bear in mind the interests of NATO as a whole in the use of cruise missiles for meeting future theatre nuclear requirements (including of course the Americans' own major contribution to the nuclear forces available to SACEUR). But I suspect that they will not have taken nearly so much account of the possible British interest in a cruise missile option for the replacement of Polaris – in good part because they will have taken it as more or less self-evident that, for the foreseeable future, an SLBM force will remain the surest form of strategic nuclear deterrent. Also, under present policy, HMG have hardly been in a position to make representations to the US Administration against foreclosing possible options for the replacement of Polaris. If Ministers should decide that that should now be done (which would probably have to be at Prime Minister to President level), it would of course present a major opportunity for putting into effect Dr Owen's idea of exploiting American "guilty conscience" in order to obtain the most generous assistance possible towards the procurement of a Polaris successor force.

22 September 1977   W J A Wilberforce
DPX 083/2   Defence Department

THE FUTURE OF THE BRITISH STRATEGIC NUCLEAR DETERRENT

Scope

1. This paper examines ways in which the British Government might maintain an independent strategic nuclear capability after the withdrawal from service in the early 1990s of the present Polaris force of ballistic-missile-firing submarines (SSBNs). The functions of a British strategic nuclear deterrent are:

(a) to contribute to the overall strategic nuclear capability of the North Atlantic Alliance and to be available for use by SACEUR, under the direction of the NATO Defence Planning Committee, in implementing his Scheduled Strike Programme of nuclear attacks on military and industrial targets in Eastern Europe and the Soviet Union in the event of general war; and

(b) to constitute an independent deterrent against any attack on the United Kingdom, by demonstrating the ability of a British Government to inflict massive nuclear retaliation on the territory of a aggressor. (It is assumed that in practice the only potential aggressor is the Soviet Union.)

2. The paper takes into account the financial implications of particular options for maintaining a strategic nuclear capability. But it does not address the question of whether, taken overall, this would be a desirable use of the resources likely to be available for defence. Nor does it address the other major questions of policy which are inherent in considering options for a successor force to Polaris: namely, of whether Britain should remain a nuclear weapon power at all; or of whether the function of British possession of nuclear weapons should be confined to a contribution to NATO's nuclear capability (function (a) above, but not function (b)). As to the latter question, the arguments in favour of maintaining an independent strategic nuclear deterrent are essentially that this provides a certain measure of additional deterrence against at least the initial use by the Soviet Union of nuclear weapons in attacking the United Kingdom in the event of war in the NATO area; and that it constitutes a basis for an alternative means of ensuring the defence of Western Europe in the event of changes in United States policy making this necessary in the long term. In addition there would be important questions of status (especially in relation to France), and of the effect on other European allies (especially the Federal Republic of Germany) in any decision to renounce the maintenance of an independent strategic nuclear deterrent. These questions are no more than noted here; and the rest of this paper takes, as its fundamental assumption, a requirement to maintain an independent deterrent.

Criteria for Effectiveness

3. The two elements which are crucial to the viability of a strategic nuclear force are:-

   (a) the assured ability of the system or systems in question to avoid destruction in a first nuclear or conventional strike and thus to threaten and execute second-strike retaliation; and
   (b) the range of targets open to the force and the degree of damage which it is capable of inflicting on them.

'Assured' ability is currently interpreted as a 100% cast iron certainty that the system will survive a first strike and that it will hit the target it is aimed at. This criterion is different from that applied to any other weapons system. In most other areas of warfare, effectiveness is measured in terms of Single-Shot Kill Probability (SSKP) or Circular Error Probability (CEP), and ratios of 80% assurance, rather than 100% certainty, are commonly accepted. In logic there is no reason why such ratios might not be applied to a nuclear system. Indeed one could pose the fundamental psychological question of deterrence not in the current terms of 'Can we be absolutely sure that our system will reach its targets?' but rather in terms of 'Can the Russians be absolutely sure that it will not?'.

4. Similarly, the question of what range of targets is required is also open to argument. The current criterion is that the ability to inflict massive destruction on Moscow itself is essential. Dr Owen has already expressed doubts about this and has suggested to the Prime Minister that the JIC should examine the question again. The paper does not therefore accept the Moscow criterion as axiomatic but allows for an alternative criterion, which is defined as the ability to destroy 10 other major cities in the Western Soviet Union.

5. Within the present and prospective state of military technology the following are the ways in which a strategic nuclear attack could be delivered by Britain against the Soviet Union:-

    (i)   by manned aircraft delivering bombs or missiles;
    (ii) by ballistic missiles, either
        (a) ground launched, or
        (b) submarine launched;
    (iii) by cruise missiles, either
        (a) air launched,
        (b) ground launched,
        (c) sea launched, or
        (d) submarine launched.

(For the purposes of this paper the theoretical option of air-launched ballistic missiles is ignored.) The following paragraphs describe in general terms the capabilities of each of these systems, estimate the likely cost to Britain of procuring them in sufficient numbers and, where appropriate, describe ways in which they might be procured.

Manned Aircraft

6. Before the introduction of Polaris, manned bomber aircraft (the Victor and Vulcan force) constituted the only British means of delivering nuclear strikes against Soviet territory. Some Vulcans still remain in service and could, in theory at any rate, be used for strategic strike purposes. All the other nuclear powers also still retain a strategic bomber capability. Nonetheless no nuclear power has thought it sensible to rely on manned aircraft alone for strategic purposes, and the recent American decision to cancel the B-1 suggests that the concept of using manned aircraft to deliver nuclear bombs (or short-range stand-off missiles) is unlikely to survive for long, other than as a supplementary delivery means. The reason lies in the vulnerability and

the cost of manned aircraft. Most Soviet cities are now protected by anti-aircraft defences (either surface-to-air missiles or interceptor aircraft), and the general air defence environment of Central and Northern Europe in the 1990s will make it extremely difficult for manned aircraft to penetrate far into Soviet territory without unacceptable loss ratios. Manned aircraft moreover are vulnerable while on the ground (more so in Europe than in the USA); and in order to ensure the ability to survive a first-strike attack, it would be necessary to maintain in the air a force of aircraft sufficiently large to have a reasonable prospect of penetrating Soviet air defences and delivering a wide enough spread of nuclear strikes, either on Moscow or on other targets in Western Russia. Even so, the bomber bases would remain a prime attraction for a Soviet first-strike attack, thus failing to serve the deterrent purpose.

7. Quite how large the force would need to be – and how many aircraft would need to be kept in the air at all times – could not be stated without detailed military study. Given the likely price of a modern penetrating bomber (the B-1 was expected to cost around $101 million per unit) and the cost of maintaining both aircraft and aircrews devoted to this single purpose, it would mean the expenditure of a large sum of money for a rather limited assurance of capability, resting on an operational concept that involved a loss ratio that would very probably be unacceptable.

8. Some of the disadvantages of manned aircraft can however be mitigated by giving them a longer-range stand-off capability, whereby they can deliver a missile from somewhere outside the range of enemy radar or air defences. Further discussion of this option is therefore left to paragraph 33 of the paper on Air-Launched Cruise Missiles (ALCMs).

Ballistic Missiles

9. The advantages of ballistic missiles as a strategic nuclear delivery system are their speed and the fact that they spend much of their flight outside the earth's atmosphere. The only period after their launch during which it is possible to intercept them is the final phase of their flight just before and after their re-entry into the earth's atmosphere. Their interception and destruction during this phase can only be accomplished by an expensive and complex anti-ballistic missile defence system. At present only one such system exists in the world, the Soviet ABM complex based on the GALOSH missile, which protects Moscow and the area within a radius of 350 miles around it. Under the terms of the US/Soviet ABM Treaty of 1972 (and the Protocol of 1974) the Russians are limited to a single ABM system. They can however improve the range of its radar to around 500 miles

from Moscow, which would enable them to provide some, albeit limited, protection to other major cities such as Leningrad and Kiev; and they can increase the number of missiles deployed from the present 64 to 100. There is however no evidence so far that the Russians are planning to extend and improve their ABM system in this way.

10. The ABM Treaty is due for review later this year, but this is expected to be a limited and technical affair. It seems likely, unless the SALT process should break down altogether, that the Treaty will continue in force for the foreseeable future, since it is fundamental to strategic stability, and since the US and the USSR have a strong common interest in avoiding a costly and complex arms race in ABM systems. It is unlikely, however, that the Americans, who have abandoned their own ABM system, could get the Treaty tightened so as to ban all ABM sites altogether. The Russians would probably be reluctant to agree to this, since it would leave Moscow more vulnerable to nuclear attack by China (or by Britain or France), as well as to accidental or unauthorised launch. For planning purposes, therefore, we should take it that during the 1990s the Russians would still be maintaining their single ABM complex; and it would be prudent, also, to assume that they might extend its range to some 500 miles from the centre of Moscow.

11. ABM defences are not infallible and there must be room for some doubt about the real capability of the Soviet GALOSH system. But even assuming the worst-case performance by the incoming ballistic missile and the best-case performance by the ABM system, the latter can be penetrated in two ways: either by saturation attack, delivering more re-entry vehicles than the ABM system is capable of detecting and destroying, or by equipping re-entry vehicles with a sufficient number of decoys and other devices to confuse the ABM system. The Americans, who have a superfluity of ballistic missile re-entry vehicles, including independently targettable ones, can reckon on being able to penetrate the Moscow ABM defences simply by aiming enough of their missiles simultaneously on Moscow. We cannot, however, and so have had to undertake the Polaris improvement project, in order to maintain assurance that a single Polaris submarine could hit Moscow.

12. Given the extreme difficulty of frustrating a ballistic missile attack once it has been launched, the crucial factor affecting the capability of a ballistic missile system is its vulnerability to pre-emptive strike. In both its ground launch and the submarine launched modes it could, in certain circumstances, be destroyed by nuclear, and, in theory at any rate, even by conventional attack. The following paragraphs describe the relative vulnerability of the two launch modes.

Ground Launched Ballistic Missiles

13. Ground Launched Ballistic Missiles can either be deployed in hardened shelters (as the Americans have done with their Minuteman ICBM system and as the French have done with their IRBM complex), or in mobile launch vehicles. Neither method would be suitable for Britain. No form of hardening can guarantee immunity from a Soviet counter-force attack; and a ballistic missile system based in permanent silos would, if it were to contain the number of missiles that would give the assurance of enough surviving to inflict substantial destruction on Soviet territory (and especially if it were required to be capable of penetrating the Moscow ABM defences), need to be dispersed over a number of different sites. Precisely how many sites would be required in order to give the force a reasonable assurance of surviving a pre-emptive strike is open to question. But 10 to 15 would probably be the absolute minimum. The chances of a British Government being able to find space in Britain for this number of sites, each of which would, on the analogy of the French Plateau d'Abion site, require some square miles of land, would seem to be minimal. This option is not therefore considered further.

14. Similar difficulties apply to the idea of a mobile ground launched system. Such a system could be moved about the country by road or rail and thus escape detection in any permanent location (as the Russians apparently intend with some of their new SS20 IRBMs). But in a small and crowded island like Britain, the idea of significant numbers of large ballistic missiles and their even larger launch platforms travelling about the country is just not feasible. An alternative form of mobility, which the Americans are thinking of adopting for their next generation MX ICBM, is that of a special rail-track system contained within a specific area which would be large enough to be immune to complete devastation in any first strike. It might theoretically be possible to find an area of country in Britain large enough for this purpose (for example, somewhere in Scotland). But the practical and environmental problems really rule out this option too.

Submarine Launched Ballistic Missiles (SLBMs)

15. SLBMs are protected by the relative invulnerability of nuclear-powered submarines to detection and tracking. The extent of this invulnerability in the future is open to question. At present it is considered acceptable for us to rely, for deterrent purposes, on the maintenance on station of only a single Polaris submarine (although in practice there are two submarines deployed for between 50% and 75% of the time), since the chances of the Russians being able to track or detect an SSBN once it moves into deep water away from its home port are not reckoned to be significant. But the

Russians are investing heavily in sonar technology and in other anti-submarine warfare techniques and it would be unwise to assume that the offensive/defensive correlation in anti-submarine warfare will remain static. It seems unlikely that Soviet detection techniques will improve to the point where continual tracking of an SSBN will be possible. (If this were to happen, then the whole concept of using submarines as launch platforms for ballistic missiles would be called into question; and there is no evidence that the Americans or Russians are losing faith in this respect, though neither side has all its eggs in this basket in the way that we do.) But the chances of the occasional detection of an SSBN will increase. If the SSBN detected were the only one on patrol at the time, then the necessary invulnerability to a first strike, would be lost. The chances of two or more such detections happening simultaneously is however remote. It would probably be prudent therefore, for planning purposes, to assume that the maintenance on station in the 1990s and thereafter of only a single SSBN by Britain would not constitute a significant assurance of invulnerability to pre-emptive strike; and that the composition of any SLBM force should therefore be based on a requirement to have two submarines on station at any one time. (There are of course other factors affecting the number of submarines required on station, particularly the judgement on the number of missiles which are required to be fired simultaneously.) The implication of this requirement for the total size of an SLBM force is difficult to assess. At present it is held to be impossible, with a force of only 4 submarines, to guarantee the continual deployment of two vessels at a time. But improvements in reactor core technology and in the efficiency of repair and refitting facilities might well allow for the permanent deployment in the 1990s of two submarines from a total force of 4. If not, then 5 would be required.

   16. The danger of improvements in Soviet ASW capability will also mean that any SSBN operating in the 1990s and thereafter will need to be quieter than the present Polaris vessels, and the patrol area may need to be limited to deeper water than is at present the case. It would be prudent to assume therefore that if submarines are chosen as the launch vehicle for a future British deterrent force then:-

   (a) the vessels themselves will need to be less susceptible to detection than our present Polaris fleet or the similar United States Lafayette class of submarine in which Poseidon is installed; and

   (b) subject to detailed hydrographic study, the range of the missiles might need to be increased to, say, 3,000 miles. (The range of the present Polaris missile is 2,460 miles, as is that of Poseidon, but the latter carries a much heavier payload and so offers the possibility of a trade-off to increase the range at the expense of the payload, whereas in the case of Polaris we are having to accept a reduction in the range in order to increase its limited payload.)

Characteristics of a Future SSBN Force

17. It will, in any event, be necessary to procure both new boats and new missiles for a future deterrent force. The hull life of the present vessels comes to an end from around 1993 onwards. The present set of missiles is also programmed for an in-service life which would finish around then: although it might theoretically be possible to maintain them in service for longer, it would be expensive and uneconomic to do so; it would also probably no longer be possible by then to procure spare parts or replacements for the missiles from the Americans, whose own Polaris production lines have already closed down and whose last Polaris-carrying submarines will have been phased out in the early 1980s. The characteristics of the vessels and missiles required for a new SSBN deterrent force are as follows.

Vessels

18. As indicated in paragraph 16 above, the submarine will need to be quieter (and no doubt more sophisticated in some other respects) than the current classes of British and United States submarines. But, for the number and weight of the missiles it will have to carry, it should not need to be any larger in size than the present Polaris vessels or the United States Lafayette class. Once the present run of Lafayette class vessels is completed, the future American SSBN fleet will be based on the Trident submarine which will not only be quieter and technically more advanced than its predecessors, but will be significantly greater in size since it is designed to carry 24 of the large Trident II missiles whose range will be ▮▮▮▮▮▮▮▮▮. The submarine element of a future British deterrent force would probably need to incorporate some of the technology of Trident; but this could be achieved by a design which would be in essence a development of the existing Polaris/Lafayette class of vessel rather than a switch to a fundamentally new concept.

Missiles

19. The range of the missile required for a future deterrent force will probably, for the reason given in paragraph 16 above, need to be somewhat greater than that of the current Polaris and Poseidon missiles, but will not need to be as great as that of the Trident I or Trident II missiles whose ranges are expected to be around ▮▮▮ and ▮▮▮ miles respectively. The Poseidon missile would offer the opportunity of obtaining extra range by reducing its

payload, though the extent to which this could be done would depend on the number and nature of the re-entry vehicles the missile had to carry. As regards the number of missiles and re-entry vehicles required, the critical factor is the judgement of whether the ability to penetrate the Moscow ABM defences is essential. If it were not, and the destruction of ten other major Soviet cities were considered an adequate capability, then a constantly deployed force of 32 missiles (i.e. two boat-loads) each with three re-entry vehicles, along the lines of the present Polaris force, would be enough. But if the destruction of Moscow were considered an essential requirement, then it would be necessary either to increase the number of re-entry vehicles (e.g. to 10 per missile) in order to saturate the ABM defences, or to adopt measures (e.g. maneuverable RVs, or the use of decoys) to confuse the defence. The best choice would require detailed technical study, taking into account the range factor (mentioned above) as well as cost.

20. The present American Poseidon missiles are configured for 10 to 14 re-entry vehicles each with a warhead of up to ▮▮▮▮, and should thus provide the necessary scope. It would not however be necessary for the re-entry vehicles to be independently targettable (MIRVed) as are the American ones. It would make little sense, given the small size of any future British SSBN force, to cater for the complex and sophisticated targetting options for which the Americans originally developed the MIRV technique. Moreover, because of the SALT II sub-ceiling on MIRVed systems (and irrespective of the exact language of any 'non-circumvention' provision, or its interpretation by the Russians in a 'no-transfer' sense), it seems very unlikely that the Americans would feel able to give us MIRV systems or technology. This would almost certainly appear too contrary to the spirit, if not the letter, of SALT agreements (and the consequent strengthening of the Soviet case for British systems to be counted in SALT would be to our own disadvantage). For similar reasons, if the Americans were ready to give us the Poseidon missile technology (less the MIRVed front end), it might be on condition that we took advantage of the additional payload to increase the range of our missiles rather than to increase significantly the number of deliverable warheads. In this case, if we stayed with 3 RVs, we would need (under the Moscow option) to equip them with decoys or with a capability for maneuvering to avoid the ABM defences. The development of the technique (MARVing) for this is already quite far advanced in the United States, and the capability is likely to be incorporated in the re-entry vehicles of all Trident missiles and possibly retrofitted to Poseidon. Some believe that it would not be too difficult to develop an adequate system ourselves.

Warheads

21. The choice of warhead for a future deterrent force would be determined by the constraints on warhead development imposed by a Comprehensive Test Ban Treaty. If no such Treaty is negotiated, then it will be possible to design and develop a warhead of whatever yield, weight or type seems most appropriate. But if a CTB is in force, then use will have to be made of proved British warhead designs or variants of them which will not require fresh testing. Given, however, that we shall already have the proven capacity to produce both ███████ and ███████ warheads for the Polaris force, this will probably not be a major problem. But it will mean that the missile and its re-entry vehicles will need to be designed or adapted to fit an existing warhead type rather than vice versa. There is no reason to believe that this could not be done with the Poseidon missile; but this is an additional technical constraint to be taken into account.

Cost

22. The four Polaris submarines currently in service were constructed in British shipyards to a basically American design and the missiles were bought off the shelf from an American manufacturer under the terms of the favourable Polaris Sales Agreement. The cost of procuring the Polaris force was £353 million at 1963 prices, which is the equivalent of £1,180 million at 1977 prices. This figure included around £155 million (£520 million at 1977 prices) for the construction of the four boats and around £52 million (£170 million at 1977 prices) for the purchase of the missiles, the remainder being spent on various test and logistic facilities. The initial procurement cost of a replacement SSBN system would depend very much on how it was procured. The cheapest method would undoubtedly be a repeat of the Polaris arrangement, i.e. the construction in Britain of submarines incorporating American technology, and the purchase off the shelf of American missiles. If, however, the Poseidon missile were chosen, there might be a case for manufacturing it in Britain under license, in order to have the assurance of full life-cycle support for the system and of the continued availability of spare parts when the American Poseidon production lines were run down. (But, again in the SALT context, the US Administration might be unwilling to assist us towards a capability for manufacturing long-range ballistic missiles in Britain, since this could be held to be a significant enhancement of our strategic nuclear capability, going beyond the simple and more easily justifiable replacement of the Polaris force.)

23. There is no guarantee of course that the Americans would be willing to repeat the generous Polaris arrangement; although the chances of

something on those lines would seem *prima facie*, in the present state of Anglo/US relations to be quite fair, we are not yet in a position to explore them even tentatively. Assuming that a Polaris-type arrangement were possible, the procurement price in real terms would still be considerably higher than in the mid 1960s, since construction costs for submarines have gone up and the new weapons system would be more sophisticated than Polaris. An academic study done in 1973 assessed procurement costs *per boat* (assuming the construction of new boats and the direct purchase of the missiles) of various possible future SSBN forces as follows:

	At 1973 $ prices	*At 1977 £ prices*
Polaris	$ 215 million	£ 197 million
Poseidon	$ 360 million	£ 329 million
Trident I	$ 420 million	£ 384 million
Trident II	$1000 million	£ 913 million

On this basis, the cost of an improved Polaris/Lafayette class boat equipped with unMIRVed Poseidon missiles might be somewhere around £350 million at 1977 prices, making £1,400 million for 4 boats. But that was in 1973; and real costs have continued to rise (perhaps more sharply even) since then. By comparison, a current academic study puts the cost of procuring a new 4-boat SSBN force with a capability similar to Polaris at around £2,000 million.

24. If American assistance in the procurement of a new generation of SSBN forces were not available the alternatives would be either national development or some kind of collaborative arrangement with the French. There is in Britain plenty of experience in constructing nuclear-powered submarines of both the SSBN and the SSN type. But, since giving up space vehicle development, Britain has had no experience of research, development or production relevant to ballistic missiles, other than with warheads and parts of their associated re-entry vehicles; and it would be a very major undertaking to establish such a capability in order to replace Polaris. Even the limited work done on the Polaris re-entry vehicle has proved extremely expensive (though it could be regarded as having restored at least the nucleus of a British industrial capability in this field). It might be possible to spread the cost of a new ballistic missile system by collaboration with France, drawing on the considerable experience which the French have in the field. But the existing generation of French ballistic missiles is inferior in performance to Polaris, and we do not know how advanced their future missile programme will be. The present French Defence Minister has speculated privately about

the possibility of Britain and France co-operating in the strategic nuclear field, by drawing on British expertise in the construction of nuclear-powered submarines and French expertise in the manufacture of missiles. *Prima facie*, such collaboration would not seem likely, in terms either of cost or of effectiveness, to present as attractive an option as US assistance for a new British SSBN force. But it is not inconceivable that a basis could be found – suiting the major political and strategic interests of the USA as well as Britain and France – for combining Anglo/French collaboration with the use of US technology, e.g. of the Poseidon missile. (It should be noted, of course, that any Anglo/French collaboration in this field would require US consent because of the US technology we already possess.) Possibilities of this kind, however, cannot profitably be explored even in internal studies until the general requirements for a new British strategic force have been clarified.

25. Even if procured with American assistance on favourable terms similar to those for Polaris, and even if expenditure on it were spread over 10–12 years, a new generation SSBN force would be an enormous investment. It would moreover be an investment limited in application since an SSBN cannot be used for any purpose other than nuclear strike. Total expenditure on equipment in the defence budget for 1977/78 is £2,350 million. The present forward equipment programme for the 1980s makes no provision for expenditure on a replacement for Polaris; and if a new SSBN force were required to come into service in the early 1990s, much of the expenditure on it would be incurred at a time when there would already be heavy demands on the equipment programme. All three Services have major projects scheduled for the 1980s: the Navy has its through-deck cruisers and its continuing programme of hunter-killer submarine (SSN) construction; the Air Force has the MRCA and the eventual Jaguar/Harrier replacement; and the Army has the Main Battle Tank to replace Chieftain. If an SSBN programme had to be accommodated as well, it would seem likely that either there would have to be an increase in real terms in the defence budget over a number of years, or some other things currently planned would have to be given up. This financial strain might be eased by spreading out the development and production programme for the replacement SSBN force as far as was safe – and the limits to which we could continue to reply on the present Polaris vessels and missiles will be an important point to review with as much exactitude as possible. But even then, new problems of concurrency of expenditure might arise.

Cruise Missiles

26. Cruise missiles of one type or another have been in the inventories of the United States and the Soviet Union since the early 1950s. Three recent technological developments however have radically changed the capabilities of the weapon:–

(a) the development of small nuclear warheads which enable a missile no more than 20 feet in length to carry a warhead generating 200 kilotons of explosive power (like the warhead used on the re-entry vehicles of the present Polaris missiles);

(b) the introduction of micro-computerisation techniques which enable great amounts of information to be stored in a very small space; and

(c) the development of a guidance system based on digitalised mapping which enables the missile to be targetted over land with great accuracy at long ranges.

27. For the strategic nuclear role the three key issues with advanced cruise missiles are:–

(i)   Is the accuracy of cruise missiles good enough to ensure that they will reach their designated targets?

(ii) Can they be intercepted on their way?

(iii) In what numbers would they be required and what would they cost?

28. On accuracy, the American systems already under development with the TERCOM guidance system have a circular error probability of 200 feet, and it is possible that the introduction of Scene Matching Area Correlation (SMAC) techniques for the final phase of the missile's flight (this involves the installation in the missile's computer of a digitalised photograph of the target area which is locked onto the actual terrain as it appears through a television camera carried in the missile's nose) might reduce this to between 3 and 17 metres. But there are problems, which will need to be examined, about getting SLCMs and ALCMs onto the start of a low attitude course over land, in which the TERCOM guidance system could ensure such extreme accuracy.

29. As regards penetration capabilities, the first generation of these advanced cruise missiles travel at sub-sonic speeds and are therefore liable, if detected on enemy radars, to be shot down by surface-to-air missiles or aircraft. The ease of detection by radar depends critically on the observable features of the missile, particularly its radar cross-section. There have been speculative references to cruise missiles eventually having a radar cross-section as small as that of a seagull, and thus being virtually undetect-

able. Whether anything as small as this can be achieved in the foreseeable future is not yet clear. Recent exchanges with the Americans have suggested a radar cross-section of ▓▓ square metres for the cruise missiles currently under development (compared with the cross-section of a tactical aircraft of between ▓▓ and ▓ square metres). Even with radar cross-sections of this order or lower, and with super-sonic speeds, it is not possible to guarantee that in the long run cruise missiles will be incapable of interception. Most cities in the Soviet Union, and particularly Moscow, are already surrounded by air defences, and it is likely that the Russians will increase their investment in this field in the future, with the result that of all the potential targets for cruise missiles, Soviet cities will be the most difficult to hit. Cruise missiles are moreover susceptible to electronic counter-measures (ECM) and it is not yet clear to what extent it will be possible to give them the anti-ECM capability which modern aircraft possess.

30. It is impossible therefore to offer any confident prediction at this stage of cruise missiles' penetration capabilities. One might hazard a guess that if the radar cross-section of a cruise missile could be brought significantly below ▓▓, then something like at least a quarter of the missiles launched could be relied upon to reach their targets. (On this basis a target requirement for 20–25 missiles would necessitate the launch of 80–100). But in the present state of knowledge of cruise missiles' capabilities and vulnerabilities, it would be rash to assert on their behalf the kind of assured capability for destroying Moscow (or ten other Soviet cities) which would be achievable by an improved British SSBN force. American confidence in the penetration capability of the ALCMs to be carried by B-52s should be seen against the background of the vastly greater size (and capacity for defence suppression) of the US strategic forces, end of the use of ALCMs as just one component in a retaliatory second-strike. Current and prospective discussions at technical level with the Americans, and studies being carried out at the MOD's Defence Operational Analysis Establishment, should enable a better judgement to be made of cruise missiles' strategic capabilities by the end of the year.

31. The cruise missile can be launched either from the ground, from aircraft, from surface ships or from submarines. The relative advantages and disadvantages of each of these modes of launch are as follows:

Ground Launched Cruise Missiles (GLCMs)

32. A GLCM does not require an expensive launch platform and is thus the cheapest option. It can be installed in permanent sites or it can be maintained on mobile vehicles, either road or rail. If the number of fixed

sites were small, they would be vulnerable to pre-emptive strike, and in a small island and an open society like Britain it would be difficult to keep secret the existence of such sites. Dispersal in a large number of sites would increase the chances; but then there would be problems over the need for secure storage in peacetime of the associated warheads; and in practice probably only RAF airfields, of which there are a fair number but whose location is known, could be used. Another option would be to keep some GLCMs in mobile deployment at all times, and to rely (as NATO does with many weapons in Germany) on dispersing the rest from central storage in a crisis. Then the Russians could not feel confident of launching a successful pre-emptive strike, unless they were prepared to 'take out' the whole of Britain. Cruise missiles do not require large launch-platforms like ballistic missiles and could thus, in theory, be moved around the country by road or rail. But there would be environmental and security difficulties about doing so; and this concept (though not to be ruled out) is probably more suited to application on the Continent than in Britain. Also, some of the guidance problems associated with SLCMs and ALCMs would arise with GLCMs which had to be launched across the North Sea before attaining their low-attitude overland TERCOM-guided flight path. And the flight path of GLCMs launched from Britain would take them directly across the heavily defended area of Central Europe in order to reach Soviet targets. This would probably mean that, in order to maintain an assured penetration capability, considerably more cruise missiles would be required than under other modes.

33. It is as yet unclear how GLCMs (and indeed, all modes of cruise missile) will in the end be constrained by arms control arrangements. The Americans have indicated their willingness to see included in the three-year Protocol to a SALT II agreement a temporary moratorium on the testing and deployment of ground-launched and sea-launched cruise missiles with a range of over 600 km. A restriction on testing of this kind would not prevent the development of any mode of cruise missile, since a long-range missile destined for ground- or sea-launch could have its range and accuracy tested by being launched as an ALCM from a heavy bomber (where the range restriction is 2,500km), and the ground or sea launching mechanism could be tested separately at up to 600 km range. But if the restriction were, in SALT III, to become a permanent ban on GLCMs over 600 km – and there is obviously a risk of this – then it would not be possible for Britain to rely on them for strategic purposes unless we were prepared to dissociate ourselves from this particular SALT provision. It would be politically extremely difficult for a British Government to do this, even with the SALT agreement

being formally only a bilateral one between the United States and the Soviet Union; and we would, among other things, be cutting ourselves off from any possibility of US assistance with GLCMs. It should also be noted that even a limitation of the range of GLCMs to 2,500 km (the maximum range limit at present under discussion in SALT for any mode of cruise missile) would not be quite enough to allow them to be used for strategic purposes from Britain.

Air Launched Cruise Missiles (ALCMs)

34. The advantages of the air launched mode are that the missile can be conveyed supersonically nearer to its target before initial launch, thus reducing the time during which it is liable to interception; that the aircraft is recallable at the last moment; and that an enemy cannot be confident of the direction from which the missile will come. As against this, the aircraft carrying the missile could itself be vulnerable; and there is little logic in building an expensive manned aircraft in order to carry a vehicle which is itself capable of flight. The Americans' enthusiasm for the ALCM is a reflection of the fact that they have a large fleet of B-52 strategic bombers anyway, as one component of their strategic triad, which (if it were not for the ALCM) they would have had to replace, at greater cost, by the B-1. But all the aircraft currently planned for our own inventory for the 1990s will be assigned to other tasks, and any use of them to carry cruise missiles for strategic strike could only be at the expense of their other missions. There would in any case be likely to be technical difficulties in adapting their missile pods to take ALCMs. Moreover it is highly likely that if cruise missiles are covered in some way by SALT II or subsequent SALT agreements, one of the relevant provisions will be a limitation of the range of ALCMs to 600 km except when deployed on heavy bombers, when it would be 2,500 km. The degree of American commitment to a limitation provision of this kind on ALCMs is strong (because it precludes the deployment of long-range ALCMs on the controversial Soviet Backfire aircraft, so long as the Russians refuse to have this counted as a heavy bomber). None of the aircraft currently envisaged as part of the RAF's inventory for the 1990s could be classified as heavy bombers in SALT terms. But the Americans are considering whether in SALT II they need to redefine 'heavy bombers' so as to keep open the option of using wide-bodied transport aircraft as future ALCM carriers, which would then be a possible option for us too. Also, without proper operational study, it should not be concluded that a 600 km limitation would entirely rule out the use of ALCMs for strategic purposes with an aircraft such as the MRCA. The cost-effectiveness of both these possible options might deserve consideration.

Ship Launched Cruise Missiles

35. The advantage of surface vessels as a launch platform is that they are mobile and that, at any rate in the case of major capital ships, they have their own built-in defence system. On the other hand, the installation of cruise missiles on existing, or planned, ships can only be at the expense of other aspects of their armament and, unless cruise missiles were to be installed on a very wide range of vessels (and it is doubtful whether this would technically be possible), it would be difficult to guarantee the invulnerability to pre-emptive strike of those few vessels on which they were installed. Indeed, the vulnerability of surface vessels today to submarine and missile attack is such as really to rule out any ship-based option for the purposes of an assured second-strike capability.

Submarine Launched Cruise Missiles (SLCMs)

36. Submarines are the launch platform least vulnerable to pre-emptive strike. The installation of long-range cruise missiles in our existing SSN fleet would be technically feasible. But the number of missiles which could be installed on each boat would be limited and would involve a commensurate reduction in the number of torpedoes, or anti-ship missiles, which the submarine would otherwise have carried. At present, the SSN fleet is scheduled to number 17 by the end of the 1980s: four of the vessels will have 6 torpedo tubes carrying 31 torpedoes or Sub-Harpoon missiles, and 13 will have 5 tubes carrying 24 torpedoes or Sub-Harpoon missiles, the total torpedo/missile carrying capability of the fleet thus being 436. If cruise missiles were to be installed on submarines, the alternatives would be either:

(a) To maintain the present SSN construction programme but to pre-empt a certain proportion, say a third, of the available torpedo tubes for cruise missiles, by equipping certain SSNs exclusively with cruise missiles (which would undoubtedly be better than installing cruise missiles on all SSNs in addition to torpedoes and anti-ship missiles). This would mean that the maximum number of cruise missiles would be around 145 and that the capability of the SSN fleet for anti-submarine and anti-surface ship warfare would be correspondingly diminished by a third.

(b) To construct at least 4 or 5 more SSNs so as to provide an SSN fleet capable of delivering strategic nuclear strikes but without detriment to its anti-submarine and anti-surface ship attack role. Although nuclear attack submarines cost less than ballistic-missile-firing submarines, they are still expensive: the current procurement cost for an SSN is around £150 million.

37. The arms control constraints on the use of SLCMs for strategic strike would be similar to those on GLCMs (see paragraph 31 above), except that it is more probable that the Americans would be willing to see the range of SLCMs permanently constrained. The Americans have no particular need for a land-attack cruise missile capability in their SSNs since they already have a sufficient number of SSBNs capable of performing the task. (Indeed, in these circumstances, and since there are more important US coastal targets than Soviet ones exposed to SLCM attack, it would even suit the Americans for the SLCM range-limit to be lower than 600 km, down to whatever range was required for their use in an anti-ship role.)

38. It would be possible to deploy cruise missiles in a combination of different launch modes as part of a strategic nuclear force. It is possible moreover that cruise missiles may be considered an attractive option for British forces for other forms of strike, for example theatre nuclear strike or deep conventional strike against fixed targets. The same missile could be used for any of these purposes: the only differences would be in the warhead, the amount of fuel carried and in the particular flight programme fed into the guidance system. It is not yet clear whether the cruise missile will in fact be cost-effective for use in these other roles. But if it is, then there could be economies of scale in relying, for a strategic nuclear capability, on missiles and delivery modes which had other applications as well in the British forces. There might also be marginal political advantages in this, as compared with the choice of a 'new-generation' ballistic missile system as a straight successor to Polaris.

Warheads

39. As far as is known, there would not be any major problems over installing British warheads (without the need for testing) into cruise missiles; and the amount of extra research and development required for adapting the warheads would probably not be all that high, though it would presumably be necessary to design a new fusing mechanism.

Cost

40. Cruise missiles are under active development only in the United States. A figure of $750,000 has been much quoted as the unit cost for a cruise missile. But it is not clear whether this figure relates simply to the production cost or whether it includes also an allowance for the expenditure on research and development. If one took three times this figure as a crude basis for calculating the cost of a complete cruise missile programme (through the acquisition of American missiles), the cost of a force of 500 GLCMs might

be £692.5 million; while a force of 5 boatloads of SLCMs might cost £750 million for the vessels and £159 million for the missiles, i.e. a total of £909 million. With ALCMs, the critical factor would be the number of aircraft additional to the RAF's projected holdings which would be required. An extra 50 MRCAs, for example, would cost around £500 million, and their missiles (at 2 each) £128.5 million, i.e. a total of £628.5 million.

41. Procuring cruise missiles from the United States, either by straight purchase or by manufacture under licence, would probably be the cheapest way of acquiring the system. But it may be feasible for us to develop a cruise missile of our own. The fuel and engine technology involved is not particularly complex, and British Aerospace have already designed and are about to start manufacturing, a short-range air-launched cruise missile for use against surface ships (the P3T). The computerisation and map digitalisation techniques are within our existing technological capabilities (indeed we do a good deal of the Americans' work for them already in this field) and will be incorporated in part into the terrain-following radar system to be installed in the MRCA. The guidance system would require new development but British Aerospace have already produced a design study for a Terrain Profile Matching System (TERPROM) using similar techniques to the American TERCOM system but with a claimed greater potential for accuracy. (British Aerospace are also working on a design study for an eventual supersonic cruise missile, but it is not yet clear whether this would be a cost-effective development: the construction techniques would be more complex, and the unit costs therefore higher; and it may be that it would be more cost-effective to get the radar cross-section of cruise missiles smaller, and thus make them more difficult to detect, rather than to try to increase their speeds.) British Aerospace are said to be fairly confident that they could, if necessary, manufacture a long-range cruise missile with a sufficiently accurate guidance system without any need for American assistance. But this should be taken with a large grain of salt. It is true that information on the detailed geography of the Western Soviet Union is already available for use in a TERCOM-type system and there would probably not be any need to rely on American satellite information for that. But for SLCMs and ALCMs there would be complex guidance and control problems in directing the initial flight of the missile (from a moving launch platform) over a considerable distance e.g. of sea, so that the TERCOM would take over at the correct point over land. Whether we could provide our own solution to these problems, at any reasonable cost, must be open to question. (And it should also be noted that, if the US Navy did not go for full development of a long-range SLCM – as, for reasons explained earlier, it might not – the alternative of

a buy of US technological solutions to these problems would not be available.) It must be said, therefore, that studies on cruise missiles in the MOD and among British manufacturers, principally British Aerospace, are still at much too early a stage for anyone to take a confident view of the ability of British industry on its own to develop and produce a cost-effective system.

42. A third alternative, in addition to purchase from the Americans or national development, might be collaboration on a European basis. There is considerable interest in cruise missile technology in Europe, particularly in France and Germany, and the Franco/German EUROMISSILE consortium is believed already to be doing some design work in this field. The French have included cruise missiles on the agenda for the first Anglo/French/German meeting of Defence Ministers in November, under the heading of equipment matters. It is the general aim of British Aerospace to secure accession to EUROMISSILE as an equal partner, and collaboration with the French and Germans on cruise missiles might therefore fit in well with British Aerospace's overall industrial policy (the P3T missile already under development will have a French engine). But this, of course, ignores the major political implications of any such collaboration connected with a system for British strategic nuclear delivery. These would have to be considered fully at a later stage, if this possible option of collaboration on a cruise missile system appeared, after further technical study, to deserve inclusion in a refined range of options for providing a successor to Polaris.

Conclusions

43. It is not the purpose of this paper to offer any firm recommendations on the procurement of a replacement for Polaris, not least because the lack of information on many aspects of the various weapons systems which might be used make it unrealistic to offer anything but very general or hypothetical assertions about their likely cost or capability. But the following are the main conclusions which might be drawn from the above analysis:–

(i)   A force of 4–5 modern ballistic-missile-firing submarines would probably be the most reliable and effective way of ensuring a continuing independent strategic nuclear capability, particularly if the ability to destroy Moscow is maintained as a fundamental requirement. But its cost, even on the most favourable terms, would be extremely high in relation to the resources which seem likely to be allocated to defence equipment.

(ii) It is not yet clear whether cruise missiles, in some mode or combination of modes, could provide a sufficiently reliable means of inflicting strategic nuclear strike, or, if so, whether they could do so

at a relatively cheap price. But there is at least a reasonable possibility, deserving full examination, that cruise missiles might offer a
cost-effective means of maintaining a strategic nuclear capability,
at a price significantly below what would be required for an SLBM
force.

(iii) It is not yet possible to assess definitely the relative attractions of
different types of launch modes for British cruise missiles in the
strategic nuclear role. In general, GLCMs would be cheapest since
they would not require any additional launch platforms. But they
would be the most vulnerable to attack both before and after their
launch (and thus would need to be procured in greater quantities)
and there would be practical difficulties over their deployment.
ALCMs would be liable to similar vulnerability problems, and would
be more expensive (depending on the number of extra aircraft
required). SLCMs would be the most reliable in terms of invulnerability to first strike, and probably also in penetration capability, but
would also be the most expensive because of the need to construct
additional submarines to carry them.

(iv) Assuming that cruise missiles are technically capable of providing
a satisfactory strategic nuclear capability, a system which could be
used for other military purposes as well (such as theatre nuclear
strike or conventional interdiction) should offer economies of scale
– though this is less likely to apply to SLCMs than to GLCMs and
ALCMs.

(v) If the possibility of our wishing to use cruise missiles, in some
form or other, as a replacement for Polaris is established politically,
there will be a strong British interest in ensuring that no potentially
attractive options are. foreclosed, at least permanently, by SALT
limitations.

Defence Department

22 September 1977

DOCUMENT 2

PS/PUS
Sir A Duff
Mr Crowe

Military Nuclear Issues

The Secretary of State has now approved the record of the meeting on Monday 17 October prepared by Mr Lever and seen and amended by Messrs Wilberforce and Moberly. Indeed he commented that it was a very good record. However, because of the great sensitivity of the subject matter and in particular his own personal opinions as recorded, he wishes to restrict the record to the present single copy. I am therefore marking it to the PUS, Sir A Duff and Mr Crowe, who should return it to me. In case of need it can always be consulted in this office. It will, naturally, form part of the supporting papers for the forthcoming meeting with the Prime Minister, Chancellor of the Exchequer and Mr Mulley.

E. A. J. Fergusson

25 October 1977

cc. Mr Moberly   )
Mr Wilberforce) minute only
Mr Lever   )

DRAFT RECORD

SUMMARY RECORD OF A MEETING ON MILITARY NUCLEAR ISSUES IN THE SECRETARY OF STATE'S OFFICE AT 10.15 AM ON MONDAY 17 OCTOBER, 1977

Present
Secretary of State
PUS
Sir A Duff
Mr Moberly
Mr Wilberforce
Mr Crowe
Mr Fergusson
Mr Lever

The Moscow Criterion

Dr Owen said that the central issue in deciding whether to proceed with the Chevaline programme and how to maintain a continuing British strategic capability was the judgement whether it was essential for a British deterrent force to have the assured capability to destroy Moscow. He asked for the views of the meeting on the validity of this Moscow criterion. In the subsequent discussion the following points were made:–

(a) The purely military rationale for a British nuclear deterrent had always been less clear cut than the political one. It was hard to envisage any military role for a British deterrent force outside the North Atlantic Alliance. But within the Alliance such a force could act as a "trigger" mechanism for frustrating possible Soviet attempts to detach the American nuclear commitment to Europe. For this "trigger" purpose the ability to destroy Moscow was not essential.

(b) A nuclear capability gave Britain, and Western Europe generally, the confidence in peacetime to withstand Soviet political and economic pressure. There was no reason to believe that the Moscow criterion was vital for this purpose. But ope renunciation of it might cause the Russians to doubt whether the deterrent carried conviction in the minds of British Ministers.

(c) It was difficult to predict what the deterrent requirement, both political and military, might be in the 21st century. It might be premature to assume that Western Europe would in no circumstances require its own ability to destroy Moscow. Moreover, given possible improvements in Soviet city defences, it was important not to under-estimate the capability which would be required in 20 or 25 years time even to inflict, for example, substantial damage on 10 major Soviet cities other than Moscow.

(d) It was perhaps misleading to pose the requirement for the Moscow criterion in too absolute terms. What was important was not whether we could be 100% certain that in all circumstances a British deterrent force could hit Moscow, but rather whether the Russians could be 100% certain that it could not. A less than 100% of probability might be quite adequate for deterrent purposes; and in any event a second-class deterrent would be better than none at all.

3. Dr Owen said that he did not himself accept the Moscow criterion. He believed firmly that Britain should retain a nuclear capability and that this should encompass the capability to inflict substantial damage on the Soviet Union. The factors which, he had concluded over many years of

Ministerial and back-bench consideration, weighed in favour of a British nuclear capability were the dangers of decoupling, the advantage of multiple decision-making within the Alliance, and the fact that the possession by both Britain and France of nuclear deterrent forces made it less likely that the FRG would eventually decide on a nuclear force of its own (a decision which could carry the seeds of a Third World War). He saw no reason however to insist that a British deterrent force must have the specific ability to hit Moscow and there was a danger that if the Moscow requirement were regarded as overriding, there would be an implication that nothing less would serve at all. But the requirement for a British deterrent force was different from that of the two superpowers. Whatever their calculations vis-à-vis the United States, it was unthinkable that the Russians should put even one of their major cities at risk simply in order to threaten the United Kingdom. To insist that a British deterrent must be able to destroy Moscow, and must therefore compete in sophistication with the deterrent forces of the superpowers, was to accept a commitment to a never-ending roller coaster of technology and cost. He did not believe that this was feasible or desirable.

Chevaline

4. Dr Owen said that he saw no reason to challenge the decision to complete the programme for hardening the Polaris warheads so as to reduce their vulnerability to a generalised nuclear blast from the Soviet ABM defences. He thought it important however that, in taking a decision on the future of the complete Chevaline project, Ministers should be given a clear and detailed break-down of the costs on the one hand of the hardening programme and on the other of the other two elements of Chevaline, namely the addition of decoys and the separation of the warheads in space. It would be of interest also to know by how much the costs of the programme had escalated in real terms since its inception. Other factors which were relevant were the extent to which the hardening of the warheads alone would improve Polaris' penetration capability and what degree of assurance of penetration this would represent by comparison to the 100% certainty attainable by the complete programme. He also expressed considerable anxiety about the effect of the programme on the range of the Polaris missile. It was clear that the Americans were deeply worried about the need for their SSBNs to have more extensive areas of deep waters in which to operate, hence their decision to introduce Trident submarines with ranges of 4,000 and even possibly 6,000 miles. He wondered whether it was not an unacceptable risk to allow the range of Polaris to be reduced significantly (by 500 nautical miles) below its present 2,450 nautical miles. It was

agreed in subsequent discussion that the question of range was of major
significance and that it would be important to establish whether the loss of
Polaris' present range due to Chevaline was due primarily to the hardening
element of the programme or to the other two elements. It was pointed
out that introduction of the new lightweight warhead would recover 80
nautical miles of lost range, but this would need the nuclear test planned for
March 1978. The Ministry of Defence seemed content to accept for the next
decade or so the reduction in range which would accrue from Chevaline,
but it was not clear to what extent future improvements in Soviet sonar and
associated technology would limit the areas in which SSBNs could safely be
deployed. It was recognised that, given that British SSBNs operated from
a single port, the major point of potential vulnerability was the ability of
Soviet submarines to trail them continually from their initial egress from
port and that this trailing ability would not be affected by increases in their
operational range. But the dangers of a random detection of a single SSBN
in shallow water in future would be likely to increase as well.

5. It was agreed that news of a decision by British Ministers to cancel the
Chevaline programme would be bound to leak and that the fact that this
cancellation implied the abandonment of the Moscow criterion would be
likely to become public as well. It did not seem that the hardening element
of the programme alone could be represented as fulfilling the programme
to improve Polaris' capability. It would be quite wrong however to cancel
Chevaline purely on financial grounds: if the programme, or at any rate two
main elements of it, were to be abandoned, it would be vital to ensure that
the money thereby saved was not removed from the defence budget. There
was moreover a psychological problem in that the morale of the Royal Navy,
and particularly the SSBN crews, was geared at present very firmly towards
the maintenance of the Moscow criterion. It was possible however, that the
Chiefs of Staff, including the Navy, might be reconciled to the abandonment
of the project if the money saved were used to improve the capability of the
Services elsewhere, for example by starting studies and design and development work on cruise missiles (though it was not clear whether the likely
time-scale for any alternative project eg over cash-flows, would permit this).
Dr Owen said that, although he thought that the Chevaline programme
was conceptually misguided and ought to have been abandoned in 1974, he
nonetheless recognised the psychological and political factors which would
be involved in its cancellation and he thought that they might well weigh
decisively in Ministers' minds.

Studies on a Polaris Successor System

6. <u>Dr Owen</u> said that he was inclined to agree to the continuation of Chevaline because of the psychological factors involved and because he recognised the need for a certain continuity in national defence policy. But he would never accept a case for a new generation SSBN/SLBM system to replace Polaris. It was out of the question for Britain to contemplate acquiring a sophisticated and expensive system like Trident, even in the unlikely event that the Americans were prepared to supply it; and it was unrealistic to think in terms of introducing for the 1990s a Poseidon-type system which would by then already be some 25 years old. In any case, there was no need for a decision on that to do about replacing Polaris for another three years or so. Dr Owen added that he would therefore oppose any suggestion of an inter-Departmental examination of the feasibility of a new SSBN/SLBM system. Nor could he accept the idea of a general study on how to replace Polaris which would include such a system as one of the possible options. If the Ministry of Defence staffs were allowed to consider the possibility of a new ballistic missile force and if the Moscow criterion were retained then the result of their study would be a foregone conclusion: they would place an unrealistic emphasis on the need for a highly sophisticated deterrent force and would fail to give adequate attention to the feasibility and utility of a lesser degree of strategic nuclear capability. What was needed at this stage was a full examination of cruise missile options to see what kind of a strategic nuclear capability they could supply and at what cost. Only when such a study has been done, and proper cost estimates were available, should Ministers take any decision on what was to happen when Polaris was withdrawn from service and on whether any work was needed on a future ballistic missile system in the light of known cruise missile options. There might, in any event, be scope for prolonging Polaris' life, for example by giving up in normal peacetime circumstances the notion of continuous patrolling.

Cruise Missiles

7. <u>Dr Owen</u> said that he did not accept the thesis in the Chatham House paper that 17 additional submarines would be required if Britain were to rely on submarine-launched cruise missiles (SLCMs) for deterrent purposes. This did not mean that he opposed the idea of more submarines for the Royal Navy. He was himself an advocate of a larger hunter-killer submarine (SSN) programme at the expense of the present investment in capital ships, particularly the three through-deck cruisers whose vulnerability made them a very questionable investment. But even the existing SSN fleet might on

its own provide a suitable launch platform for cruise missiles, particularly if its torpedo-carrying capability were reduced. It was pointed out in subsequent discussion that torpedoes were the only means at present by which one submarine could attack another and that submarines were a major element in NATO's overall anti-submarines warfare capability. If an SSN had no torpedo-carrying capability at all it would be limited to missions of land attack or anti-surface ship. It was however the Soviet submarine fleet which posed the greatest danger to NATO at sea: already the Royal Navy's capability for meeting this threat had been diminished by the decision to install the Sub-Harpoon missile in SSNs and to pre-empt half their existing torpedo-carrying capacity for the purpose. Careful study would be needed of the effect of introducing a mix of torpedoes, anti-ship missiles and long-range cruise missiles into the SSN force in the future. There were also other modes of cruise missile launch which might prove attractive, for example, air or ground.

8. Dr Owen said he was sceptical about ground-launched cruise missiles (GLCMs), not least because of the arms control implications. He thought that it was very likely that a third stage of SALT would be under way by mid-1978 and that cruise missiles would inevitably be one of the main features of discussion there. There was no way in which they could be completely excluded. The main Soviet concern was likely to be to ensure that cruise missiles of a kind capable of threatening Soviet territory did not come under German control. If this concern was to be met some kind of a ban on GLCMs was a likely result. Dr Owen added that he himself saw advantage in not allowing the Germans to move into the field of rocket technology. The effect on the Russians could be very destabilising, as had been shown by their recent concern over German rocket testing in Zaire. He wondered whether it would not be feasible to seek to draw a distinction between GLCMs and SLCMs so as to ensure that arms control limitations bore on the former rather than the latter. It was agreed that more studies were needed on how cruise missile limitations could be applied in ways which did not prejudice British interests. It seemed however that the use of air-launched cruise missiles (ALCMs) other than on heavy bombers had already been effectively foreclosed by the Americans. But if the Americans were considering the use of wide-bodied aircraft as a delivery system for ALCMs it might be worth Britain doing the same. There was a danger however that the Americans, who had clearly discussed the question at much greater length with the Russians that they had admitted publicly to their Allies, might foreclose the possibilities still further. Care would also be needed about the non-circumvention/no transfer aspects of SALT. If the main Soviet concern was about

Germany, it might be possible to devise wording which would exclude the FRG from receiving nuclear technology but which would leave existing Anglo/American arrangements intact. It was agreed that the Americans might not be able to maintain their present stance against any no transfer provision.

Theatre Nuclear Weapons

9. Dr Owen said that in his judgement enhanced radiation warheads (ERWs) were a dead issue. The United States Administration was split about the wisdom of producing them and the Europeans were unenthusiastic about receiving them. The problem was how the proposal could decently be killed off. The Americans seemed to be thinking of doing this via the MBFR negotiations but this needed careful watching. He was not prepared himself to champion the cause on ERWs and thought that Britain should adopt a low profile. The public line should be simply that no decision had been taken either by the Americans or the Europeans. Dr Owen added that he thought that the Alliance's whole policy on theatre nuclear weapons needed re-examination and that the FCO ought to do more to challenge some of the Ministry of Defence's interpretations of this policy. It was absurd for NATO to pretend that there were any circumstances where large numbers of these weapons would be used in Europe simply in order to demonstrate the Alliance's political will to escalate the level of a conflict. He himself saw a possible need for some kind of intermediate nuclear capability and he was sympathetic to the idea of the demonstrative use, in certain circumstances, of nuclear weapons. But some of the arguments which were put forward for retaining NATO's present extensive holdings in the theatre nuclear field simply did not hold water.

Non-Proliferation/Peaceful Nuclear Explosions

10. Dr Owen said that he had been surprised, during his visit to Moscow, by Mr Gromyko's apparent unawareness of the link between non-proliferation and peaceful nuclear explosions. The Russians did not seem to realise that if they insisted on using nuclear explosions for peaceful purposes, then a country like South Africa could hardly be prevented from doing the same. He wondered whether, in the Comprehensive Test Ban (CTB) discussions, enough had been made of this argument. The PUS added that this point would be likely to come up during the Indian Prime Minister's forthcoming visit to the Soviet Union. It was agreed that this argument might be deployed more extensively and that it might have more effect on the Russians than other arguments against PNE.

DOCUMENT 3

PM/79/11
Prime Minister

Chevaline

1. In his minute to you of 18 January Fred Mulley has argued that the Chevaline project should now be funded to completion.

2. As you know, while I have never accepted the operational requirement for taking out Moscow, I have felt that we could not cancel Chevaline, having gone so far on the project. Its escalating cost is a cause for concern, as is the chance that the Russians may deploy a new terminal air-defence missile as early as 1983. This underlines the difficulty for the UK of trying to mirror the operational strategy of the United States. We have not got the resources to keep up with technological modifications and adaptations to the sophisticated defence systems that the Soviets can deploy if they wish around Moscow. It would be useful to have a more detailed assessment of the impact of this on Chevaline's effectiveness, and I think we should therefore look at Chevaline again in six months' time. But I broadly share Fred Mulley's view that a decision to cancel Chevaline at this stage would immediately become public and the resultant controversy would undermine the credibility of our deterrent.

3. In his minute of 26 January, Denis Healey has suggested that the case for extending Polaris life so as to extract the maximum benefit from Chevaline should now be examined. I strongly support him. I thought we had decided formally at our last meeting that we should seriously consider the option of extending the life of the present 4 Polaris boats to see if we could keep their missile systems in service, until at least the late 1990s and possibly even longer, if necessary by purchasing the US stock of missiles, cannibalising them and re-motoring the existing missiles. This decision is not reflected in the minutes, and I have raised this with Sir John Hunt. The minutes refer only to a modernised Polaris A3, which is something different. I hope you will agree to make it explicit in the minutes that one of the options is extending the life of the Polaris A3 missile, and that this should be discussed by Sir Clive Rose and Professor Mason.

4. I am sending copies of this minute to the Chancellor of the Exchequer, the Defence Secretary and Sir John Hunt.

DAVID OWEN
Foreign and Commonwealth Office

DOCUMENT 4

Mr Stephen

PUBLIC DISCUSSION OF NUCLEAR ISSUES

1. I read with interest the record, a copy of which you kindly sent to Defence Department, of the discussion at the meeting of the Labour Party International Committee on 7 March.

2. I was very struck by one of the enclosures to your record, namely the note prepared by the Committee's Secretariat on Mr Mulley's letter of 25 November 1977 about nuclear weapons policy and defence expenditure. The paper is a very competent and perceptive piece of work and exposes a number of (intentional) ambiguities in Mr Mulley's earlier letter. For example:

   a) The paper draws attention, in paragraphs 1 and 9, to the misleading impression given by the use of the phrase "maintain the effectiveness of our existing nuclear deterrent", which is the stock answer given by Ministers to any questions about our current strategic nuclear programme. In fact, of course, as the paper implies, we are not just ensuring that the current stocks of missiles and warheads are in good working order. We are engaged, at great expense (the figures quoted in paragraph 4 of the paper are a massive underestimate), in a Polaris Improvement Programme which gives our missiles a significantly new capability.

   b) Similarly, on cruise missiles (paragraph 3): the assertion that "we have no plans to develop or acquire such missiles" (which is the stock answer given by MOD Ministers and spokesmen on the subject) is true as far as it goes in that no decision has yet been taken on whether British forces should be equipped with them. But it is a bit specious in that it might be thought to infer that the Government is unlikely to want to develop or acquire such systems in the future. If this were so, there would be no need, as the paper points out, for us to express concern to the Americans, as we regularly do in our consultations on SALT, about the dangers of having certain types of Western cruise missile options foreclosed by arms control arrangements. In fact, of course, although we have no "plans" as such, both British Aerospace and the MOD Procurement Executive are conducting design studies on the industrial and technical problems involved and the Defence Operational Requirements Staff and the Defence Policy Staff are examining the operational requirements and capabilities of cruise missiles. As the Secretariat's paper indicates several current British development programmes, for example the terrain following radar developed for the MRCA and the air breathing engine developed for the P3T missile, involve technology which would be relevant for long-range cruise missiles (although this is incidental to their original purpose and not a matter of conscious policy by the MOL). It is thus a little disingenuous to imply that we have little or no interest in the system. There is, at the very least, a greater then evens likelihood that we shall one day wish to deploy cruise missiles in some form with British forces.

3. There are certain other issues on which the Secretariat's paper is less well-informed. The Polaris Improvement Programme is no longer code-named Antelope (paragraph 1) and it certainly has not been abandoned (paragraph 2). And the reference in paragraph 3(a) to the "Marconi-developed underwater to surface guided weapon" is presumably to Sub-Martel, a project which was abandoned a couple of years ago when we decided to buy the American Sub-Harpoon system instead. But on the whole the paper is an impressive document. My main reason for drawing it to your attention, however, is its concluding paragraph which complains of the impossibility of having any sensible debate in Britain about nuclear weapons policy because of the limitations on access to information. This complaint is a little exaggerated: the academic press manages to sustain a reasonably informed commentary on British nuclear policy, of the recent paper by Ian Smart at Chatham House on the Future of the British Strategic Nuclear Deterrent. But precious little of this seems to percolate through to the general political arena. And the accusation that this is due to Government reluctance to publicise information or to enter into public debate is perfectly justified: successive British Governments have maintained a rigid refusal to discuss the details of our military nuclear programmes, because of the fears of the political sensitivity of the issue and an apparent belief that it is not one which lends itself to the normal process of political debate. (It is this fear, rather than any problem of technical security which has been responsible for Governmental policy: the very high security classification which is put on almost anything to do with British nuclear programmes is quite unjustified by any real "threat to the national interest": we regularly classify things Top Secret which the Americans cheerfully dish out in unclassified public of Congressional briefings.)

4. I wonder though whether it will be realistic to sustain this restriction on political discussion in the future. Although there is no need for the present Government to take any immediate major decisions on nuclear weapons policy, many such decisions will need to be made within the

next, say, 2–3 years, for example on the replacement or non-replacement of Polaris, the acquisition of cruise missiles in one mode or another, the future of British theatre nuclear forces, general British attitudes towards arms control arrangements on intermediate-range nuclear systems, etc. And if these decisions are to be taken sensibly, they will need a fair degree of technical and official level preparation. Such preparation has in some instances already started, but in a very secret and restricted forum. I do not myself believe that by limiting consideration of issues of this kind to a tiny handful of officials, usually and inevitably those who have some particular kind of axe to grind, Ministers necessarily get the best advice. For do I think it natural or healthy that these decisions should be prepared, virtually uniquely within the Government apparatus, without any kind of concomitant public or parliamentary discussion.

5. It may in any case not be possible to avoid such discussion altogether. Political circumstances are different now to what they were in the late 1940s and early 1950s when the original decisions on the British nuclear programme were taken, and even to what they were in 1962–63 when the decision on Polaris was pushed through. The fact, *inter alia*, that the Secretariat of the Labour Party International Committee can produce (albeit, I imagine, aided by outside expertise) a reasonably well-informed critique of current Ministerial pronouncements on nuclear weapons policy, surely suggests that no Government will be able to get away with "slipping through" decisions on nuclear weapons in the way that as possible in the past. It seems to me that whatever this, or its successor, Government decides to do about our nuclear weapons programme, there is bound to be enormous public and political interest. The choice is therefore likely to be between an informed political debate in which the facts, options and choices are set out and discussed (perhaps in a manner not wholly dissimilar to the debate about nuclear energy) and a debate founded on rumour, misinformation, conspiracy theories and mistrust. Despite the political sensitivity and technical complexity of some of the issues I wonder whether the former situation would not be more likely to produce a rational outcome than the latter.

6. I realise, of course, that this is probably not Dr Owen's own current view. He has, I believe, hinted that a decision on the retention of some kind of strategic nuclear capability by Britain through the acquisition of cruise missiles might best be taken by not referring overtly to the strategic role of such systems at all but by anchoring them firmly in the theatre context. There are, of course, disadvantages to this approach in terms of deterrence (it would be difficult for a future British Government to refer publicly to the strategic deterrent value of cruise missiles if those missiles had been

procured ostensibly only for theatre nuclear purposes). But it seems to me that there is a political danger as well.

7. Cruise missiles seem likely to become the next focus of Soviet "peace" and disarmament propaganda following the neutron bomb. There may well therefore be a sustained political campaign against them which could spill over into domestic political opposition in Britain to acquisition of them in any form. It may not therefore be politically realistic to think in terms of slipping through a strategic cruise missile capability if cruise missiles themselves are under political attack. The best way in which such an attack could be met would be by making available sufficient facts and figures about them and their characteristics, and about comparable systems on the Soviet side, to show why British acquisition of them for the theatre nuclear or conventional strike role may turn out to be a sensible and cost-effective way of maintaining our defence capabilities. But this would require a much greater degree of openness on the part of the Government than is customary and would inevitably lead to the exposure of the role of cruise missiles in the strategic nuclear field as well.

8. I wonder also whether the political sensitivity of nuclear military issues has not sometimes been misrepresented. There is within the Parliamentary Labour Party a minority of MPs who are opposed to any kind of expenditure on armaments, whether nuclear or conventional. There are others who are implacably opposed to British possession of nuclear weapons. They, and their supporters within the Party as a whole, will react forcefully against anything the Government does in the field of nuclear weapons policy, other than complete renunciation. It will not make any difference what particular decision the Government takes or whether it takes it openly or secretly, their opposition will remain a fact of political life; and given that sooner or later a decision will have to be announced, they can be relied upon at some stage to create a row about it. There is no way, surely, in which this row can be avoided. The political problem is therefore more one of whether the Government should try to prepare public and political opinion for future decisions on nuclear weapons, by encouraging discussion of, and making facts available about, the various options; or whether it would be more prudent to try to avoid public discussion until the decisions have been taken and then hope that the resultant political fuss will be containable.

9. It is of course a matter of political judgement which course to take. But the work done by the NEC Working Party on Defence Spending and the Arms Trade and the paper by the International Secretariat on Mr Mulley's letter on nuclear weapons policy suggest that there will in any event be a degree of debate within the Labour Party on these issues while the Government

is making up its mind, and that it will be difficult to present any eventual decisions, for example on cruise missiles, in too disingenuous a light. There is moreover a danger that even if the Government tries to play down or conceal the fact that it is studying certain future nuclear weapons options, news that they are doing so will nonetheless leak and will lead to a good deal of misleading and misinformed publicity. This in turn might lead to a political row in which the Government appear in something of a conspiratorial and underhand light and might in the end be forced to make public what it was doing anyway.

10. By contrast the risks of proceeding on a more open basis from the beginning might not turn out to be so great. It is true that it would give those elements in the Party implacably opposed to any British nuclear capability the opportunity to make a lot of noise. But they are likely to do this anyway and their political credibility may well be eroded if they are unable (as is likely to be the case) to engage in any rational debate on the subject. It is interesting that both the French Socialist Party and the French Communist Party have managed in recent months to debate openly their defence policies, including their nuclear policies, and reach conclusions which involved radical changes of direction from their previous postures. Is it really the case that the British Labour Party is incapable of conducting such a debate or that the result would inevitably be such as to cause the Government major embarrassment? Of course, the resolutions endorsed at the Party Conference and passed throughout the year by CLPs do not show much evidence of a very detailed or sophisticated interest in defence matters. But they are not necessarily typical of the way a serious political debate would be conducted if the Government were to generate public discussion of some of the issues involved. Although it would no doubt be unrealistic to expect the Party ever to reach similar conclusions to the Government, the divergence might not be impossibly wide and the fact that the issues had been reasonably openly discussed might take a good deal of wine out of the sails of those opposed to the Government's policies.

11. If such a debate does ever take place it seems to be that Dr Owen would be best placed to take the lead in it, partly because of his personal interest and experience in the subject and partly because it could more effectively be broached from an arms control and security perspective (which lies within his responsibility as Foreign Secretary) rather than from a military one. Questions such as how far reductions in US and Soviet strategic systems should go (i.e. President Carter's 50% proposal); whether there should be a negotiation on theatre nuclear, grey area systems; how cruise missiles fit into the SALT regime; whether British nuclear forces could or should be included

in SALT in any way; are all ones where decisions will be required over the next few years and where it would be natural for there to be a wide degree of public and political interest. Discussion of these issues would overlap to some extent into questions of Britain's nuclear defence policy to some extent into questions of Britain's nuclear defence policy generally. Given the manner in which Dr Owen has already encouraged public discussion of disarmament issues, it would be quite consistent for him to stimulate a wider-ranging discussion of nuclear arms control problems as well. He could do this by taking some appropriate occasion (for example the address which he has agreed in principle to give later this year to the International Institute for Strategic Studies) to make a major speech on the future of SALT and British interests therein in which he might spell out the various options and the factors affecting them, making clear that the Government had not yet made up its mind which course to follow but was taking an active interest in the subject. It would of course be necessary to secure the Defence Secretary's agreement to broaching these topics publicly; but provided that Dr Owen geared his remarks primarily to the arms control and disarmament implications and emphasised that in most cases no final Government decisions had been taken, I doubt whether he would object. I doubt also whether a speech of this kind would give rise to undue political difficulty even in a pre-election period.

12. I have not discussed this idea elsewhere in the Department and am therefore sending this minute to you on a personal basis. But if you think that a speech of this kind would be useful, I could discuss it with Mr Wilberforce and others and perhaps draft a submission to Dr Owen suggesting the outline which such a speech might take.

16 March 1978   P Lever

Defence Department

DOCUMENT 5

CONFIDENTIAL

Private Secretary

MEETING WITH MR VANCE, 23 APRIL: SALT

1. In his account of his discussions in Moscow Mr Vance will no doubt give an indication of how close the two sides now are to a SALT II agreement. Previous American estimates were that conclusion of the agreement could probably not be expected before July. In addition Dr Owen may wish to put the following more specific questions:-

   i)   Timing of Ratification and Future Negotiations
       If an agreement is signed sometime this summer (or whenever), how long would the process of ratification by the Senate be expected to take? And do the Americans anticipate that the SALT III negotiations would begin before the process of ratification on the American side is completed. (HM Ambassador in Washington has suggested that getting a SALT II agreement ratified by the Senate will be no easy task, though President Carter's recent success with the Panama Canal Treaty may increase the Administration's confidence in this respect) and that ratification would therefore not be likely to take place until well into 1979. It has never been clear, however, whether the SALT III negotiations, the guiding principles for which will be incorporated into the SALT II agreement, would have to wait on the Senate's ratification or whether they might follow on very shortly after the conclusion of a SALT II agreement on the understanding that the agreement would in due course be ratified.

  ii)   Cruise Missiles
       Has there been any discussion with the Russians on what will happen when the envisaged three year Protocol on cruise missiles expires? The Protocol precludes the deployment of cruise missiles in any mode with a range of over 600 kilometres except that Airlaunched Cruise Missiles of up to 2,500 kilometres range may be deployed with heavy bombers, although they will, when so deployed, be counted as part of the sub-ceiling on MIRVed ballistic missiles of 1320 systems. During the period of this Protocol the testing of cruise missiles of all kinds up to a range of 2,500 kilometres from heavy bombers will however still be permitted. The Americans have

insisted that the Protocol is a temporary measure only and that when it expires all options are still open. It would be surprising however if the Russians were to acquiesce in the unrestrained deployment of cruise missiles in three years time, and it would seem highly likely that they will press for some kind of limitation on the deployment of cruise missiles to be made permanent. There is, of course, a strong British interest in ensuring that potential cruise missile options, for example long range submarine launched cruise missiles, are not closed off to the Allies before their military value has been properly studied.

iii) The Statement of Principles for SALT III
Will the Statement of Principles for SALT III include any reference to the inclusion in the negotiations of Forward Based Systems or other "grey areas" weapons? Hitherto, the Russians have sought to include in the Statement of Principles a reference to the need to take FBS into account. The Americans have responded by saying that if there is to be any such reference, there must be a reference to the need to discuss also Soviet nuclear systems targeted upon Western Europe. The Russians have implied that if FBS is not covered in an agreed Statement of Principles they might wish, at the occasion of the conclusion of a SALT II agreement, to make some unilateral declaration on the subject. The Americans have replied that in that case they would themselves make a unilateral declaration about Soviet systems directed at Europe.

21 April 1978   P Lever

DOCUMENT 6

Private Secretary

NATO AND DISARMAMENT

1. At our meeting yesterday the Secretary of State asked that I should submit any comments I might have on the draft memorandum for the DOP (which I have now seen attached to Mr Mallaby's submission of 8 May) on possible improvements in NATO machinery for dealing with arms control matters.

2. I have one suggestion. The draft proposes that the Allies should seek to make better use of existing NATO machinery. But there might be value in introducing some slight organisational changes. For example, the Senior Political Committee (SPC) of the Alliance was established some 10 years or so ago largely because deputy permanent representatives found themselves with very little work to do. It now spends virtually the whole of its time on MBFR and deals with few other subjects on any kind of regular basis (the normal business of political consultation and exchange takes place, other than at Council level, in the ordinary Political Committee). It would be perfectly appropriate therefore to rename the SPC the "NATO Arms Control and Disarmament Committee" – or something similar – and to give it the kind of broader remit to discuss arms control topics envisaged in para 4(b) of Mr Mallaby's submission. To rename the Committee in this way would have presentational attraction in that it would symbolise NATO's perma-nent serious and institutional interest in disarmament; and would ensure that discussion of these topics in the Alliance took place in a forum in which, although the military side of the house is represented on the SPC is a Grade 3 officer from the Diplomatic Service). Such a change would not however mean any overall increase in the size of NATO bureaucracy.

3. The announcement of a change of this kind might appropriately be included in the reference in the Washington Summit communiqué to greater NATO attention to arms control matters. If the Secretary of State sees merit in the idea an additional sentence could be inserted in the DOP memorandum at the end of para 4(b) along the lines of "In particular, the Senior Political Committee of NATO, which already spends the bulk of its time discussing MBFR, could be renamed the "NATO Arms Control and Disarmament Committee" and given a broader remit for this purpose".

9 May 1978   P Lever

DOCUMENT 7

Private Secretary

VIEWS IN THE UNITED STATES ON SECURITY POLICY ISSUES

1. During my stay in the United States last week, I called on a number of people in the Administration, in academic institutions and on the Senate and Congressional staffs, to discuss various arms control and defence policy questions. Many of the points we covered were of a somewhat specialised nature and will be incorporated in the wider study which the Secretary of State has requested on British security policy. But the following are some general impressions of present thinking in the United States on certain current issues:-

(a) SALT

There is general agreement both inside and outside the Administration that SALT has been oversold, ie that it has been invested with a central importance for the overall management of Soviet/American relations which it cannot by itself sustain now and which it will certainly be unable to do in future. It seems to be recognised that the problems of handling the Russians need to be tackled individually as they arise, albeit on the basis of a coherent policy framework, and that the continuing SALT dialogue, important though it is, will henceforth be but one strand among many. Moreover, SALT will not even "solve" the problem of American, or Soviet, strategic nuclear planning. Whatever the fate of the SALT II agreement (and the general consensus seems to be that although such an agreement would be rejected decisively by the Senate if submitted now, the new Senate will in the end probably ratify it by the middle of 1979, albeit at a certain price), the United States Administration will face difficult decisions on the MX missile, the B1 bomber (which is far from dead) and the Trident submarine programme. SALT will provide a framework within which these decisions can be made but will not in itself make them any easier.

(b) Grey Area Systems

No one in the Administration seems to know what sort of theatre nuclear/grey area arms control agreement the Germans think they can attain, nor how the concept of parity would be relevant to it. Nevertheless, the fact that the Germans seem to hanker after some

114

kind of negotiation in this field is taken very seriously by the Americans and there is considerable regret and disappointment that the United States' major European allies, the Germans and ourselves, seem to be at odds over this issue. Although intellectually the Administration tends to agree with our own assessment that, on the basis of the weapons systems currently deployed, the asymmetry of theatre nuclear/grey area capability between East and West seems to rule out the possibility of a viable balanced agreement, nonetheless the general receptiveness in Washington to German concerns is such that the Americans will probably go along with a proposal for setting up negotiations in this field if the Germans pursue the idea. The concern of the present Administration to show sensitivity towards German wishes in the politico/military field was emphasised to me over and over again.

(c) Cruise Missiles

Those in the academic arms control community who favour the idea of some kind of grey area negotiation assume that any grey area agreement would reflect the introduction into Europe of substantial numbers of nuclear capable cruise missiles. Indeed, they thought that a desire to limit the numbers of cruise missiles deployed in Europe, and if possible to inhibit their acquisition by the Europeans, particularly the Germans, would be the only factor which might induce the Russians to take part in such a negotiation. On the actual capabilities of cruise missiles there seemed to be some general agreement, even among the arms controllers at MIT who are generally sceptical about new weapons systems, that cruise missiles would constitute a viable and cost-effective means of delivering nuclear strikes against Soviet territory. The most significant warning which was offered was that if cruise missiles were introduced on the Western side, the Soviet Union would develop various forms of area and points defence against them, which in turn would lead to a continuing competition in technological innovation between cruise missiles and counter-missile defences. For the United States, involvement in such continuing competition might be acceptable. But for the Europeans, the prospect of having to up-date and modernise any cruise missile force every few years or so might be a daunting prospect.

(d) The British Nuclear Deterrent

There was considerable interest outside the Administration in the future of the British nuclear deterrent. The current Chevaline project, about whose purpose and nature people were surprisingly accurately informed, was widely regarded as a nonsense. Nobody took the Soviet ABM system seriously and nobody suggested that there was any real need to alter the existing British Polaris force in order to cope with it. It seemed to people inconceivable that the Russians would ever regard their ABM system as capable of guaranteeing Moscow invulnerability against attack even by one submarine load of Polaris missiles. As regards any successor to Polaris, opinions varied: one arms control expert at MIT asked whether the British Government had not considered simply letting its strategic nuclear capability expire or, if it was going to be kept going till, say, around the turn of the century, why the British Government did not press as hard as it could internationally for strategic nuclear disarmament on as wide and far-reaching a scale as possible. By contrast, a (formerly British) professor at Tufts University thought that the possession of a nuclear deterrent was the single most important diplomatic asset which the British Government possessed and that it would be madness ever to throw it away.

(e) MBFR

No serious analytical work seems to be being done on MBFR either inside or outside the Administration and, before the announcement of the recent Soviet move in the negotiation, there was little serious interest in the subject in the United States. Representatives of ACDA said that the Americans felt inhibited about offering new ideas on MBFR for fear of seeming to pressurise their European allies, particularly the Germans. It was easier for the Americans nowadays to react to European ideas in this field than proffer any of their own.

(f) Defence Equipments and Doctrines

There is considerable interest both inside and outside the Pentagon in the more effective use of infantry including reserve formations to occupy ground in Central Europe and in the more mobile use of tank formations. In addition, there is considerable scepticism about using expensive multi-role manned aircraft for deep-strike or ground support behind enemy lines. Many of the tasks for which the British MOD seems to envisage the need for a successor aircraft to the Jaguar and Harrier could perhaps be done by a combination of better ground based artillery (including multiple rocket launchers), small reconnaissance and ordinance carry RPNs and perhaps a much simpler and more unsophisticated anti-tank aircraft provided it were available in large numbers.

12 June 1978   P Lever

DOCUMENT 8

PM/78/73
PRIME MINISTER

Nuclear Weapons Policy

1. I have, as you know, for some years taken a close interest in our nuclear weapons policy. I attach a paper which I have prepared, setting out some of the broader issues involved in terms both of NATO doctrines and our own nuclear weapons requirements. The conclusions which I draw from this are mine. I have deliberately not put the paper to the Department since they are involved in preparing the options paper for the next Government. This paper is being prepared without reference to Ministers so I do not know what ideas my own officials are putting forward. You may however find that some of the ideas in this paper are worth exploring and I hope you might consider asking for some work along these lines to be done so as to ensure that these points are covered by the officials' paper.

2. As regards NATO doctrines, we should make a greater effort to impress upon our allies the unreality of some of NATO's current assumptions about the way in which nuclear weapons might be used. I do not believe that responsible political leaders in the West would ever contemplate using nuclear weapons for limited battlefield purposes. The initiation of nuclear war would be such an awesome step that no rational politician would contemplate it other than in circumstances where the very survival of his country was at stake; and in this case we in NATO would surely only think of using nuclear weapons, initially perhaps in a demonstrative manner, against the Soviet Union itself. The Alliance's very large holdings of short-range nuclear systems seems to me to be of no real use to us whatever, unless we take the view that because the Russians have such systems, we must as well.

3. As a contribution towards reducing NATO's emphasis on short-range nuclear weapons, I believe that we in Britain could appropriately allow our independent national ability for tactical nuclear warfare to be phased out. I cannot conceive of any circumstances in which we would use our tactical bombs and depth bombs independently of NATO (the argument that, if we have an independent strategic nuclear capability, we need an independent tactical nuclear capability as well seems to me to be nonsense); and I cannot see that having a distinctive British capability in this particular area is of any benefit to the Alliance as a whole. To withdraw our bombs from service would

not only save us some money, it would also, more usefully, relieve some of the pressure on our supplies of weapons-grade plutonium. At the same time we might consider withdrawing from some of our two-key arrangements with the Americans for access to US warheads for our surface battlefield systems. The justification for these arrangements is that they reinforce deterrence by enabling a number of allies to share responsibility for nuclear release. But insofar as this consideration is valid, it surely applies only to nations defending their own territory. On the Central Front there is a political case for the Germans, Belgians and Dutch having this facility (though I think it would be more logical to apply it to long-range systems than to short-range ones), but I can see no good reason why we should be involved as well.

4. As to our own strategic nuclear capability, my main concern is that before any decisions are taken, we should explore thoroughly and without prejudice all the possible options open to us. For example, I believe that it is sometimes assumed (though I do not know whether the group of officials currently looking at this problem has accepted this assumption) that 1993 or thereabouts represents some kind of date after which our Polaris force will no longer be viable. But, as the attached papers indicates, it is not impossible that ways could be found of prolonging the force's active life beyond the year 2000. There is evidence that the hull life can be extended and we could buy in extra stocks of Polaris missiles, and possibly also abandon the idea of unaccompanied deep-water patrolling in favour of coastal patrols. Prolonging the life of Polaris in this way would give us at least an extra seven years breathing space and would enable us to get full advantage from our considerable investment in Chevaline. I believe, therefore, that this option should be seriously studied and that we should not take it for granted that the force needs to be replaced by any particular date.

5. Another area in which I hope we can soon engage in specific studies is that of cruise missiles. I realise that there are still a number of uncertainties over some of the technical aspects of these systems. But from what we know of the present state of the art, there seems to be a good possibility that cruise missiles installed on our SSN hunter-killer submarines could be a valuable and cost-effective supplement both to our strategic nuclear capability and to our capability for attacking surface ships. I hope, therefore, that any studies which are done on cruise missiles will look at the full spectrum of their potential. We need, I believe, to get a lot more information from the Americans about their Tomahawk programme, perhaps by approaching them at a high level to express our interest in it; and we need to consider whether the introduction of cruise missiles into an enlarged SSN fleet, in addition to or in part replacement of the currently planned mix of

torpedoes and Sub-Harpoon missiles would not be a cost-effective way of enhancing both our strategic nuclear and our conventional naval capability. It is as dual capable systems that cruise missiles seem to be likely, not least politically to be most attractive.

6. Finally, there is one issue on which thinking about this subject has confirmed my earlier beliefs: I do not accept that a British strategic nuclear force needs to have the kind of 100 per cent assured capability for destroying Moscow which has hitherto been the basis of our planning. We have tended in the past to identify our own criteria for deterrence too closely with those which are appropriate to the Americans. This was, I believe, a mistake. For the distinctive national and European political and military role for which a British deterrent is justified (and it is this, rather than the need to contribute to NATO which is, in my view, the ultimate justification for our being a nuclear power) I believe that the ability to destroy, say, half a dozen major cities in the Soviet Union is perfectly adequate.

7. As to the drafting of the Manifesto you need no advice from me. There will however be an attempt to close off the cruise missile option. I believe this would be a more serious development than language which said we would not purchase a second generation of Polaris submarines and I believe we ought to be able to confuse the issue by pointing to the submarine to ship version of the US Tomahawk cruise missile. Indeed the political attraction of this system is its dual purpose role – submarine to ship and submarine to land; a conventional weapons systems as well as a strategic nuclear weapons system.

DAVID OWEN

Foreign and Commonwealth Office
31 July 1978

[A handwritten comment made by the Prime Minister on David Owen's memo on 18 August read: 'A remarkable piece of work if, as I gather, Dr Owen has prepared this himself. It can go later on to officials but before it does I should want to have a talk with the FOCS [Foreign and Commonwealth Secretary] (and be reminded of the present position of the officials' work).']

NUCLEAR WEAPONS POLICY

Introduction

1. Nuclear weapons represent, because of their unique destructive power, the great potential threat to world security. For Britain, involvement in a nuclear war, even on a limited scale, would be a disaster unparalleled in our history. The avoidance of nuclear war is therefore a central preoccupation of British foreign policy. This in turn means that the role of nuclear

weapons in maintaining our security deserves the most careful scrutiny and analysis.

2. This paper discusses some of the issues involved. It is divided into three sections, namely:–

a) What doctrines for the use of nuclear weapons should NATO as a whole espouse and what sort of weapons does it require?

b) What is the case for an independent British nuclear capability and what sort of capability should it be?

(c) What are the particular options for a future British nuclear force?

A. THE GENERAL NATO REQUIREMENT

3. According to current NATO doctrine nuclear weapons serve the broad political purpose of deterring any kind of attack on the territory or forces of NATO countries in the North Atlantic area. Under the agreed Allied strategy of flexible response NATO would be prepared to use its nuclear forces, including if necessary its massively destructive strategic nuclear forces, against an aggressor whose attack could not be repelled by non-nuclear means. The conventional defence forces of NATO, although much improved since the early 1950s when NATO was out-numbered 5 or even 10 : 1 by the Warsaw Pact, are still not considered by NATO governments to be capable of sustaining indefinitely a viable defence against a Warsaw Pact conventional invasion. NATO has refused therefore to subscribe to a doctrine of using nuclear weapons only in response to a nuclear attack and has insisted on retaining the option of initiating the first use of nuclear weapons. (The Soviet Union, by contrast, has, like China, said that it will never be the first country to use nuclear weapons.) Indeed, most discussions in the Alliance on concepts for the use of nuclear weapons assume that it will be NATO which will take the initiative, at a time and in a manner of its own choosing, in escalating if necessary a future East–West conflict to the nuclear level.

4. It is further assumed in NATO that the credibility of deterrence requires the maintenance of a very wide spectrum of nuclear capability. The range of nuclear options currently available to the Alliance, and the systems associated with them, include the following:–

a) Limited and local tactical use in the immediate battlefield area (LANCE missiles, nuclear artillery and short-range dual capable aircraft);

b) the mining of geographical choke points on NATO territory (Atomic Demolition Munitions);

c) Air Defence (Nike Hercules missiles);

TABLE 1A

THE CURRENT NATO STOCKPILE OF NUCLEAR WEAPONS

I　UNITED STATES CENTRAL STRATEGIC FORCES
(Not all of these are formally assigned to NATO)

Intercontinental Ballistic Missiles	1054	(450 Minuteman II, 550 Minuteman III & 54 Titan II)
Ballistic Missile Firing Submarines	41	(31 Poseidon, 16 Polaris)
London Range Bombers	373	(B 52s)

II　EUROPEAN BASED STRATEGIC FORCES
(ie forces capable of inflicting major damage on targets on Soviet territory)

Ballistic Missile Firing Submarines		4	(Polaris) British warheads
	[French	5	M2/M20 MSBS] French warheads
Medium Range Bombers	British	212	(56 Vulcans & 156 Fllls) British warheads for Vulcans American warheads for Fllls
	American		
	[French	32	(Mirage 1VA)] French warheads
Medium Range Ballistic Missiles	[French	18	(52 SSBs)] French warheads

III　MEDIUM RANGE THEATRE STRIKE SYSTEMS
(range between 100 and 1,000 miles)

Surface to Surface Missiles	US & FRG	135	Pershing (81 US launchers 59 German launchers) American warheads
Aircraft (all dual capable)	US, UK, FRG, ▮▮▮▮	about 1000	(F4, F109, Buccaneer Jaguar American warheads for F4 and f109 British Warheads for Buccaneer & Jaguar

IV　BATTLEFIELD SYSTEMS (range under 100 miles)

Artillery	US, UK, FRG, ▮▮▮▮	about 1000	(8" & 155m American warheads) (LANCE & HONEST JOHN)
Surface to Surface Missiles	US, UK, FRG, ▮▮▮▮	200	

V　MISCELLAENOUS
Surface to Air Missiles　　　　　　　　　　NIKE HERCULES
Atomic Demolition Munitions
Nuclear Depth Bombs
Nuclear Torpedoes

TABLE 1B

THE CURRENT WARSAW PACT STOCKPILE OF NUCLEAR WEAPONS

I	SOVIET CENTRAL STRATEGIC FORCES		
	Intercontinental Ballistic Missiles	1477	
	Ballistic Missile Firing Submarines	62	(Delta Yankee class)
	Long Range Bombers	135	
II	SOVIET STRATEGIC FORCES TARGETTED ON WESTERN EUROPE		
	Ballistic Missiles	591	(484 SS4s, 87 SS5s, & 20 SS20s)
	Ballistic Missile Firing Submarines	20	(Golf class)
	Aircraft	510	(48 Blinder/Badger 30 Backfire)
III	WARSAW PACT MEDIUM RANGE STRIKE FORCES (range between 100 and 1000 miles)		
	Surface to Surface Missiles	612	(144 Scaleboard, 968 Sand B)
	Aircraft (all dual capable	?2000	
IV	BATTLEFIELD SYSTEMS (range under 100 miles)		
	Artillery	432	203mm & 240mm
	Surface to Surface Missiles	about 980	Sand A and Frog

   d) Anti-submarine warfare (nuclear depth bombs carried on aircraft and helicopters);
   e) Deeper interdiction strikes against military targets in and behind the battle area but outside Soviet territory (Pershing missiles, F4 aircraft);
   f) Limited nuclear strikes on local military targets in the Soviet Union (F111 and Vulcan aircraft);
   g) Strikes against Soviet strategic military targets and against major Soviet cities (ICBMs, SLBMs and strategic bombers).

Table 1A sets out the current NATO stockpile of nuclear weapons; and Table 1B the Warsaw Pact stockpile.

   5. NATO has not however succeeded in formulating a coherent doctrine for all these various options. The Provisional Political Guidelines for the Initial Defensive Tactical Use of Nuclear Weapons by NATO, approved by Defence Ministers in 1970, stated that NATO's objective of maintaining or restoring the security of the NATO area would be achieved by making a potential aggressor desist from an attack "either because of the military defeat of his forces or through a realisation that unacceptable risks may be involved". The Guidelines went on to set out a number of ways in which NATO might introduce nuclear weapons into a conflict, (including the demonstrative use of a single weapon not aimed at a military target; the use of atomic demolition

munitions; the use of nuclear weapons in an air defence role; battlefield use; use in an extended geographical area; and maritime use). They concluded that the most appropriate term of initial use by NATO would vary according to the particular circumstances; but that it should in general not involve targets in the Soviet Union itself.

6. Further studies were set in hand to examine the practical consequences of introducing nuclear weapons on the battlefield. The results of these studies showed however that, if the Warsaw Pact was prepared to use nuclear weapons on a similar scale in response to NATO's initial use, it would be impossible for NATO to impose a military defeat. The result of a two-sided exchange of nuclear weapons on the battlefield was shown to be simply an accentuation of the trend of the preceding or associated conventional battle, albeit at a much higher level of attrition and destruction. Thus if NATO was already losing a conventional war, the consequences of introducing nuclear weapons would be to cause it to lose even faster if the Russians responded in kind. An extended nuclear exchange might lead to a temporary pause in the fighting – a shock effect while the two sides regrouped and brought forward whatever forces they had left – but victory, if it could be termed such, would eventually accrue to the side with the great number of readily available reserves and this would invariably be the Warsaw Pact.

7. Studies on the notion of unacceptable risk have necessarily been more speculative. But the Provisional Political Guidelines themselves recognised that any initial use of nuclear weapons by NATO should be designed to "convince the enemy of NATO's evident readiness should aggression continue to escalate the conflict if necessary to all out nuclear war". Given that Warsaw Pact forces are trained and equipped to fight in a combined nuclear/conventional environment and that Soviet military doctrine specifically recognises the possibility of prolonged limited nuclear warfare, it would be rash to assume that anything short of a nuclear attack on the Soviet Union itself would necessarily be regarded by the Russians as unacceptable.

8. NATO's own studies have shown therefore that many of the nuclear systems which NATO currently possesses, particularly the short-range battlefield systems and the systems which could only be used on or over NATO's own territory (which in all account for nearly 70% of the nuclear warheads stockpiled in Europe), are of little or no use in satisfying the criteria of "military defeat" or "unacceptable risk". But it has proved impossible within the Alliance to secure agreement on an alternative rationale for NATO's nuclear weapons requirements. The Alliance's military authorities, both national and international, are reluctant to admit that many of the nuclear systems they have deployed are of no real utility; and at the political

level, though some recognise privately that current plans are inadequate, there has been little enthusiasm for facing up to the challenge of redefining the conceptual framework of deterrence.

9. There are however dangers in accepting too complacently the status quo. NATO's current stockpile of nuclear systems is large and expensive to maintain (there are, for example, enough US troops involved in guarding nuclear storage sites in Europe to man two full divisions); new procurements of nuclear systems are being contemplated; and the possible inclusion of certain systems in arms control negotiations is already being discussed. It will be impossible for Allied governments to take sensible decisions in these areas without a more rational overall policy on nuclear weapons requirements. The following paragraphs suggest what the basis of this policy should be.

10. The three factors which NATO must take into account in planning its nuclear weapon capabilities are:–

   a) The need to pose a credible deterrent to any form of Soviet aggression.
   b) The need to allow for a reasonable degree of flexibility and control in managing a crisis.
   c) The need not to allow the Soviet Union to acquire forms of nuclear capability to which NATO has no appropriate specific counter.

11. For the purposes of deterrence the principal requirement for NATO is a survivable capability for delivering nuclear strikes against the territory of the Soviet Union including its major cities and its industrial and military installations. It is unlikely that the Soviet Union would be seriously deterred from launching or maintaining a major attack against the West simply by the risk of incurring nuclear strikes on the territory of its Warsaw Pact allies, even if such strikes were directed specifically against Soviet forces, let alone by the prospect of NATO using nuclear weapons on its own territory. Insofar as a more limited capability for nuclear warfare contributes to deterrence it does so only by holding out the further risk of nuclear retaliation against the Soviet Union itself.

12. The need for a reasonable degree of flexibility means it would be undesirable for the Alliance to be limited to a capability for delivering nuclear strikes only against major strategic targets in the Soviet Union. There is also a need for the Alliance to be able to attack, on a more selective basis, local military targets, for example, airfields, bridge-heads, railway marshalling yards and so on in the Soviet Western military districts. It is questionable however, how far this requirement for flexibility need be extended. It is extremely doubtful whether the Allies gain anything of significance in terms

of their ability to maintain political control in a potential East–West conflict by their massive holdings of short-range battlefield nuclear weapons. If the Soviet Union were to launch an all out attack on Western Europe it would probably use its own nuclear weapons from the start, in which case NATO should be ready to respond straightaway with strikes against targets on Soviet territory: a limited battlefield nuclear exchange would achieve nothing. In the case of an all out conventional attack by the Warsaw Pact (which of all the possible scenarios for a conflict is probably the least likely) the additional time which limited nuclear battlefield use would gain would be marginal. The Soviet Union would presumably have calculated, in launching such an attack, that NATO would not be prepared to use nuclear weapons against Soviet territory in response and it would be necessary for NATO to demonstrate that this was a misreading of NATO's resolve. The only politically feasible response would be by an early demonstrative nuclear explosion somewhere on the territory of the Soviet Union but avoiding major population centres or military targets. If this failed it would be necessary to launch strikes against local military targets in the Soviet Union's western military districts. It is very doubtful whether, in the event of an all out conventional attack, NATO would gain any negotiating time by initiating a phase of short-range battlefield nuclear warfare: assuming that the Soviet Union responded in kind the effect would simply be to intensify and accelerate the conflict, thus causing NATO to reach exhaustion point quicker than would otherwise have been the case and it would risk escalating the nuclear exchange to strategic weapons.

13. In the context of "accidental" hostilities in Europe, it is unlikely that short-range tactical nuclear weapons will be of any relevance whatsoever. If a war does occur in Europe, it is most likely to start not from a major Warsaw Pact attack, nuclear or conventional, short-warning or long-warning, against NATO but from miscalculation and misjudgement of some local incident. (For example, an internal uprising in the GDR might lead to the deployment there of additional Soviet troops for internal security purposes and to fighting between the Soviet occupation forces and parts of the GDR army; the FRG might, because of the increased tension on its eastern border, proceed to mobilisation and ask for NATO reinforcements; armed East German refugees might begin to cross the inner German border and be pursued by Soviet troops who would in turn be engaged by NATO forces; the Russians might fear that an attack on them was imminent and take some kind of pre-emptive action; the conflict could thus begin to escalate without either of the two sides having at any stage decided specifically to attack the other or having any actual military ambitions outside their own borders.)

14. Under this sort of scenario NATO would be primarily concerned with the political management of the crisis and with reassuring the Russians that NATO did not harbour any aggressive or subversive intentions. So long as there were signs that the Russians were not hell-bent on the complete subjugation of western Europe but were simply reacting nervously and irresponsibly to a threat to their own internal security, NATO would have no interest in escalating the crisis to the nuclear level. The employment of a local nuclear battlefield weapon or set of weapons would only make things worse, by provoking the Russians into a wider nuclear exchange. If it proved impossible to defuse the situation and restore stability by political means, it might be thought appropriate for NATO, as in the case of a full-scale conventional invasion, to launch a one-off demonstrative nuclear strike somewhere remote on Soviet territory (though even this would be extremely risky); but otherwise nuclear weapons would have no useful role to play.

Countering Soviet Capabilities

15. The requirement for countering Soviet capabilities is more complex. It need not be interpreted as implying that there must be a western nuclear delivery system precisely comparable with anything which the Russians have (any more than the Russians have chosen to imitate every single Western technological development). Nor does it mean that there should be a Western nuclear system actually targeted on every Soviet one, in the way that some American ICBMs are targeted on Soviet missile silos and vice versa. Rather, it is a political requirement that there should be no major perceived asymmetries between the nuclear forces of the two sides. At the moment there are two types of asymmetry which are causing political concern in the West, namely:-

   a) The alleged prospective ability of the Soviet land-based missile force to take out all or most American minuteman missiles in a disarming first strike, which is not matched by any comparable ability on the Western side. This is tied in with the "throw weight" argument whereby SALT II would allow an increase in Soviet nuclear megatonnage.

   b) The capability which the Soviet Union has for inflicting assured nuclear destruction on Western Europe with systems, such as the SS20 missile and the Backfire bomber which are separate from Soviet strategic forces targeted on the United States and which are not subject to any form of arms control limitation.

16. Neither of these asymmetries presents a critical military problem. In the case of the alleged vulnerability of their land-based missiles (and it is questionable whether technically the Russians could ever realistically hope to succeed in a pre-emptive first strike against them), the Americans would still have available the other two legs of the strategic nuclear triad, their bomber force and their submarines. And in the case of Soviet systems targeted against Western Europe, NATO has, in addition to its F111 and Vulcan aircraft, American and British SSBNs assigned to the integrated command structure and targeted on the Soviet Union through SACEUR's Scheduled Strike Programme. Nonetheless, in each case there are political apprehensions. Some Americans argue that the vulnerability of the land-based missile force means a reduction in the ability of the United States to maintain control in a nuclear conflict, in that the land-based missiles are capable of more selective, discreet and controlled targeting than either bombers or submarines; that their elimination would mean that the United States would have no further nuclear options left than all out strategic strikes on Soviet cities or military/industrial targets; and that this loss of flexibility might weaken the confidence of the European Allies in the maintenance of the US nuclear guarantee.

17. Some Europeans, particularly West Germans, believe that the Soviet Union's capability for attacking Western Europe with a class of nuclear weapons separate from its central strategic forces targeted on the United States represents a political threat to which NATO cannot afford not to respond. There are many counter arguments but the fear in Europe is genuine, though at present largely unspoken. It nevertheless needs to be faced and is a factor in considering the role of British and French nuclear forces.

Force Structure

18. In political and military terms therefore the nuclear forces which NATO should aim to deploy are:-

i)   A sufficient number of survivable strategic nuclear missiles capable of inflicting assured destruction on Soviet cities and major industrial assets;

ii) Other nuclear delivery vehicles (missiles or bombers) capable of delivering more precisely targeted strikes against Soviet military installations including local targets in the western military districts;

iii) A European-based nuclear capability, separate from the US-based central strategic capability, able to inflict a degree of destruction on the Soviet Union comparable to the Soviet IR/MRBM and bomber threat to Western Europe.

19. The first two of these three requirements are satisfied by the present US triad of strategic nuclear bombers, land-based missiles and nuclear submarines. Of these three elements the submarine force occupies a key position because of its invulnerability to pre-emptive strike. There is a strong Allied interest therefore in ensuring the continued invulnerability of this force either through technological improvement to it – such as the introduction of quieter boats with longer ranges – or by arms control arrangements which limit the likelihood of SSBNs being detected and tracked ██████████ ██████████ or both. There are however for the present still command and control problems over nuclear submarines which limit the extent to which they can be used for complex targeting purposes. There will therefore for the foreseeable future be an Allied requirement for additional means of central strategic nuclear delivery. From a European perspective however there is no overriding reason why this additional requirement should involve both strategic bombers and land-based missiles. Nor does there seem any fundamental reason why the land-based missile component should have the same degree of invulnerability as the submarine force. Nonetheless American domestic preoccupation over the vulnerability of the Minutemen silos is likely to continue and the US Administration will probably feel obliged to do something to enhance their survivability, either by introducing a new mobile ICBM force such as the MX or, just conceivably, by introducing certain point defence systems for individual silos.

20. The third requirement is the area where NATO's present nuclear forces are open to criticism. French nuclear forces are still seen as being totally independent, though this is becoming generally less so. They are unlikely to give much reassurance to the Germans. The 4 British Polaris submarines are committed to NATO and are seen as being European in a way that US Polaris and Poseidon submarines are not. 56 British Vulcan bombers are based in Britain, but it is unlikely that the Vulcans could be used for attacks on more than a few very local military targets at the edge of the Soviet Union's western military districts; they do not pose a credible threat to Soviet cities or industrial or strategic military installations. The 156 American F111 aircraft stationed in Britain are not seen as being part of a European capability by those who fear an American "decoupling" from Europe.

21. If NATO's European based capability against the Soviet Union is to be strengthened the options would include:–

  i)   A new force of intermediate range ballistic missiles, based in Germany under double key arrangements, of greater accuracy range and survivability than the present Pershing force and replacing it on a one for one basis subject to whatever limitations on Pershing emerge from MBFR.

ii) A force of long range ground (over 2,000 km) launched cruise missiles (perhaps up to 500 launchers) based in Germany under double key arrangements.

iii) The installation of air-launched cruise missiles on strike aircraft such as the F111 Mirage and the Tornado or on special wide bodied aircraft (the use of ALCMs in the European theatre in this way has however been considerably inhibited by the limitations which the Americans have accepted in the SALT II Treaty).

iv) The deployment of cruise missiles on British and French nuclear powered submarines.

22. The remainder of NATO's present nuclear capability, i.e. all the short-range ASW and air defence systems, could in theory be allowed simply to wither away. In practice there would probably be certain constraints upon this. So long as the Soviet Union retained numbers of battlefield nuclear systems NATO would probably not feel able to do away completely with all its Lance missiles, nuclear artillery and nuclear capable aircraft, (though it could without cost get rid of its atomic demolition munitions, nuclear air defence missiles and nuclear depth bombs to which there are no real Soviet equivalents). In any case many of the delivery systems concerned are dual capable and would be required for conventional defence purposes. But a considerable reduction of the present stockpile of 7,000 warheads (5,000 of them in West Germany) could be achieved and considerable economies made in training personnel to guard, operate and service the present systems.

23. In the long run some kind of East–West understanding, not necessarily a formally negotiated one, on short-range nuclear systems might be attainable. NATO might announce, as part of its basic doctrine for nuclear weapons, that it was not willing to fight a limited battlefield nuclear war; that it rejected the notion that tactical nuclear weapons could be used for purely military purposes; that the value of nuclear weapons was in terms of deterring the Soviet Union from launching or pursuing any kind of attack against the West; and that therefore NATO would henceforth plan its nuclear capability and adapts its nuclear planning solely in order to pose a threat to Soviet territory. If it became clear that this doctrine was being accompanied by a de-emphasising and thinning out of NATO's short-range nuclear systems, the Soviet Union might eventually follow suit and reduce its own short-range nuclear capability. Provided that this process of de-emphasis did not involve any weakening of NATO's conventional capabilities, and provided that it was accompanied by a strengthening of the Alliance's European-based long-range nuclear strike capability it ought also to be acceptable to Western political and public opinion. Indeed, insofar as

it offered a rational and responsible conceptual basis for NATO's nuclear posture it ought, by contrast with the current misunderstood and misinterpreted policy on theatre nuclear weapons, increase public confidence in the Alliance's overall defence doctrines.

24. A change of nuclear doctrine and force structure of this kind by NATO would also facilitate the pursuit of arms control arrangements. At the lower end of the nuclear spectrum, formal arrangements would be difficult to achieve because of problems over dual capability, categorisation and verification (though it might be possible in due course to discuss certain very generalised limitations, such as a prohibition on the carriage of nuclear weapons on surface ships or on the use of nuclear capable artillery). But at the more important strategic or near-strategic level, an improvement by NATO in its European-based nuclear capability will, paradoxically, be a major help in the search for a controlled and stable East-West nuclear balance. One. of the major difficulties which will confront the negotiators in future rounds of SALT is the impossibility of dealing, in a negotiation which is supposedly about the central strategic balance between the United States and the Soviet Union, with systems which pose a strategic threat to the non-US members of NATO or which pose a strategic, or near-strategic threat to the Soviet Union from outside US territory. The Soviet Union is likely, in SALT III, to want to discuss US-forward based systems and British and French strategic nuclear forces. Some European members of NATO want SALT III, or some negotiation associated with it, to discuss Soviet "strategic" nuclear systems targetted on Western Europe. Under existing force structures it will be impossible to meet these concerns: the Soviet capability against Western Europe is so vastly greater, in both numbers and quality, than NATO's European based capability against the Soviet Union that no arms control arrangement in this area will be possible; and so long as this area of nuclear capability remains unconstrained both the United States and the Soviet Union will find it difficult to contemplate any very far-reaching further reductions in their central strategic forces.

25. An enhancement of NATO's European based nuclear capability against the Soviet Union would remove this difficulty. It would become feasible to negotiate a controlled East–West balance in strategic nuclear forces at the European level, either as an adjunct to SALT or even in a separate negotiation, since the capabilities of the two sides would be more evenly matched. The form which such a balance might take would, of course, depend partly on the form of NATO's force planning decisions. But if, for example, NATO decided to opt for a long-range cruise missile force based partly on the ground in Germany and partly in British, and possibly French,

submarines, it could offer to negotiate an arms control arrangement whereby the size of this force, together with the British and French SSBN forces and US, French and British long-range bomber aircraft would be numerically equal to the Soviet Union's holdings of SS 20, SS4 and 5 (if they remained in service) missiles, Backfire and Blinder/Badger (if they remained in service) aircraft, Golf Class SSBNs and SSM3 cruise missiles carrying submarines, ie all nuclear systems not covered in SALT with a range of over 2,000 kilometres. Other more specific limitations on individual forms of capability could also perhaps be discussed. It would be important for NATO, in improving its European based nuclear capability to try to avoid generating a further acceleration of the nuclear arms race in this area. Any procurement decision should therefore ideally be accompanied by a simultaneous offer to negotiate a controlled balance (and perhaps by an offer to discuss informally the possibility of removing altogether certain short-range nuclear systems). But without some kind of improvement by NATO in this area, it is unlikely that any arms control negotiation will be possible.

B. BRITISH NUCLEAR WEAPONS POLICY

The need for an independent nuclear capability

26. The general Alliance requirements for nuclear weapons and particularly the arguments for changing the balance of the European based nuclear capability provides a background against which to assess Britain's own future nuclear weapons policy. But it is only a partial background. Britain possesses nuclear weapons for political and military reasons and for national as well as European reasons. It cannot be seen therefore solely as a contribution to NATO's overall defence posture.

The need to contribute to NATO

27. The present British nuclear forces consist of 4 Polaris submarines, 56 Vulcan bombers; Buccaneer and Jaguar dual-capable aircraft; Lance surface to surface missiles and dual capable artillery; and nuclear depth bombs. The warheads for Polaris, the bombs for the Vulcans, Buccaneers and Jaguars and some of the depth bombs are British made; the remainder are American, held under two key arrangements. The British nuclear forces represent only 5% of the Alliance's total nuclear capability. There is no reason to suppose that the US would not be able, if necessary, to assign extra nuclear assets to SACUER to replace any gaps in his targeting requirements which the disappearance of the British nuclear contribution might cause. In numerical terms the British nuclear contribution is thus relatively insignificant.

28. It can be argued however that the existence of the British nuclear forces is of significant political benefit to the Alliance. There are two particular reasons:

a) the existence of a second centre of nuclear decision making within NATO constitutes a complicating and inhibiting factor in Soviet calculations and this adds to deterrence;

b) the readiness of Britain to commit its nuclear forces to the defence of Western Europe might in certain circumstances act as a "trigger" which would strengthen the resolve of the US to do the same.

The validity of these arguments is difficult to assess. It is hard to know whether the Russians would really believe that Britain would use its own nuclear forces – and thus risk complete national destruction – to defend other European countries, in circumstances where the Americans were refusing to do so; or whether the Americans would seriously allow themselves to be swayed against their own judgment in using nuclear weapons by a British threat to escalate unilaterally. We do know that the Federal Chancellor, Helmut Schmidt, does attach importance to the maintenance of a British nuclear contribution in the form of an independent nuclear capability. It is clear that a significant section of German opinion would regard it as politically damaging for us to renounce our nuclear status at a time when the specific Soviet threat against Western Europe is being increased. But it would probably be fair to assume that they would not attach such a high value to it that they would wish us to retain it in all circumstances and at any price. If therefore the maintenance of our nuclear capability required major new capital investment which could only be achieved by some major reduction in our contribution to other areas of the Alliance's defence effort our Allies would hesitate before pressing us to remain a nuclear power. There is however no evidence that our Allies attach particular value to the form or quality of the British nuclear contribution. At present the British nuclear Polaris forces are targeted, under SACEUR's Scheduled Strike Programme ████████████████████████████

██

████ There would thus be no need, in NATO terms, for any future British nuclear force to be more effective in range, yield or penetration capability than the present one.

The National Security Requirement

29. In order to assess the requirement for any "last resort" guarantee of national security it is necessary to examine the particular circumstances in which this security might be at risk, and where the possession by Britain of

nuclear weapons might consitute a significant asset. There are broadly two types of circumstance in which this might be the case:–

a) a threatened Soviet attack against the UK which the Alliance as a whole was unwilling, or unable, to deter by virtue of its collective defence capability;

b) the degree to which the territory of the UK would be subject to attack in the event of a general East–West war in Europe.

30. It is the first of these which is usually cited as the fundamental national security justification for a British nuclear deterrent. It is argued that if one day NATO were to collapse, the possession by Britain of a nuclear deterrent would be necessary in order to deter the Soviet Union from using its massively superior conventional and nuclear forces to attack Britain. The "ccollapse" of NATO would for this purpose, not mean necessarily that the Alliance had ceased to exist or that its forces had been defeated in a war. It could also apply to circumstances where the American commitment to the physical defence of Europe had become conspicuously weakened, for example by the withdrawal of large numbers of US forces, both nuclear and conventional, back to the US and/or by the emergence of domestic pressures in the US against any involvement in "foreign" wars. In such circumstances, even if, formally speaking, the US Administration remained committed to its North Atlantic Treaty obligations, a British Government might judge that this commitment would no longer be credible in the eyes of the Soviet Union; that the Soviet leadership would probably not expect American nuclear weapons to be used unless American territory itself came under attack; and that therefore the maintenance of British security depended on our ability to pose an alternative nuclear deterrent to the Soviet Union.

31. The validity of this justification for a national nuclear capability depends on a judgement on the plausibility of a NATO "collapse". No one could seriously argue in present circumstances, that it is in any sense a likely occurrence. But clearly it cannot be dismissed as utterly inconceivable. If such a collapse were to take place Britain's security would indeed be seriously at risk whether or not we possessed an independent deterrent capability. The consequences of a NATO collapse would be so serious that, it could be argued, no British Government should fail to cater for such an eventuality.

32. A collapse of NATO is not however the only scenario in which our possession of a nuclear capability would affect our security interests. It would also do so in the case of a general East–West war, either conventional or nuclear in Europe, in which British forces were involved. It is likely that the Russians would, in the context of such a war, contemplate specific action

against the territory of the UK. They might calculate however that a British ability to to use nuclear weapons in retaliation meant that the risks involved in extending the theatre of operations to include the UK were unacceptably great. If therefore the Soviet Union was, for whatever reason, launching widespread theatre nuclear strikes against Western Europe, it might deliberately avoid targets in the UK for fear that this might provoke a British national nuclear reaction against Soviet territory. Similarly the Soviet Union might in a conventional conflict refrain from using against its targets, or at any rate against major civilian targets, in Britain for fear that this too might provoke nuclear retaliation.

33. The idea that the possession of nuclear weapons offers a country a kind of "sanctuary" in the event of a general war was one of the tenets of Gaullist defence philosophy. It has been called into question by President Giscard who has recognised that in the event of a major war in Central Europe, France, even though outside NATO's integrated military organisation, could not expect automatically to remain uninvolved. Nonetheless, the prospect of nuclear retaliation against its own territory is the critical factor which the Soviet leadership would bear in mind in calculating the potential risks and gains of any form of military activity in Europe. It would be foolish for Britain to assume any automatic immunity to attack. But our geographical position means that we are, in a sense, less crucially involved in a land/air battle on the Central Front; and there might therefore be circumstances in which the possession of a nuclear capability by Britain would mitigate the extent to which British territory came under Soviet attack. This would apply particularly in the case of an "accidental" East–West conflict, for example, the sort of scenario set out in paragraph 13 above.

34. One thing which is clear however is that the only form of independent nuclear capability which would be of any use to Britain for safeguarding its national security is the ability to strike targets on Soviet territory; and that there would be no value whatever in this context in an independent capability for short range nuclear strike. There are no circumstances in which Britain might sensibly think of using short range tactical nuclear weapons independently of NATO as a whole; and none of the short range systems which Britain now possesses, either land, sea or air, would be of any miltary utility in defending the UK itself. Indeed, even within NATO's existing nuclear doctrine, there is no real argument for a British contribution in the short range field. Insofar as NATO has a requirement for short range nuclear systems at all (and the first part of this paper suggests that there is none and that the only real argument for them is the need to maintain some counterpart to the short-range Soviet capability) there are good political reasons for

ensuring that some of the relevant delivery vehicles are European rather than American. A sharing of responsibility for nuclear delivery both enhances deterrence externally by emphasising the common commitment of the Allies to NATO's declared nuclear policies; and satisfies the internal aspirations of certain Allied countries, particularly the FRG, for participation in common nuclear defence arrangements. But the logic of these arguments suggests that that it is more sensible to include in such arrangements those European countries whose actual territory is most likely to be subject to attack. In the case of a Warsaw Pact invasion of Central Europe, this means the FRG, the Netherlands and Belgium. There is no particular reason why British surface-to-surface missiles, artillery or battlefield support aircraft should be used to deliver tactical nuclear strikes, rather than German, Dutch or Belgian under dual key arrangements. Indeed one means of reducing NATO's holdings of short-range systems might be to confine them henceforth to national forces operating in their own territory.

35. There remains however the question of what particular form of capability against Soviet territory an independent British nuclear capability ought to have. Clearly this must, in order to constitute a credible deterrent, include the ability to inflict major damage on civil and industrial targets. The interpretation of "major damage" is however debatable. Hitherto, it has been assumed as axiomatic that it must include the capability for taking out the city of Moscow. This in turn poses considerable technical problems since Moscow, uniquely among targets in the Soviet Union, is protected by an Anti-Ballistic Missile defence system. The system is however not very efficient and is not frequently tested which gives the impression that the Soviet authorities do not attach great importance to its effectiveness.

36. The technical justification for this programme is that in certain hypothetical situations it would be theoretically possible for the Moscow ABM defence system to destroy before their arrival all the 48 re-entry vehicles which a single Polaris SLBM is capable of firing. This is a deliber-ately worst case analysis. It is relatively unusual for there to be only a single Polaris submarine on station at any one time (at present for between 50 and 75% of the time there are two on station, sometimes three, and it would probably be feasible to put an extra boat on patrol at any time on fairly short notice in the case of any developing East–West crisis). And, in any event, it supposes an extraordinary degree of confidence by the Russians in the capabilities of their Galosh ABM system. This system is old, is not regularly tested and is assessed by the Americans as only partially operational. It represents, moreover, a degree of technological capability markedly inferior to the American SAFEGUARD system which was de-activated five years ago

on the grounds that it was not a worthwhile investment. It seems unlilkely that the Russians would regard it as giving them a 100% guarantee of Moscow's immunity to attack from even a single boatload of Polaris missiles; and it is quite legitimate to pose the fundamental question of deterrence not in terms of "can we be absolutely sure that our missiles would reach their targets" but rather in terms of "could the Russians be absolutely sure that they would not".

37. But even if the invulnerability of Moscow could be assured, it is questionable whether the Russians would be prepared to risk the destruction of their other major cities or industrial assets. This is inevitably a matter of subjective assessent. But it is one which needs to be made in relation to the somewhat limited circumstances of a possible Soviet attack on the UK under the scenarios presented in paragraph 29 above. The judgement by the Russians of what they might be prepared to risk in return for the gains which would accrue from an attack on Britain would be a very different matter from their judgement of the gains and risks involved in a general attack on Western Europe or on the US. It is hard to see how, on any rational calculation, the military or other benefits which they would obtain from an attack on the UK alone would compensate for the loss of, say, ███████████████ ███

38. The broad technical requirements for a British nuclear deterrent force are thus:–

a) it must be invulnerable to an initial pre-emptive strike;
b) it should be capable of inflicting assured destruction on a number of major Soviet cities;
c) it would be valuable (though not in the last resort essential) if it could pose sufficient of a threat to Moscow for the Russians to not feel absolutely confident in Moscow's invulnerability;
d) it should also be capable of being targeted, in accordance wirh SACEUR's Scheduled Strike Programme, ███████████████ ███████████████████████████

Political Aspects

39. In addition to these security considerations there are certain broader political issues relative to the future of the British nuclear deterrent. It is sometimes claimed that the possession of nuclear weapons is an accepted international index of political power which enables the country concerned to play a greater role in international affairs than its economic or conventional military strength would otherwise warrant; and that the renunciation by Britain of a nuclear status would in the long run severely diminish our

general influence on world affairs, including, for instance, our retention of a permanent seat on the UN Security Council. It is sometimes argued, in the contrary sense, that renunciation would constitute a catalyst to international arms control efforts, would be a major step in arresting the further horizontal proliferation of nuclear weapons and would invest the renouncing country with a very considerable moral authority which would increase its political influence. Experience shows that this political "halo" effect might last for a year or so but would soon wear off.

40. It is difficult to assess these claims. But it seems unlikely that such validity as they may have is of any more than marginal significance by comparison with the security considerations. The one political factor which does however bear some weight is the effect of a renunciation of our nuclear status on our relations with our European partners and Allies, in particular France and the FRG. A situation in which France was left as the only European nuclear power would undoubtedly enhance French prestige and authority and this would be likely to have some spin-off in terms of an increased French ability to dominate European political discussions and perhaps also, to some extent, Community affairs. This would in turn arouse German anxieties. The Germans do not look to our deterrent for direct nuclear protection and they do not in any sense regard it, either on its own or in association with the French nuclear capability, as the embryo for some future European nuclear force which might if necessary subsitute for the American nuclear guarantee. Nonetheless, they would, given their present anxieties about the improvements in the Soviet Union's intermediate range nuclear forces, be concerned at the disappearance of such a distinctive part of NATO's European nuclear capability. In some sections of German public opinion this could lead to a resurgence of demands that the FRG should acquire some kind of indigenous capability of its own. The acquisition of such a capability, which is of course precluded both by the Revised Brussels Treaty of 1959 and by German signature of the Non-Proliferation Treaty, would be the most destabilising development in Europe since the end of the Second World War.

C. <u>BRITISH NUCLEAR WEAPONS POLICY</u>

<u>POSSIBLE OPTIONS</u>

41. Against this background the following paragraphs set out the implications, including the cost implications, of certain specific options for future British nuclear weapons policy. These are:-

   i) Abandonment of an independent nuclear capability altogether.
   ii) Low cost option: retaining in service the present nuclear force.

iii) Low/medium cost option: re-equipping the present Polaris boats with new missiles.

iv) Variable cost option: acquisition of a force of long-range cruise missiles.

v) High cost option: acquisition of a force of 4 or 5 new SSBNs.

OPTION ONE: ABANDONMENT

42. Under this option we could decide either to allow our present nuclear forces gradually to be withdrawn from service, starting with the Vulcan bombers in the early 1980s and ending with the withdrawal of the. last Polaris submarine in, say, 1990; or we could withdraw them from service altogether at an earlier date. Early withdrawal would save some money. The present cost of the Polaris force is some £93m a year and there is some £359 million of the Chevaline programme still unspent (though up to ½ or ¾ of this might need to be paid in cancellation fees). There would also be some small savings on a premature phase-out of the Vulcan bomber force (which is due any way to be withdrawn from service by 1983) and on the closure of nuclear research and development establishments. But the total amounts involved would be small. They would not enable us to achieve any very significant improvements to our defence capabilities elsewhere. In cost terms the main benefit of the abandonment of a nuclear capability is that there would be no requirement for accommodating within the present set of long term costings expenditure, which is not currently planned, for developing any new nuclear system.

43. In security terms, we would lose the benefits set out in paragraphs 29 and 32 above which an independent nuclear capability gives us. There would be few, if any, compensating security advantages. It might be argued that the removal of the British Polaris base and Vulcan airfields, would lessen the Russians' interest in Britain as a target for nuclear attack. But so long as other major military assets, including bases for US strike aircraft and reinforcement forces as well as the US SSBN base at Holy Loch (although it is possible that this may no longer be required by the Americans when their Trident 2 submarines come into service in the 1990s) remain, it is unlikely that the Russians' military interest will significantly decline. Britain would therefore almost certainly be involved in any widespread hostilities, either nuclear or conventional, which took place in Europe. Politically, the consequences would be as described in paragraphs 39 to 40 above.

OPTION TWO: RUNNING ON THE PRESENT NUCLEAR FORCE

44. The present Polaris submarine force entered service in 1968. It is argued by the Ministry of Defence that by around 1993, when the first of the boats will have been in service for 25 years, it will become impractical

to retain them, or their missiles, in service. There is however no conclusive basis for this assumption. The experience obtained so far by the US Navy of corrosion and hull fatigue in over 100 submarine hulls, including vessels which have been in the water and subject to depth cycling for as long as 23 years, suggests that with proper maintenance and preservation the life of an SSBN hull can be prolonged virtually indefinitely. It might of course be necessary, from time to time, to replace parts of the vessels' propulsion and auxiliary machinery as well as some of its communications and fire control equipment. But in principle there is no reason why the 4 Polaris boats cannot be kept in service until past the end of this century. There is a long history of successfully stretching the life of ships and other military equipment against the technical arguments of the Ministry of Defence.

45.   There would however be a potential problem of their increased vulnerability to detection and tracking. This problem of vulnerability will apply to all submarines even the quieter modern versions, though SSBNs do not operate at high speeds. The Russians are investing heavily in sonar technology and in other anti-submarine warfare (ASW) techniques and there is bound by the end of the 1980s to be a considerable improvement in their ability to locate and track submarines both from the air, from surface ships (including their large fleet of intelligence-gathering trawlers) and with hunter-killer submarines of their own. It is not yet clear how far this improvement will seriously jeopardise the survivability of the Polaris force. But there are a number of palliative measures which could be taken to lessen this threat. One possible option, for example, would be to abandon the notion of unaccompanied deep water patrol. Even with its present missiles a Polaris SSBN can deliver strikes against a wide range of Soviet cities, including Moscow, from within British coastal waters, ie from within the range of protection of British-based aircraft and naval support. It is unlikely that at a time of crisis or war, the Russians would be able to operate their own aircraft intelligence gatherers or naval vessels with impunity in or around the British Isles. There would thus be scope for developing tactical procedures for safeguarding the invulnerability of such Polaris boats as might be on patrol. It might, for example, be feasible to use British surface ships, hunter-killer submarines and aircraft to seal off the Irish Sea, or a maritime box area west of Scotland so as to deny the Russians the precise knowledge of the location of the vessel which they need in order to be able to target it accurately by either conventional or nuclear strike.

46.   The possible vulnerability of Polaris or any successor means that there is a very strong British interest in developing international arms control arrangements aimed at facilitating the survivability of SSBNs. This is not something which has hitherto featured in the SALT discussions, in part

because under the existing state of the ASW art neither the American nor the Soviet SSBN fleets are significantly threatened. But as ASW technology develops there may be a degree of common interest between the two super-powers in ensuring that submarine based ballistic missile forces do not become subject to the same degree of instability and potential vulnerability as now affects land-based missiles. Neither side could afford to allow the other to develop a first strike capability against SSBNs; and if there was any danger of such a capability becoming attainable, both sides might see merit in discussing possible measures to prevent it (just as the prospect of a poten-tial defence system against ballistic missiles generally, with all the instability which this would entail, led the two sides to negotiate the ABM Treaty).

47. At the moment the Americans have a much more sophisticated and extensive ASW capability against SSBN than the Russians. The Americans sometimes justify their investment in this area on the grounds that their capability to impose significant first strike damage on the Soviet sub-marine based missile force is a balancing counterpart to the growing Soviet capability to take out a significant portion of the US Minuteman silos. The Russians may feel sufficiently threatened by this ASW capability as to see attrac-tion in negotiating on the subject. (It is only the threat of crucial American superiority in this area which is likely to induce them to negotiate; we cannot expect them to do so simply for the sake of it or in order to help us preserve the survivability of our own nuclear forces). The kind of arrangements which might be considered for negotiation could include:-

a) a ban on the active trailing (ie the use of active sonar and similar systems) of strategic ballistic missile firing submarines. Because SSBNs have certain distinguishing features, a ban on trailing them would not need to apply to other types of submarine as well. Such an arrangement would be in the nature of a confidence building measure, ie it would not actively prevent anything from happening in time of war. But, assuming that the parties to such an arrangement took it seriously, it could have an affect on their construction programmes of intelligence gatherers and active sonar trailing systems which would make it difficult for them to resume a major active trailing capability at short notice.

b) The establishment of "sanctuaries" in which all forms of anti-submarine warfare would be banned and in which SSBNs could be left to roam undisturbed. Such sanctuaries would need to be large in size (at least several 100 miles square) and would need to be located in areas, for instance the Arctic Ocean, away from normal areas of operation of naval units but within range of their potential targets.

48. Neither of these arrangements, or any others which might be considered, would be easy to achieve. But Britain would have a major interest in seeking to promote discussions on the subject. In the last resort, we have a much greater interest in ensuring the survivability of our own SSBNs than we do in maintaining our ability to interdict Soviet submarines, either ballistic or attack. Indeed, we have no interest whatever in detecting or tracking Soviet SSBNs since there is no way in which we can, or would want, to limit the Soviet Union's second strike capability.

49. Steps would also need to be taken to maintain the reliability of the missiles themselves. At present replacement parts and logistic support are provided, under the aegis of the Polaris Sales Agreement, by the Lockheed Corporation and by certain other US contractors. The production line for Polaris missiles has however already closed down and when the last American Polaris vessel is withdrawn from service in the early 1980s there will be no reason for the American contractors to maintain a facility for producing further Polaris spare parts. This suggests that if we decide to retain the Polaris fleet in service until beyond the year 2,000, we should approach the US Government and ask to buy in as many as possible of their several hundred surplus Polaris missiles and associated spare parts which we could cannabilise over the remaining life of our own Polaris force. There seems no reason why the Americans should not agree to this; and the costs should be small given that the equipment in question would otherwise presumably have been junked for scrap.

50. The cost of retaining Polaris in service would be at a minimum the continuation of the present £93m a year operating expenses. There would however be additional expenditure in replacing parts of the machinery and equipment of the boats during their refit periods and some extra capital expenditure (albeit small) for purchasing new missiles or missile parts. But the overall amounts involved would be relatively small and there is no reason to suppose that they could not be accommodated within the present Long Term Defence Costings. Since it would be a continuation of existing policy it would not have any new policy implications. It would leave our options open for another 5–10 years and by not pre-empting major resources still allow the cruise missile option to be explored and, if desirable, developed.

OPTION THREE: RE-EQUIPPING THE POLARIS BOATS WITH NEW MISSILES

51. Another method of improving the survivability of the Polaris force would be to equip the boats with new missiles. The alternatives would be:–

a) Poscidon;

b) Trident 1 (the Trident 2 missile would not fit inside the Polaris tubes);

c) a new design.

Poseidon, when fitted with its 10 to 14 MIRVs has a range of some 2,500 miles ie very similar to that of the original Polaris A3 missile but greater than the range of the Chevaline variant of Polaris whose range is only around 2,000 miles. Without its MIRVed warheads the range of Poseidon would presumably be significantly increased, perhaps by up to 500 miles. There would be no overriding reason why we should want a MIRV capability for our nuclear deterrent. MiRVing is useful primarily as a means of attacking a wide range of targets with a single missile, ie it is particularly useful in the context of a complex counter-force strategy against hardened military targets. Given that the principal targetting requirement for a British deterrent force would be the much simpler anti-city role, there would be no need for this. A Poseidon missile with the existing British re-entry vehicles would thus meet our needs. On the other hand, Poseidon itself will be becoming obsolete by the end of the 1980s and there would seem little advantage in procuring a system which the Americans themselves are already beginning to phase. out. We should in due course face the same problems over continued logistic and spare parts support as we would over Polaris itself.

52. By contrast, the Trident 1 missile would have a significantly longer range ████████████████████ when equipped with a MIRVed pay-load and probably even longer if fitted with a simpler and lighter front-end. Trident I missiles will enter service with the US submarine force in the early 1980s and will initially be retro-fitted into submarines which had previously carried Poseidon. The technical feasibility of fitting Trident into a Polaris vessel has never been examined but given that Poseidon tubes are the same size as Polaris tubes, there ought to be no difficulty.

53. A new design would mean either a national programme or some form of collaboration with France. A national programme would be a major undertaking given that we have no industrial experience (apart from some spin-off from the Chevaline programme) of designing missiles. We would presumably not think of embarking upon such a programme unless the Americans refused to supply us either Poseidon or Trident. It is extremely doubtful whether we could carry such a programme through other than at enormous cost. Collaboration with France might lessen the financial penalties but the present French missiles are inferior in performance even to Polaris and would almost certainly not be compatible with its tubes. It seems likely that the adaptation of them for this purpose would either be feasible or cost-effective.

54. The advantage of installing new missiles on the Polaris boats would be to lengthen their range and thus to increase the area of deep water available for patrolling in which they could hope to escape detection and tracking. This would only be necessary if and when it became clear that the Soviet ASW capability was so effective that the Russians would have a reasonable degree of confidence of being able to take out in a first pre-emptive strike any Polaris which was on patrol in the currently available deep water patrol areas; and if the alternative tactic of coastal water patrolling or protection by surface ships was thought not to be feasible or to be too expensive.

55. The costs are difficult to estimate. The Polaris missiles were purchased from the United States under particularly favourable terms – actual production costs plus a nominal R and D levy of only 5%. It is by no means certain that the US Administration would be willing, or would be allowed by Congress, to offer us such financially advantageous terms again. Even if they did, there would still be costs incurred in Britain in converting the fire control machinery and test instrumentation systems. The extent of these extra costs would depend partly on whether the new missiles were procured with a MTRV capability, in which case the targetting control requirements would be more complex and expensive. But on the basis of information available in the US a rough estimate of re-equipping the Polaris boats with Poseidon or Trident might be, assuming the conversion of all four boats and the procurement of around 100 missiles:–

Poseidon:	around £1200m
Trident:	around £1600m

If these figures prove to be of the right order of magnitude it would be a better buy to purchase the Trident missile.

OPTION FOUR: CRUISE MISSILES

56. Cruise missiles of the kind currently under development in the US (ie equipped with small nuclear warheads capable of generating up to 200 kilotons of explosive power and with computerised precision guidance systems) have not yet been deployed. It is difficult therefore to offer any reliable prediction of their capabilities and thus of the numbers or types of them which might be appropriate for a British independent deterrent force. It is clear however that the accuracy which the Terrain Contour Matching (TERCOM guidance system offers (a circular error probability of something like 200 ft is adequate for strikes against major Soviet cities; and it seems likely that the introduction of Scene Matching Area Correlation (SMAC) techniques for the final phase of the missile's flight (this involves the

installation in the missile's computer of a digitalised photograph of the target area which is locked to the actual terrain as it appears through a television camera carried in the missile's nose) may reduce this to between 10 and 15 ft., ie accurate enough for use against local military targets as well.

57. The problem in cruise missiles lies in their penetration capability Whereas it is impossible to stop a ballistic missile in flight with anything other than a very complex and sophisticated anti-ballistic missile and associated tracking radar system, cruise missiles, which in the form in which they are currently under active development travel at subsonic speeds, can in theory be shot down by an aircraft, an ordinary surface to air missile or even an air defence gun. They need however to be detected first; and this is not easy. The cruise missiles currently under development in the US have a radar cross section ███████████████████████████████████████ ███████████████████████████████████ and they fly at very low levels. Locating, tracking and destroying them will thus be an extremely hazardous business. If it proves possible to reduce the radar cross section of cruise missiles still further, and/or give them a supersonic capability, it seems likely that the chances of their being intercepted will be relatively small (though still finite). In the present state of cruise missile technology however, it would be imprudent to rely with any confidence on the ability of a single cruise missile to reach a given target and any cruise missile mission would need to have a margin of error of something like 4 or 5 to 1. Much would depend however on the particular target to be attacked. Cruise missiles which had to travel across the densely defended area of Central Europe in order to reach a target which was itself defended by point air defence systems would be more vulnerable to interception than cruise missiles which travelled across relatively remote areas and were targetted on a largely undefended city or industrial plant. Attacking Moscow in a direct line from Britain might require something approaching a saturation approach; whereas attacking, say, █████████████ from somewhere at sea would not.

58. Cruise missiles can be launched from the ground, from the air, from surface ships or from submarines. Ground-launched cruise missiles, in the numbers in which they would be required (probably around 500 or so) would need to be installed either on fixed sites, such as RAF airfields of which there are a fair number, or on mobile launchers. If in fixed sites they would, even if their shelters were hardened, be vulnerable to a pre-emptive strike. Even a wide dispersal of missiles among different sites (which would itself cause problems over the need for secure storage in peacetime of the associated warheads) would not wholly obviate this risk. The location of all airfields in Britain is known (as would be the location of any other fixed sites

which might be chosen) and the Russians would have enough independently targettablc re-entry vehicles to be able to launch a simultaneous first strike on all of them). Mobile launchers, either on road or on rail, would ease the survivability problem. But it is questionable whether they would be feasible on environmental and security grounds on a small and crowded island like Britain. Surface ships would also be vulnerable to a first strike. In order to give a naval cruise missile force even a modicum of survivability, it would be necessary to install cruise missiles on almost every major surface ship in the fleet which could only be at the expense of other aspects of their armament and would be extremely expensive.

59. The most feasible cruise missile options for Britain would thus be either installation on aircraft or on submarines. The advantages of the air launched mode are that the missile can be conveyed supersonically nearer to its target before initial launch, thus reducing the time during which it is liable to interception; that the aircraft is recallable at the last moment and that the enemy cannot be confident of the direction from which the missile will come. As against this, the aircraft carrying the missile would itself be vulnerable; and there is little logic in using an expensive manned aircraft in order to carry a vehicle which is itself capable of flight (the Americans' interest in the ALCM is a reflection of the fact that they have a large fleet of B52 strategic bombers anyway, which if it were not for the ALCM they would have to replace at much greater cost with the B1). All the aircraft currently planned for the RAF's inventory for the 1980s and 1990s are assigned to other tasks and any use of them to carry cruise missiles for strategic strike could only be at the expense of these other missions. It might be possible to use ALCMs as a means of prolonging the in-service life of the Vulcan and Buccaneer strike aircraft which are due to be phased out when the IDS version of the Tornado comes into service from 1979/80 onwards; and this could prove to be a valuable enhancement of NATO's long range strike capability against local military targets in the Soviet Union's western military districts. But these aircraft are already old (though no older than the B52) and it would be unrealistic to expect to retain them in service much beyond the early 1990s. This could therefore only be a temporary, and probably only partial solution.

60. There would moreover be arms control complications in installing cruise missiles in aircraft. The SALT II treaty will contain, as one of its provisions, a limitation on the range of ALCMs to 600km except when deployed on heavy bombers when it will be 2,500km (and such heavy bombers will count within the SALT II sub-ceiling on Mirved systems). The only aircraft which will be in service in the RAF in the 1980s which might count as a heavy bomber would be the Vulcan (though even this is

doubtful). The Tornado, because of its range limitations, would not be able to get within 600km of Soviet territory when based in Britain (and even from bases in Germany would only be able to get within 600km of a fairly narrow band of Soviet territory). The range of the Buccaneer is somewhat better and it would, when based in Germany, be able to get within 600km ▉▉▉▉▉▉▉▉▉▉▉▉▉▉▉▉▉▉▉▉▉▉▉ Moscow ▉▉▉▉).Thus, if we wanted to use ALCMs for strategic nuclear purposes, we would be obliged either to introduce a new fleet of heavy aircraft (perhaps a variant of some wide-bodied civilian aircraft) or breach the provisions of the SALT II treaty, in which case we would not be able to receive any form of American assistance.

61. The particular cruise missile option which seems therefore most attractive for strategic purposes is their installation in submarines. Submarines are the launch platform least vulnerable to pre-emptive strike. The installation of long range cruise missiles in our existing SSN fleet would be technically feasible in that the dimensions of cruise missiles are compatible with normal torpedo tubes. But the number of missiles that could be installed on each boat would involve a commensurate reduction in the number of torpedos or conventional anti-ship missiles which the submarine would otherwise have carried. At present the SSN fleet is scheduled to number 17 by the end of the 1980s, 4 of these vessels will have 6 torpedo tubes carrying 31 torpedos or Sub-Harpoon missiles and 13 will have 5 tubes carrying 24 torpedos or missiles. The total torpedo/missile carrying capability of the fleet will thus be 436. If cruise missiles were to be installed on the SSNs the alternatives could be:-

a) To maintain the present SSN construction programme but to pre-empt a certain proportion, say a third, of the available tubes for cruise missiles either by equipping certain SSNs exclusively with cruise missiles or by installing a limited number of cruise missiles in every SSN. This would mean that the maximum number of cruise missiles carried would be around 145 and that the capability of the SSN fleet for anti-submarine and anti-surface ship warfare would be correspondingly diminished by a third.

b) To abandon the Sub-Harpoon programme and to try to acquire a cruise missile with variable guidance and warhead modules which would be suitable for use both in the short range anti-ship role and in the long range strategic strike role, thus achieving economies of space (this ought to be technically feasible since the American Navy is developing a cruise missile, the Tomahawk, in 2 variants of just this kind).

c) To increase the construction programme of SSNs so as to provide a SSN fleet capable of delivering strategic nuclear strikes without detriment to its existing planned anti-submarine and anti-surface ship role.

62. One advantage of using SSNs is that they will be required as part of our conventional naval capability anyway. There are strong arguments at present for improving the cost-effectiveness of our general purpose naval forces by increasing the size of the SSN fleet and reducing proposed procurements of major surface ships. Hitherto the SSN force has suffered because of the inadequacy of its armament: the existing anti-ship torpedoes which it carries are among the oldest designs of weapons systems in our armed forces and SSNs have therefore been thought of mainly as ASW systems. The introduction of the Sub-Harpoon missile, and/or of an anti-ship cruise missile will radically change this; SSNs may possibly come to be regarded as the most cost-effective means of attacking surface ships. There may thus be scope for achieving considerable economies of scale in increasing the size of the SSN fleet as a dual capable force, providing both an enhanced anti-surface ship capability and a strategic nuclear deterrent. In considering the cost-effectiveness of a submarine launched cruise missile deterrent option it would be appropriate therefore to consider at the same time the cost-effectiveness of increasing the size of the SSN force for anti-ship strike, and for general anti-submarine warfare, by comparison with other naval systems.

63. A further feature of an SLCM option is that it could be combined with any one of the other options discussed above with some gain in flexibility and perhaps also in cost. For example, it might well be operationally and financially attractive to combine running on the Polaris force with the introduction of a fairly small force of nuclear armed cruise missiles, perhaps equivalent to no more than two boatloads of missiles (ie not enough to constitute an adequate deterrent force in themselves) in order to achieve, at relatively low cost, a more survivable and flexible force than either SSBNs or SLCMs alone could provide.

64. The cost of a submarine launched cruise missile force would depend on what method of installation was chosen. But the basic cost parameters would be:–

Missiles: about £600,000 each if procured at American prices with a fairly token R & D levy. Perhaps three times this if developed nationally.

Fire-control, command and communications equipment: around £20.50m per boat.

Boats: around £180m each.

The range of cost of a submarine launched cruise missile force could therefore be from £100m for a small force of 50 cruise missiles bought off the shelf
and installed in existing SSNs (coupled with the retention of Polaris) up to
around £2,500m for a force of 10 boats with missiles produced in Britain
either from a national design or under license.

OPTION FIVE: A NEW SSBN FORCE

65. A complete new SSBN force would combine the advantages of
upgrading the missiles (Option Three) with the asset of new and quieter
submarine hulls. It would almost certainly be the most technically effective
of all the options; it would also be the most expensive and the most politically visible (Option Two, and albeit more disingenuously Option Three,
could be represented as simply improvements to the existing force; Option
Four could be presented as a multi-purpose force without any specific
ascription to strategic nuclear strike; but Option Five would be unmistak-
ably the introduction of a new strategic nuclear deterrent). Its total capital
investment cost would be somewhere in the region of £3,000 million. Even
spread over period of years this would represent a major burden on the
defence budget which could not, short of a very considerable increase in
defence expenditure, be met without compensatory reductions elsewhere in
the defence programme. To introduce a force of this kind would therefore
imply a marked change of emphasis in defence priorities.

DOCUMENT 9

PM/78/138

<u>PRIME MINISTER</u>

Future of the British Deterrent

1. I have read with interest the first two parts [of the Duff–Mason Report], enclosed with Sir John Hunt's minute of 7 December, of the group of officials' study on the future of the British nuclear deterrent. I understand we can expect to receive Part 3 before we meet on Wednesday. This is a pity since I do not think that the theoretical and practical aspects of the problem can feasibly be considered in isolation from one another. I have two general comments on the work which has been submitted to Ministers so far.

2. Firstly, I think that the presentation focuses too narrowly on "strategic" nuclear weapons rather than on the role of nuclear weapons in general. Indeed, the use of the term "strategic" is itself a source of confusion and inconsistency throughout the papers. For example, in paragraph 9 of the paper on the politico/military requirement it is stated that "it is not credible that Western strategic nuclear forces would be used in response to Warsaw Pact aggression involving a markedly lower level of force". Yet paragraph 6 recognises that "in recent years United States' policy has placed increased emphasis on the need for flexibility in the targetting of strategic forces". It is impossible to draw a precise dividing line between "strategic" and "theatre" nuclear weapons. For example, I am not sure what paragraph 17 means, "if we decided not to proceed with a further strategic force we would eventually cease to be a NWS". If it means we lost the ability to strike at the Soviet Union I would agree. If it means we have to have a Poseidon/Trident missile system I would not agree. The crucial distinction in my view, and I believe in Soviet strategic philosophy as well, is between nuclear systems which can inflict serious damage on the Soviet homeland and nuclear systems which cannot.

3. I think it makes more sense therefore, in considering the case for a British deterrent, to think in terms of our, and NATO's, total nuclear capability against the Soviet Union, irrespective of the means by which it is delivered or the designation which might be applied to it. I am preparing a paper setting out my own personal view on this broader basis.

4. My second comment on the officials' study is that it approaches the issue of deterrence from an excessively technical and numerical perspective, whereas I believe it should be viewed primarily in political terms,. The paper on criteria for deterrence recognises, correctly, that the deterrence judgments made by the super powers are no guide to our own requirements;

and that there can be no unique answer as to what would probably constitute unacceptable damage for the Soviet Union in relation to the limited gains from eliminating the United Kingdom. It is as hard to conceive circumstances in which we would ever alone face a decision to use nuclear weapons as that the Soviet Union would have to consider the consequences of our doing so. The three specific options listed for a British nuclear capability, all in my view impose an unnecessarily high and detailed threshold of destructive capability.

5. I do not believe that it makes sense to try to quantify criteria in this way. We have to assume that the Russian leadership will behave rationally, for if they do not we are doomed. I am not convinced that the Soviet leadership would be willing to risk even a single major Soviet city for the limited prize of an attack on Britain alone. It is their assessment of our political resolve to use nuclear weapons which will deter them, rather than the precise degree of "severe structural damage" which they judge us capable of inflicting. I accept that for our own planning purposes we need to have some minimum level of assured capability. But I think that it is enough to express this in terms of a certain number of probable Soviet casualties – and that a figure of 1 million anywhere on Soviet territory would be more than adequate. I do not therefore agree with the assertion in paragraph 14 of the paper that a capability falling short of the three options described would not constitute unacceptable damage in Soviet eyes.

6. I am copying this minute to the Chancellor of the Exchequer, the Secretary of State for Defence and Sir John Hunt.

DAVID OWEN

Foreign and Commonwealth Office
11 December 1978

DOCUMENT 10

Foreign and Commonwealth Office
London SW1A 2AH
12 December 1978

Dear Bryan,

In his minute to the Prime Minister of 11 December on the future of the British deterrent, Dr Owen said that he was preparing and would circulate a paper setting out his views on a broader basis.

I apologise for the late circulation of this paper; but Dr Owen thinks it might be useful for the participants in tomorrow's Ministerial Meeting to have it to hand.

I am copying this letter to the Private Secretaries of the Chancellor of the Exchequer and Secretary of State for Defence as well as Martin Vile (Cabinet Office).

G G H Walden
Private Secretary

B G Cartledge Esq
10 Downing Street

TOP SECRET

12.12.78

FUTURE OF THE BRITISH DETERRENT

Britain possesses nuclear weapons for political and military reasons and for national as well as European reasons. The case for a British deterrent has to be seen therefore partly as a contribution to NATO's overall defence posture. But it clearly goes much further than that.

The need to contribute to NATO

2. NATO currently maintains a wide spectrum of nuclear capability, ranging from systems geared to limited and local tactical use in the immediate battlefield area to systems capable of destroying Soviet strategic military targets and major cities. But the most significant of these, in terms of deterrence, are those systems capable of reaching the Soviet Union. NATO's own studies have shown that the result of a two-sided exchange of nuclear weapons on the battlefield is simply an accentuation of the trend of the preceding or associated conventional battle. Thus if NATO was already losing a conventional war, the military consequence of using battlefield nuclear weapons, assuming that the Russians responded in kind, would be to cause it to lose even faster. Short-range battlefield nuclear weapons cannot

help NATO "win" on the ground a war that is not winnable by conventional means. Nor can they constitute on their own an effective deterrent. It is unlikely that the Soviet Union would be seriously deterred from launching or maintaining a major attack against the West simply by the risk of incurring nuclear strikes on the territory of its Warsaw Pact allies, let alone by the prospect of NATO using nuclear weapons on its own territory. It is the risk of nuclear retaliation against the Soviet Union itself which is crucial.

3. NATO needs, however, to have a reasonable degree of flexibility in its capability for nuclear strike against the Soviet Union. It would be undesirable for the Alliance to be limited to a capability for delivering strikes only against strategic targets such as cities or missile installations. NATO needs also to be able to attack on a more selective basis local military targets, for example airfields, bridge-heads, railway marshalling yards, etc in the Soviet western military districts.

4. The present British nuclear forces consist of 4 Polaris submarines; 56 Vulcan bombers; Buccaneer and Jaguar dual-capable aircraft; Lance surface-to-surface missiles and dual-capable artillery; and nuclear depth bombs. Of these only the Polaris, Vulcan and Buccaneer (just) are capable of reaching Soviet territory. The warheads for Polaris, the bombs for the Vulcans, Buccaneers and Jaguars and some of the depth bombs are British made; 'the remainder are American, held under two-key arrangements. The British nuclear forces represent only 5% of the Alliance's total nuclear capability. There is no reason to suppose that the US would not be able, if necessary, to assign extra nuclear assets to SACEUR to replace any gaps in his targetting requirements which the disappearance of the British nuclear contribution might cause. In numerical terms the British nuclear contribution is thus relatively insignificant.

5. It can be argued however that the existence of the British nuclear forces is of significant political benefit to the Alliance. There are two particular reasons:

a) the existence of a second centre of nuclear decision-making with NATO constitutes a complicating and inhibiting factor in Soviet calculations and this adds to deterrence;
b) the readiness of Britain to commit its nuclear forces to the defence of Western Europe might in certain circumstances act as a "trigger" which would strengthen the resolve of the US to do the same.

The validity of these arguments (which are treated in paragraphs 21 to 27 of the Part I study) is difficult to assess. It is hard to know whether the Russians would really believe that Britain would use its own nuclear forces – and thus risk complete national destruction – to defend other European countries, in circumstances where the Americans were refusing to do so; or whether the Americans would seriously allow themselves to be swayed against their own judgment in using nuclear weapons by a British threat to escalate unilaterally. We do know that the Federal Chancellor, Helmut Schmidt, does attach importance to the maintenance of a British nuclear contribution in the form of an independent nuclear capability. It is clear that a significant section of German opinion would regard it as politically damaging for us to renounce our nuclear status at a time when the specific Soviet threat against Western Europe is being increased. But it would probably be fair to assume that they would not attach such a high value to it that they would wish us to retain it in all circumstances and at any price. If therefore the maintenance of our nuclear capability required major new capital investment which could only be achieved by some major reduction in our contribution to other areas of the Alliance's defence effort our Allies would hesitate before pressing us to remain a nuclear rower. There is however no evidence that our Allies attach particular value to the form or quality of the British nuclear contribution. At present the British nuclear Polaris forces are targetted, under SACEUR's Scheduled Strike Programme, ███████████████████████████

██

███. There would thus be no need, in NATO terms, for any future British nuclear force to be more effective in range, yield or penetration capability than the present one.

The National Security Requirement

6. In order to assess the requirement for any "last resort" guarantee of national security it is necessary to examine the particular circumstances in which this security might be at risk, and where the possession by Britain of nuclear weapons might constitute a significant asset. There are broadly two types of circumstance in which this might be the case:-

a) a threatened Soviet attack against the UK which the Alliance as a whole was unwilling, or unable, to deter by virtue of its collective defence capability;

b) the degree to which the territory of the UK would be subject to attack in the event of a general East–West war in Europe.

7. It is the first of these which is usually cited as the fundamental national security justification for a British nuclear deterrent. It is argued that if one day NATO were to collapse, the possession by Britain of a nuclear deterrent would be necessary in order to deter the Soviet Union from using its

massively superior conventional and nuclear forces to attack Britain. The "collapse" of NATO would, for this purpose, not mean necessarily that the Alliance had ceased to exist or that its forces had been defeated in a war. It could also apply to circumstances where the American commitment to the physical defence of Europe had become conspicuously weakened, for example by the withdrawal of large numbers of US forces, both nuclear and conventional, back to the US and/or by the emergence of domestic pressures in the US against any involvement in "foreign" wars. In such circumstances, even if, formally speaking, the US Administration remained committed to its North Atlantic Treaty obligations, a British Government might judge that this commitment would no longer be credible in the eyes of the Soviet Union; that the Soviet leadership would probably not expect American nuclear weapons to be used unless American territory itself came under attack; and that therefore the maintenance of British security depended on our ability to pose an alternative independent nuclear deterrent to the Soviet Union.

8. The validity of this justification for a national nuclear capability depends on a judgment on the plausibility of a NATO "collapse". No-one could seriously argue in present circumstances, that it is in any sense a likely occurrence. But clearly it cannot be dismissed as utterly inconceivable. If such a collapse were to take place, Britain's security would indeed be seriously at risk whether or not we possessed an independent deterrent capability. The consequences of a NATO collapse would be so serious that, it could be argued, no British Government should fail to cater for such an eventuality.

9. A collapse of NATO is not, however, the only scenario in which our possession of a nuclear capability would affect our security interests. It would also do so in the case of a general East–West war, either conventional or nuclear in Europe, in which British forces were involved. It is likely that the Russians would, in the context of such a war, contemplate specific action against the territory of the UK. They might calculate however that a British ability to use nuclear weapons in retaliation meant that the risks involved in extending the theatre of operations to include the UK were unacceptably great. If therefore the Soviet Union was, for whatever reason, launching widespread theatre nuclear strikes against Western Europe, it might deliberately avoid targets in the UK for fear that this might provoke a British national nuclear reaction against Soviet territory. Similarly the Soviet Union might in a conventional conflict refrain from large-scale strikes against targets, or at any rate against major civilian targets, in Britain for fear that this too might provoke nuclear retaliation.

10. The idea that the possession of nuclear weapons offers a country a kind of "sanctuary" in the event of a general war was one of the tenets of Gaullist defence philosophy. It has been called into question by President Giscard, who has recognised that in the event of a major war in Central Europe, France, even though outside NATO's integrated military organisation, could not expect automatically to remain uninvolved. Nonetheless, the prospect of nuclear retaliation against its own territory is the critical factor which the Soviet leadership would bear in mind in calculating the potential risks and gains of any form of military activity in Europe. It would be foolish for Britain to assume any automatic immunity to attack. But our geographical position means that we are, in a sense, less crucially involved in a land/air battle on the Central Front; and there might therefore be circumstances in which the possession of a nuclear capability by Britain would mitigate the extent to which British territory came under Soviet attack. This would apply particularly in the case of an "accidental" East–West conflict arising from clashes across the inner-German border in the event of an uprising in the GDR.

11. One thing which is clear however is that the only form of independent nuclear capability which would be of use to Britain for safeguarding its national security is the ability to strike targets on Soviet territory; and that there would be no value whatever in this context in an independent capability for short-range nuclear strike. There are no circumstances in which Britain might sensibly think of using short-range tactical nuclear weapons independently of NATO as a whole; and none of the short-range systems which Britain now possesses, either land, sea or air, would be of any military utility in defending the UK itself. Indeed, even within NATO's existing nuclear doctrine, there is no real argument for a British contribution in the short-range field. Insofar as NATO has a requirement for short-range nuclear systems at all (and the only real argument for them is the need to maintain some counterpart to the short-range Soviet capability) there are good political reasons for ensuring that some of the relevant delivery vehicles are European rather than American. A sharing of responsibility for nuclear delivery both enhances deterrence externally by emphasising the common commitment of the Allies to NATO's declared nuclear policies; and satisfies the internal aspirations of certain Allied countries, particularly the FRG, for participation in common nuclear defence arrangements. But the logic of these arguments suggests that it is more sensible to include in such arrangements those European countries whose actual territory is most likely to be subject to attack. In the case of a Warsaw Pact invasion of Central Europe, this means the FRG, the Netherlands and Belgium. There

is no particular reason why British surface-to-surface missiles, artillery or battlefield support aircraft should be used to deliver tactical nuclear strikes, rather than German, Dutch or Belgian under dual key arrangements. Indeed one means of reducing NATO's holdings of short-range systems might be to confine them henceforth to national forces operating in their own territory.

12. There remains however the question of what particular form of capability against Soviet territory an independent British nuclear capability ought to have. Clearly this must, in order to constitute a credible deterrent, include the ability to inflict major damage on civil and industrial targets. The interpretation of "major damage" is however debatable, and is inevitably a matter of subjective assessment. But it is one which needs to be made in relation to the somewhat limited circumstances of a possible Soviet attack on the UK under the sort of scenarios set out in paragraph 10 above. The judgment by the Russians of what they might be prepared to risk in return for the gains which would accrue from an attack on Britain would be a very different matter from their judgment of the gains and risks involved in a general attack on Western Europe or on the US. It is hard to see how, on any rational calculation, the military or other benefits which they would obtain from an attack on the UK alone would compensate for the loss of, say, ███████

Political Aspects

13. In addition to these security considerations there are certain broader political issues relative to the future of the British nuclear deterrent. It is sometimes claimed that the possession of nuclear weapons is an accepted international index of political power which enables the country concerned to play a greater role in international affairs than its economic or conventional military strength would otherwise warrant; and that the renunciation by Britain of a nuclear status would in the long run severely diminish our general influence on world affairs including for example, our retention of a permanent seat on the UN Security Council. It is also sometimes argued, in the contrary sense, that renunciation would constitute a catalyst to international arms control efforts, would be a major step in arresting the further horizontal proliferation of nuclear weapons and would invest the renouncing country with a very considerable moral authority which would increase its political influence. Experience shows that this political "halo" effect might last for a year or so but would soon wear off.

14. It is difficult to assess these claims. But it seems unlikely that such validity as they may have is of any more than marginal significance by comparison with the security considerations. The one political factor

which does however bear some weight is the effect of a renunciation of our nuclear status on our relations with our European partners and Allies, in particular France and the FRG. A situation in which France was left as the only European nuclear power would undoubtedly enhance French prestige and authority and this would be likely to have some spin-off in terms of an increased French ability to dominate European political discussions and perhaps also, to some extent, Community affairs. This would in turn arouse German anxieties. The Germans do not look to our deterrent for direct nuclear protection and they do not in any sense regard it, either on its own or in association with the French nuclear capability, as the embryo for some future European nuclear force which might if necessary substitute for the American nuclear guarantee. Nonetheless, they would, given their present anxieties about the improvements in the Soviet Union's intermediate range nuclear forces, be concerned at the disappearance of such a distinctive part of NATO's European nuclear capability. In some sections of German public opinion this could lead to a resurgence of demands that the FRG should acquire some kind of indigenous capability of its own. The acquisition of such a capability, which is of course precluded both by the Revised Brussels Treaty of 1954 and by German adherence to the Non-Proliferation Treaty, would be the most destabilising development in Europe since the end of the Second World War.

DOCUMENT 11

TOP SECRET

PM/78/145

<u>PRIME MINISTER</u>

Future of the British Deterrent

1. As my minute of 11 December makes clear, I am not convinced by the contention in the earlier parts of the officials' paper that the ability to destroy at least ten major cities, or inflict damage on 30 major targets, ████████ ███████, is the minimum criterion for a British deterrent. It follows therefore that I do not accept the requirements which Part III of the study now postulates for numbers of detonations and missiles. Indeed, I believe that some of the force options which the Part III study suggests are unrealistic in relation to the financial resources likely to be available for the nuclear deterrent aspect of the defence equipment budget over the next 10–15 years. The "smaller, cheaper force using cruise missiles" to which Sir John Hunt refers in paragraph 5 of his covering minute is an option which not only needs further study, but is intrinsically more attractive than the officials' paper allows.

2. The paper argues that attacks on ten cities (criteria option 3a) requires more than 300 cruise missiles to be launched to give a 50% chance of achieving the specified damage. If we accept fewer cities as our criteria, then the number of cruise missiles can be reduced proportionately, though admittedly some extra allowance may need to be made for aircraft interception. The oddest aspect of the officials' paper is their advocacy of a purpose-built cruise missile carrier, of about the size of our present SSBN, to carry about 80 cruise missiles. On this basis they argue that submarine deployment will be one or two years later and that the cost will not be much different from a ballistic missile system. Paragraph 26 does mention the alternative, which I believe needs far more serious study, of deploying submarine-launched cruise missiles on existing SSNs. But it does not feature as a major part of the paper. We currently plan an SSN fleet of around 19 by the end of the 1990s. We need the SSNs anyway for non-nuclear purposes – and I have long advocated an increase in the SSN-building programme on its own merits. Equipping each of them with the ability to fire a salvo of five cruise missiles from their torpedo tubes need not be an unacceptable detraction from their other roles, and it would be possible to increase the number of cruise missiles carried by those submarines deployed on deterrent patrols.

3. Dispersing our nuclear capability over a number of submarines mitigates the major vulnerability of our present four SSBNs. The vulnerability to Soviet ASW measures of a submarine force limited to four boats is

undoubtedly growing as tracking techniques improve. As the paper argues, a force of eight submarines, allowing three on continuous patrol, adds greatly to the credibility of the force. We need to know urgently whether there are any major technical problems in installing the US Tomahawk cruise missile in our SSNs. We also need to know the nature of the command and control problems referred to in paragraph 26. I do not understand the reference to problems over a dispersed submarine-based deterrent force, while in paragraph 29 a combined ballistic and cruise missile force, using the submarine cruise missile force in a theatre role, is discussed. The command and control problem will presumably exist in whatever situation missiles are fired.

4. Fuller analysis is also required on that part of the paper which deals with the effective life of the present Polaris force. I am strongly in favour of keeping the present force in operation as long as possible. The next 10–15 years are likely to bring important developments in the politico-military and arms control field, which could alter drastically the basis on which we currently assess our national deterrent requirement. This argues for extending the life of Polaris, looking flexibly at cruise missiles and keeping our options open as long as we can. I am not convinced by the argument in the officials' paper that 1979 is the decision point.

5. US naval sources argue that the life of the Polaris submarine hulls themselves can be prolonged virtually indefinitely, and certainly to the year 2000, through replacement and upgrading of some of their ancillary and propulsion equipment. As to the possible constraints on missile life referred to in paragraph 7b of Annex A to the paper, could we not if we wished to keep Polaris going take advantage of the fact that all the American Polaris missiles will be withdrawn from service in the early 1980s, and ask the United States to make all their Polaris missiles available to us? I suspect if you put this to President Carter at Guadeloupe the answer would be yes, and you might, like Macmillan, get them at a bargain price. I also hope you could sound out President Carter on our being able to purchase Tomahawk cruise missiles. The French might be interested and the Germans might want to purchase land-based cruise missiles on a double key basis.

6. If we can in 1979 credibly decide to extend the life of the Polaris vessels, albeit at some increase in running costs, and consider deploying cruise missiles in SSNs, we will have kept open our future options at minimal cost and the subject could be re-examined in 1983.

7. I am copying this minute to Denis Healey, Fred Mulley and Sir John Hunt.

DAVID OWEN

Foreign and Commonwealth Office
19 December 1978

SECRET AND PERSONAL

British Embassy,
Washington, D.C. 20008

From the Ambassador   14 March 1979

The Rt Hon Dr David Owen MP
FCO

Dear David,

THE LIFE SPAN OF THE UK POLARIS BOATS

1. You asked me to give some thought to the question whether it would be possible to extend the existing UK Polaris system beyond its planned life which, according to Ian Smart, comes to an end about 1993. The following represents the best I can offer in the time available, given the obvious caveats on talking freely about this. There has however been an opportunity to talk round the subject again with Dick Garwin and, without disclosing the purpose in hand, we have been able to tap discreetly some of the expertise of the submariners on the British Naval Staff here, as well as a Pentagon contact who spent 20 years in the US Navy and commanded the US nuclear submarine Skipjack. I should be interested to know in due course whether the work on this subject being done in London throws up markedly different conclusions.

2. The problem may conveniently be examined in terms of:

(a) the submarine hull;
(b) the systems contained by the hull which are integral to the submarine;
(c) the missiles.

<u>Hull</u>

3. The conclusion of the Assistant Secretary of the US Navy (Research Engineering and Systems) in his letter to Garwin of 28 March, 1978, was that "hull corrosion and fatigue are not limiting considerations for extending the life of Poseidon SSBNs." The UK Polaris boats are of British design and construction. But if one assumes that the differences between them and the US Poseidon boats are not critical and that hull preservation systems and monitoring inspection programmes are comparable, there would appear to be no reason to draw a different conclusion over the UK boats. Garwin made the point that the life expectancy of the pressure hull varies as a function

of the boat's operating conditions and that a reduction of 100 feet in its normal operating depth would prolong the life of the hull by a factor of 10. As against that it may be observed that the normal operating depth of the UK boats is already only about ███████████████████████████████ ████ and that this comparatively shallow cruising depth is adopted precisely in order to minimise hull fatigue due to depth cycling. Given that the Polaris boats measure about 50 feet vertically from hull to fin and that large surface vessels have a draught of about 90 feet below the surface, there is very little safety margin for further reduction in normal cruising depth, leaving aside the question of penalty in terms of detectability. (William J Perry predicts a "potentially significant Soviet ASW problem by the 1990s").

Systems integral to the submarine

4. The argument on which the US Assistant Secretary of the Navy (RE & S) based his case to Garwin for finite life-span was basically one of cumulative technological obsolescence: "hulls would require major internal system replacement which would be tantamount to a new ship construction. In this I mean major new ship sensor and defence systems would be required, major new communication capabilities, major new propulsion and auxiliary machinery installations and other major improvements would also be required. The size and space constraints of the existing Poseidon hulls would severely limit the scope of improvement achievable". In other words there is a point for the Americans where it becomes cost-effective to replace existing boats altogether rather than to maintain them by successive component replacement with increasing penalties in terms of financial outlay, diminished time on station and lower operating standards.

5. All components wear out or give rise to increased broad-band or narrow-band noise over time. In addition to the electrical, navigation and communications equipment, internal systems which require periodic replacement include the nuclear reactor core, the secondary propulsion system, turbo-generators, coolant pumps, steam-pipe runs, and the salt water systems including the hydraulic valves. Some of these systems are relatively inaccessible and replacement therefore requires major stripping down (replacement of the hydraulic valves alone on USS Skipjack in the early 1970s cost around $1 million at then prevailing prices). SSBNs normally go in for refit for a period of 18 months once every 5 years.

6. One aspect of the integral systems not covered in the letter from the Assistant Secretary of the Navy to Garwin is the pressure container vessel of the nuclear reactor core. There is a theoretical problem here arising from the effect of long-term neutron bombardment which leads to the embrittlement

of the pressure vessel. Garwin said that there were of course considerable variations in reactor design as between different countries and it was true that no nuclear propelled boats had been at sea long enough to enable definitive conclusions to be drawn. Nevertheless it was his impression that zircalloys used in the construction of pressure vessels were proof against such effects and that if there were some deterioration over time he saw no reason in principle why replacement of the pressure vessel should not also be feasible. However, this type of major structural work must approach the point at which "replacement" becomes virtually indistinguishable from new construction with obvious implications for financial outlays. For what it is worth, the neutron bombardment effects are said to be more pronounced in hunter killer submarines than in SSBNs because the operating conditions of the former on standard missions require more frequent stops and starts of the propulsion unit.

Missiles

7. Extending the life span of the Polaris A3 missiles would require continuing access to spare parts and propellants such as is now still assured by Lockheed's assembly line in the United States under existing co-opera-tion arrangements. Lockheed are due to discontinue their own operation in the United States when the last US Navy Polaris missiles are withdrawn round about 1984/85. It is a political question whether at that time it would be open to the UK to acquire a sufficiently large number of Polaris compo-nents from the United States (existing inventory or those boosters taken out of US service) to meet continuing UK needs. Even if it were not possible to do this or if it were shown that components so acquired were to be subject to brittleness and other ageing faults, it is Garwin's view that it would in principle be well within the reach of UK technology to replicate the neces-sary components; and that the certification of such replicated parts would be easier to achieve than for example would be the case for components of nuclear warheads (which are subject to different kinds of on shelf degrada-tion) under a CTB Treaty.

8. Garwin accepts that there is a special problem about the useful life of the solid grain propellant of the Polaris booster. This is packed into the combustion chamber of the rocket in such a way as to ensure that the area of propellant burning at any given instant after ignition is of certain specified dimensions in relation to the properties of the combustion chamber which contain it. If due to age the propellant (which in texture is of a hardened rubbery quality) were to shrink or dry, cracks could occur in it which would disturb the rate of burn-up and if certain pressures were exceeded this would

cause the rocket to explode. The grain propellant's capacity to adjust to changes in temperature over time and the quality of the sealants are critical in this regard. But (as with every other product ranging from meat to film) the ageing process could be delayed by lowering the temperature under which it is stored. Storage at the temperature of a normal refrigerator could be expected to prolong the normal life by a factor of 20 and storage at deep frozen temperatures by a factor of up to 100. In addition, Garwin sees no problem in principle in manufacturing new propellant in the UK of the same specification as that which existing Polaris missiles contain.

Arguments from analogy

9. If the life span of the SSBN is dated from the time of launch, the working figure used in the conventional wisdom about the life-span of the UK boats would appear to be 25 years, since the 4 UK SSBNs were launched between February 1967 and March 1968. As against that, the median date for the launch of the first 4 French SSBNs was 1970/71: according to an authoritative article in Le Monde of 24 February, the present generation of French boats "would stay in service until the year 2000, with improvements to their manoeuvrability, warheads, depth of dive and engine noise". This suggests that the working figure for the French is 30 years. A similar figure is implied for the life of the older US nuclear hunter-killer submarines. For example, the former captain of USS Skipjack told us that the boat was launched in 1958, is still in service and has another estimated 9 years of life ahead of it (= 30 years). Some stretching of the life of certain existing US Poseidon boats is also envisaged to make good the slow-down in the rate of production of the Trident submarine, and extensive refits for these Poseidon boats will take place during the early 1980s.

10. According to Garwin the paradigm case for the life of major defence systems is the story of the B52 bomber. Garwin said that he had at an earlier point in his career been chairman of a panel appointed by the Senate to consider certain aspects of the strategic bomber force. In 1962–63 it had been alleged that the B52s could not be expected to prolong their active life beyond 1970 because of metal fatigue etc, and that it was therefore necessary to procure a new low-level near-supersonic bomber which would be more invulnerable to Soviet SAMs. However, in the event it had proved possible without great difficulty to modify the performance of the B52s in relation to fatigue factors and nearly 20 years later it was now accepted by the Air Force that B52s could fly beyond the year 2000.

Conclusion

11. I see no a priori reason why the cross-over point at which cumulative technological obsolescence makes the construction of totally new boats more cost-effective than maintaining old ones should be the same for the UK as it is for the United States. The job which the SSBN leg of the US strategic triad has to do is different in kind from that of the UK Polaris boats. Political, military and technical expectations of the US SSBN leg are also of a different order of magnitude. There are political costs for the United States Administration in not replacing SSBNs "on time" with new boats: whereas for a British Labour Government (and perhaps any British Government) there are political (among other) gains in not doing so. It may also be that the essential perceptions about the role of the UK strategic nuclear deterrent can be preserved, notwithstanding the acceptance of some penalty in terms of diminished time on station and lower operating standards. There is therefore no argument that I can see that would rule out prolongation of the life of the existing UK Polaris boats, say by a further 10 years to the year 2003, provided:

(a) rising maintenance costs are accepted;
(b) there is a practical solution to the problem of missile components; and
(c) reduction in overall operating standards is not excluded.

At the same time it should not be pretended that such a course would be anything other than a short term expedient or that it avoids for very long any of the major political, military and economic questions that surround the future of the UK deterrent.

Yours

Peter Jay

2
Nuclear Weapons Policy

Two months after taking office as Foreign and Commonwealth Secretary, I met with Lord Zuckerman, on a private basis, to discuss British nuclear strategy. He was a friend and an iconoclast on many of the fixed positions over these questions in Whitehall. At the end of the meeting he gave me a copy of two notes that he had sent to the Cabinet Secretary on 3 May 1977. As is clear from a note sent to the Cabinet Secretary the following day, copied to my private office, Lord Zuckerman let it be known that he had left the two documents (Documents 13 and 16) for my eyes only.

What these papers reveal is how exasperated Zuckerman was by the officials writing for ministers on nuclear arms control and in particular how obstructive they were being over a comprehensive test ban (CTB):

> Nowhere does the paper point out to Ministers what the UK might gain, both politically and in security, from whatever successes the USA/USSR talks might achieve. How could the Prime Minister or the Foreign Secretary be put up to argue that if in the interests of world peace the USA can accept a CTB, we can't? It's the tail trying to wag the dog! Worse than that – it could be argued that our objectives, as set out in the paper, are the very things the NPT, to which we are fully committed, was designed to prevent. Nuclear proliferation is far too serious a matter for lip service. We stand to gain a great deal if we ride with the Americans, and very little – if anything – if we obstruct their efforts.

He goes on with the withering comment:

> When I came to the discussion of 4c and 4d and discovered that the Group in effect was advising that we must oppose a CTBT because that would stop us improving the technical effectiveness of existing British nuclear forces, I could not forebear from thinking that were these forces ever used, it would not matter at all how effective they were technically. In the subsequent exchange we would be eliminated. Whether or not we shall ever have the resources to proceed to successor systems remains to be seen, but why did the Group not consider whether the cost of maintaining our options (i.e. to discourage a CTB) would be equal in long-term value to the realisation of the American aim? I am quite certain that Harold Macmillan would never have got to first base in his efforts to reach a CTB (as opposed to the PTB which he managed to achieve) if he had been advised on the lines of the present Report.

Then in his final paragraph he writes:

> If we impede President Carter's aims, do we not risk losing his support
> – whatever is said on the surface? And if the arms race goes on acceler-
> ating, where are we going to find ourselves with our limited resources? The
> worsening of US/USSR relations will surely mean a continuation of the race,
> for the Russians have certainly got as many hotheads as have the Americans –
> and we clearly have a few too. A question which should be put to Ministers is
> whether the balance of advantage for us is less a strengthening of our military
> position vis-à-vis the Russians or the Americans (indeed even the French),
> than the political kudos we might gain by helping to bring about an accom-
> modation between the two super-powers.

Lord Zuckerman's views were like a refreshing blast of cold air, but they also
carried a warning. Whitehall contained people then who had no interest in
constraining or reducing nuclear arms, but rather wished to go on testing
nuclear weapons and deploying them on ever more sophisticated means
of delivery, irrespective of cost. To combat their influence in chairing the
Cabinet Committee on Non-Proliferation I would need all the expertise and
facts I could establish and much of this would have to come from like-minded
people in Washington. After a little time and some further discussion with
other experts, I sent out ten questions for the Department to answer and
received a reply on 3 August 1977 (Document 14).

Then on 28 September 1977, quite out of the blue, while in New York
for discussions, mainly on Southern Rhodesia (Zimbabwe, as it is today),
I was given by a special courier from No. 10 a report of a very private
message from President Carter to Prime Minister Callaghan and Callaghan's
personal reply. The Prime Minister had seen Zbig Brzezinski, President
Carter's National Security Adviser, the previous day. Callaghan's reply was
held tightly and not circulated to anyone else in the Foreign Office. It was
to be delivered personally to the White House by Peter Jay, the UK's ambassador in Washington. President Carter was due to speak to the UN General
Assembly on 4 October. Callaghan was very worried that the wording in
President Carter's proposed speech went far too close to calling in question
the then flexible response of NATO's strategy, including the use of nuclear
weapons in self-defence against any overwhelming attack, whether nuclear
or conventional, on the US and its allies.

I personally found particularly difficult in the President's proposed statement the rather too grandiose wording 'renounce the use'; it seemed to me
that this would give an unwarranted sense of a totally new policy on 'no first
use', which was the prevailing NATO policy. Having read the documents I
immediately sent a handwritten note from New York to the Prime Minister
to be taken back to No. 10 by the special courier:

I entirely support your view this is a <u>dangerous</u> development, quite unnecessary – I would like to have been able to tell Cy my view but I respect your request to say <u>nothing</u>. I hope this initiative can be ditched and will <u>never</u> be revealed until the history books are opened. I think you are right to write in a low key way, but the impact of any such statement on the Germans could be very serious. If you wished I would fly back to Washington ostensibly to hear President Carter speak on the 4th but to reemphasise personally our concern. I may well arrive back in England before you read this but in case not, I think you should have this comment in my own hand. I have <u>not</u> shown it to <u>any</u> of my private staff. I may send you a private message but since on present plans I will be back myself on Friday morning, I will probably leave this and I suspect we may need to meet to discuss private conversations with Cy Vance and Henry Kissinger related to:

    Enhanced Radiation Weapons }
    Non Circumvention   } related to SALT
    Cruise Missiles   }

I hope my speech on Thursday in Chicago will help the President to see us as his <u>friends</u> and reinforce your warning.

Yours ever

DAVID

On 29 September, Callaghan sent a message to President Carter (Document 17) offering to delay my departure to enable me to talk to Cy Vance. On 30 September I had a late-night talk with Vance in New York and sent a telegram to the Prime Minister before I flew back for the Labour Party Conference. In the telegram (Document 19), I reported: 'I am hopeful that there will be some new wording and clarification which will be helpful'.

On 1 October, back in London, I sent a longer letter to the Prime Minister covering in more detail (and typed from my own manuscript note) my discussions with Vance and in particular how Zbig Brzezinski had confirmed in my presence over the telephone that Helmut Schmidt had read the questioned passage slowly two or three times and had commented he could 'live with it'. I ended up by saying of the President's words: 'I still feel that it is an unnecessary gesture and would prefer him to have given up ERWs' (Enhanced Radiation Weapons).

In the event President Carter removed the words 'renounce the' and made a few other minor changes. In view of Helmut Schmidt's moderate reaction Jim Callaghan probably over-reacted slightly, but the use of the term 'renounce' might have provoked a stronger public reaction. When the modified statement was actually delivered in the UN some German officials were mildly upset and one newspaper presented it as a pledge of non-first-use of nuclear weapons. This was described in a telegram from Bonn, dated 7 October (included here). My response to their concern about 'flexible response' and theatre use was to ask Paul Lever to write a paper on theatre nuclear weapons, the draft of which he sent to me on 18 April 1978 (Document 23). Based on this, I wrote to the Prime Minister on 30 May under the title 'NATO's Theatre Nuclear Forces' (Document 24). The Defence Secretary Fred Mulley sent a reply on 9 June 1978 (Document 25); Paul Lever sent me a note on 13 June 1978 (Document 26) on 'the predictably cautious attitude of MOD officials'.

POSTSCRIPT

It took some years for the logic of the arguments against theatre nuclear weapons to take hold. Gradually, however, theatre nuclear weapons, whether carried on ships or aeroplanes or launched from the ground, have been progressively withdrawn by successive UK governments, so that today the UK now relies only on its strategic nuclear deterrent carried in four Trident submarines. But the main lesson of all this was that for most sensible people the very idea that the Western democracies should use nuclear weapons first was anathema, and President Carter's wish to distance himself from a strategy of 'first use' of nuclear weapons was understandable. Yet it was a fact, dramatized at the time in a popular book[1] written by a former NATO commander, General Hackett, that the Soviet Union was able to punch a hole in NATO's conventional forces deployed in Germany. We therefore had to countenance the possibility of 'first use' at least as part of a deterrent strategy, even if no sane leader would in fact have deployed nuclear weapons first other than perhaps as a warning demonstration targeted on some remote area. The idea of embarking on a battlefield nuclear exchange was a recipe for nuclear escalation. (See the discussion in Section 4: Enhanced Radiation Weapons.)

---

1   General Sir John Hackett *et al.*, *The Third World War: A Future History* (London: Sidgwick & Jackson, 1978).

DOCUMENT 13

To: SIR JOHN HUNT
From: LORD ZUCKERMAN

NUCLEAR ARMS CONTROL
(GEN. 63(77) 1)

1. I take it, both from the cover note, and paras. 10 and 17, that GEN. 63(77) 1 has been prepared so that Ministers can take a view about the issues which it discusses. I fear that these have been set out in an extremely narrow and one-sided way. Having as it were given lip-service to "a general commitment to furthering arms control" (first sentence, para. 3), the document then goes on to discuss four "specific objectives" (para.4, a.b.c.d.), only to leave the impression that a CTB and a more effective NPT would be against our interests. It is interesting that the 'specific objectives' of para. 4 become transformed into our 'national objectives' in para. 8, and then in a different guise, and on the basis of easily faulted argument, "important national interests" in 10b.

2. Nowhere does the paper point out to Ministers what the UK might gain, both politically and in security, from whatever successes the USA/USSR talks might achieve. How could the Prime Minister or the Foreign Secretary be put up to argue that if in the interests of world peace the USA can accept a CTB, we can't? It's the tail trying to wag the dog! Worse than that – it could be argued that our objectives, as set out in the paper, are the very things the NPT, to which we are fully committed, was designed to prevent. Nuclear proliferation is far too serious a matter for lip-service. We stand to gain a great deal if we ride with the Americans, and very little – if anything – if we obstruct their efforts.

3. With the world as it is, the maintenance of the credibility of the Western deterrent is, of course, essential (4a). But I fail to understand the linkage between 'the field of strategic nuclear arms control', and what is called 'the balance of conventional and theatre nuclear capability' (4b also in the middle of para. 5). If theatre nuclear capability implies that there is any reality to the concept of field warfare in which nuclear weapons are used, the proposition is to my mind nonsense. I am aware that every two years or so SACEUR goes through some ritual exercise in which those concerned satisfy themselves that the presumed 7,000 weapons held in NATO's armoury are adequate for thousands of targets specified on a map. But I was under the impression that the concept of 'tactical nuclear' warfare is hardly a reality to the members of the NATO Council. It is my understanding, too, that this is

the prevailing view in the Ministry of Defence. Does the Official Group have different views? If so Ministers should surely have the matter explained to them.

4. I myself went deeply into the subject from about 1960, and my own review of the problem was followed by an independent study by Dr. Shaw, now the Head of the Byfleet organisation. Between 1962 and 1967 the Army Operational Research Group also carried out a series of war games based on actual NATO plans. All these studies led to the same conclusion – namely that the idea of tactical nuclear warfare is a nonsense. The Americans have also done numerous investigations of the problem. Alain Enthoven, who was Assistant Secretary of Defense in the Pentagon and Director of Systems Analysis published an article in 'Foreign Affairs' (April 1975), which provided a critical analysis of the question. In it he writes that tactical nuclear weapons cannot defend Europe – they can only destroy it (this was almost the same sentence which I had used in a corresponding article in 'Foreign Affairs' of 1961). He also says that 'there is no such thing as a two-sided tactical nuclear war in the sense of sustained purposive military operations, and that 'nobody knows how to fight a tactical nuclear war'. 'Twenty years of effort by many military experts', he writes, 'have failed to produce a believable doctrine for tactical nuclear warfare'. (I attach photo-copies of a couple of pages from his article [not included in this book]).

5. I was the UK member of the United Nations Group which in 1968 reported to the Secretary-General about the effects of the possible use of nuclear weapons. The report used the results of various studies which we and other countries had carried out. I have just re-read the Report to check that my memory was not at fault. It was not, as the attached photocopies (Annex B) of the relevant pages show. It therefore amazed me that the Official Group's Report implicitly takes a totally different line. I have therefore enquired whether any new studies have been carried out – of which Enthoven too would have been unaware when he published his 1975 article. The answer I have been given is none. Press and Macklen are the technical people on the Group. If they have not got convincing new evidence, I fear that they have not guided their colleagues very well.

6. The trouble, of course, is that the word "nuclear weapon" has become the reality, and that the reality which the word was once intended to imply and should imply has been buried in verbiage. On paper we differentiate between strategic and tactical nuclear weapons when such differentiation could have no political reality. The term strategic seems to be taken to imply an exchange between the USA and the USSR, or any exchange in which nuclear bombs explode over the USSR. But a tactical exchange of 'Theatre

Nuclear weapons' could mean the total elimination of almost any, or of several European countries within a matter of days. If that would not be to NATO's detriment – to use the last two words of 4b – I'd like to know what would be.

7. When I came to the discussion of 4c and 4d and discovered that the Group in effect was advising that we must oppose a CTBT because that would stop us improving the technical effectiveness of existing British nuclear forces, I could not forebear from thinking that were these forces ever used, it would not matter at all how effective they were technically. In the subsequent exchange we would be eliminated. Whether or not we shall ever have the resources to proceed to successor systems remains to be seen, but why did the Group not consider whether the cost of maintaining our options (i.e. to discourage a CTB) would be equal in long-term value to the realisation of the American aim? I am quite certain that Harold Macmillan would never have got to first base in his efforts to reach a CTB (as opposed to the PTB which he managed to achieve) if he had been advised on the lines of the present Report.

8. Para 8 also confuses me. If a CTB were to come into force, what is the evidence that the effectiveness of the nuclear forces of both sides would be diminished? If there is evidence to this effect, why should the credibility of nuclear deterrence be reduced given that the diminution in effectiveness applied to both sides? The second sentence of 8a talks about confidence. 'Whose confidence' is in question here. Is it that of our political leaders, or our military leaders, or that of our technical people whose jobs would be affected? The final sentence of 8a implies that while the Americans are not worried by the idea of a CTB we need to be. I find this fantastic.

9. I also find 8b somewhat mystifying. Obviously the Russians are going to make a thing of PNE's. But why does it matter to us? Have we ever suggested indulging in PNE's, or have we evidence which controverts the American conclusion that PNE's are useless from the point of view of civil engineering? Furthermore, it does not necessarily follow that the only practical way of accommodating the PNE problem is what's set out in this paragraph. The Americans have already suggested that PNE's should be 'internationalised'.

10. I am equally surprised by 8c. This paragraph might have been written in 1960 by the 'hard-liners' in the United States who were opposed to an atmospheric as well as a complete test ban. In this argument it is always the Russians who cheat, never us.

11. 8e is also odd. Are we to suppose that we are not already significantly behind the point reached by the Americans in nuclear weapons technology? From the point of view of deterrence, why do we need more up-to-date

information than we have? Why do we want to consider a radically new war-head? What political purpose would it serve? Are Ministers going to be advised? So far as the last sentence of 8f is concerned, where France is brought in, all I would say is that it is gross exaggeration.

12. I now come to para.10. The first question it asks is whether the balance of advantage to us is to give support in principle to the Americans in working for a CTB? But, as I have said, the question is posed without giving any indication of what we stand to gain were détente to mean something, and equally what we stand to gain if we go on with nuclear warhead development.

13. In 10b the question is asked whether the analysis in para.8 and the Annex is accepted. I would say definitely no. The 'analysis' is so superficial it is hardly worthy of the term.

14. 10c is important. We would be certain to make Harold Brown, the Secretary of Defense, smile if we approached the Americans – at whatever level – with an indication that we wanted to impede their negotiations with the Russians. If we started meddling in the way the paper suggests I am practically certain that his good offices – which we will need if negotiations fail – would not be forthcoming.

15. In my view the question which should be put is very different. It is this: "We intend to be an original party to the CTBT and we propose assisting the Americans to this end. But if negotiations fail could we have assurances that they would help us etc. etc." I am of course assuming that the etceteras would have been properly spelt out to Ministers, so that they can take decisions in the light of balanced views. I also feel, (turning to para. 14 of the paper) that the issue of non-transfer/non-circumvention should be put to Ministers in a way which will indicate what strategic aims we wish to achieve through technical developments.

16. 15d surprises me. Are we supposing that we might one day be engaged unilaterally against the Soviet Union? I imagine that they have all focal points in the UK targetted, as well as in the USA, whereas while we have a formidable force, I can hardly imagine that we could do relatively as much damage to the USSR as they can to us. The issue as stated here is an odd one.

17. The section which deals with Cruise missiles is interesting, because it suggests that the present generation under development in the States will be vulnerable to surface to air defence systems. My information does not accord with this statement. On what is it based? Furthermore, why should we concern ourselves with a range greater than 2500 km, within which Moscow falls? Once any missiles or any aircraft penetrate into Russian air space I imagine that the balloon would go up. In any event, what purpose

would Cruise missiles serve in our hands? If their actual use were limited to Western Europe, it would be the end of Western Europe. In order to deter, do we need more nuclear weapons than we already have?

18. What is said in the latter part of para. 2la is military nonsense. Given that we launched Cruise missiles against Moscow, what difference would it make if we could then release 'quick reaction alert aircraft'? What would these aircraft be supposed to be doing then? The likely reaction of the Russians to nuclear weapons on Moscow would be to take out every UK target which the Russians have on their map. And would we be launching Cruise missiles on our own – with the Americans standing-by?

19. 21d talks about the potential of Cruise missiles for European countries. What 'potential'? Para. 25 states clearly that we already have an 'overkill capacity'. Why is this matter regarded as being outside the scope of the report?

GENERAL

20. I am sure that any arguments which Ministers or officials deploy with the Americans must be well founded – and I doubt if they would be moved in their determination to seek a CTB by anything in the paper. Harold Brown, and many others, accept the view that the number of warheads deployed in the NATO armoury could be reduced significantly without affecting Western security – I have heard the figure of 1, 000 mentioned more than once. The argument against any reduction is not military, but political. The Germans for one would believe that were the Americans to withdraw nuclear warheads they might be contemplating withdrawing from Europe. If the reduction of tension, the slowing of the arms race, a CTBT, imply a lessening of the risk of nuclear war, we stand to gain. If we impede President Carter's aims, do we not risk losing his support – whatever is said on the surface? And if the arms race goes on accelerating, where are we going to find ourselves with our limited resources? The worsening of US/USSR relations will surely mean a continuation of the race, for the Russians have certainly got as many hotheads as have the Americans – and we clearly have a few too. A question which should be put to Ministers is whether the balance of advantage for us is less a strengthening of our military position vis-a-vis the Russians or the Americans (or indeed even the French), than the political kudos we might gain by helping to bring about an accommodation between the two super-powers.

S. ZUCKERMAN

3 May 1977
Z/0891

DOCUMENT 14

Questions on Defence dictated by Foreign Secretary

1. <u>SALT and the East/West Nuclear Balance</u>

Do we expect SALT to develop into a negotiation covering systems which have theatre, as well as strategic, application?

If so, what sort of SALT III agreement would we want to see, would Britain take part in the negotiation of it and what would be our principal interests at stake? In particular, what interest, if at all, do we have in cruise missiles?

2. <u>The future of the British Nuclear Deterrent</u>

Is Britain to retain any kind of national strategic nuclear deterrent in the 1990s? If so what kind will it be and how will it be procured?

3. <u>Tactical Nuclear Weapons</u>

Should not NATO adopt a more radical approach to its holdings tactical nuclear weapons and to their inclusion in arms control negotiations?

4. <u>The Prospects for MBFR</u>

How do we see the impasse in MBFR being broken? Do we really need to maintain the idea of the common ceiling in its present form?

5. <u>New Military Technology</u>

Are we taking proper account of the implications of new weapon technologies? Should we not use our limited resources to procure greater numbers of cheaper, simpler weapons rather than a few expensive vulnerable pieces of capital equipment?

6. <u>The Need for Balanced Forces</u>

Can we afford, given the likely continuation of constraints on our defence resources, to maintain our traditional insistence on "balanced" forces? Ought we not to be studying alternative mixes of capability involving a reduction of the emphasis on one of the three services?

7. <u>The Future of BAOR</u>

Do we regard the Brussels Treaty commitment to maintain an army of 55,000 over in Germany as irrevocable and infinite? Is there no scope for reducing in due course the size of BAOR and the drain on our foreign exchange reserves which it constitutes? If not how are we going to bear the financial burden?

8. <u>Teeth and Tail</u>

Are we really sure we cannot save more money on support costs for frontline troops and equipment? Why is it that other countries manage with much better personnel/equipment ratios than we or our Allies?

9. The Future of the British and European Defence Industries

What do we expect the European Programme Group actually to achieve? Should we not be developing a comprehensive strategy for safeguarding the future of our defence industries by a more systematic integration of European production arrangements?

10. Peacetime Requirements

Should we not pay more attention to the roles the Services have to play in peacetime and, where appropriate, order equipment geared specifically to these roles?

July 1977

DOCUMENT 15

CONFIDENTIAL

Private Secretary

DEFENCE QUESTIONS

1. Of the attached list of questions posed by Dr. Owen, numbers 1 and 2 (SALT, and the British Nuclear Deterrent) are the subject of separate work. The purpose of the present submission is to answer the remaining questions, 3–10, on which papers (with some supporting material) are provided in the attached folder. These answers are covered by a general paper on British defence policy. The work is largely that of the Defence Department, in consultation and collaboration with the Planning Staff; and we discussed the initial drafts in the Planning Committee.

2. There is one major point which I think it right to make at the outset. This is the need for a period of stability in the defence budget which will permit the Ministry of Defence to plan ahead against the background of an assured level of resources. The 1974 Defence Review was supposed to do just this. But in practice it has been followed by a succession of reductions in the planned forward levels of expenditure, which have obliged the MOD to live from hand to mouth, preoccupied with working out where savings could be made with the least damage. The resultant uncertainty has, in our view, become a really important factor militating against any proper forward thinking on defence policy. In the case of the Army the effect of this has been compounded by the overstrain resulting from the Northern Ireland commitment. In practical (as opposed to policy) terms this has also impaired the training and general state of readiness of the Army to meet its NATO responsibilities.

3. If some assurance of stability in the resources available for defence is a badly needed condition for proper defence planning today, it does not of course follow that it will of itself guarantee planning or decision-making of high quality. We have good liaison with the MOD over day-today business, but the fact is that (whether or not wholly because of the budgetary difficulties through which they have been passing) the Ministry of Defence are at the moment quite without any staff resources devoted to conceptual thinking on problems that lie ahead of the daily workload. For example, it is 18 months since the subjects of cruise missiles, and the conventional implications of new military technology, emerged over the horizon; but even today we have had no adequate MOD contribution on either. Some people in the MOD are very conscious of this weakness; and effects are currently being made to restore a capability in the MOD for "general studies". We are giving discreet

support to this since, without such a capability in the MOD, we cannot make from the FCO the primarily political input we ought to be making on emerging politico-military issues. On the other hand, although useful forward-looking work might be done in this way, it cannot be regarded as the whole answer to getting better decision-making in defence policy.

4. It is not easy to judge what other steps might best be taken within the framework of the division of ministerial responsibility. On special occasions, use can be made of an interdepartmental working party, including FCO and Treasury officials, as for the preparation of the 1974 Defence Review. But this is not a formula for regular use. We can also influence MOD thinking occasionally through the Cabinet Office working group on military nuclear matters (GEN 63) which has done some useful work on SALT and CTB; but its scope is limited. Proceeding from the attached papers there are two approaches which might be worth pursuing. The first is outlined in paragraph 10 of paper No. 6. It rests on the thesis that it is probably in considering major equipment options that the greatest scope exists for the exercise of deliberate choice in defence policy-making today, and that consideration of major equipment options provides the opportunity for considering the role which British Forces are expected to perform in a particular field as well as the technical requirements expected of the equipment to be produced for those roles. Moreover, major equipment decisions not only involve a large expenditure of public funds (with a frequent tendency for the first estimates of costs to escalate) but also, increasingly, important political factors in the choice of collaborative partners. On these grounds there would be a clear case for both Treasury and FCO participation in consideration of major equipment options at options at both the official and ministerial level. Some such participation does exist today, at both levels; but it is limited in the sense that we only become involved after the Ministry of Defence have effectively decided on their objectives in developing new equipment and the argument has become one of means rather than ends. It would therefore be better to seek to establish a procedure whereby the four senior Ministers most concerned (Prime Minister, Defence Secretary, Foreign and Common-wealth Secretary and Chancellor) would consider and discuss all major new equipment programmes *before* the stage even of limited development was reached. The preparatory work at official level would have to be done inter-departmentally (possibly under Cabinet Office auspices) to ensure that the right questions were presented to Ministers.

5. If Dr. Owen approved of this idea, two matters for political judgement arise. The first is whether, given the pressure on senior Ministers, now is the time to suggest putting on them this extra burden of inevitably quite

detailed consideration of complex defence equipment choices. The other is whether the best approach to getting the procedure established would lie at the political level, in discussion with the Prime Minister and Chancellor, or whether we should try to prepare the ground first at official level with the Cabinet-Office and Treasury, in either case before the idea is put to the MOD. Personally, I incline to the former course.

6. The second idea which arises from these papers relates to the future of European collaboration in defence procurement (paper No. 9). It is expected that Mr. Mulley will have a tripartite private meeting in Paris in early November with his French and German counterparts, at which equipment questions will be probably the major topic. Because of the political as well as military importance of this European collaboration, the prospect of this meeting could offer Dr. Owen a natural opportunity to raise with Mr. Mulley some of the questions in paper No. 9 – perhaps particularly the worrying lack of new collaborative projects with either the French or the Germans; and to suggest that a general paper on the future of European equipment collaboration should be produced for discussion in DOP before Mr. Mulley's tripartite meeting in November. (This would also be relevant to a suggestion by Sir N. Henderson that industrial collaboration, including the defence field, should be a major theme of the next Anglo–French summit.) There might well be some resistance to this idea from Mr. Mulley and his Ministry. (We have had the recent case in which Mr. Mulley responded negatively to Dr. Owen's suggestion that we should put Mr. Jay in Washington into bat on the subject of a transatlantic dialogue in advance of Dr. Gilbert's visit to Washington in September.) But the idea seems worth Dr. Owen's consideration. It could also provide a lead-in to the proposal discussed in paragraphs 4 and 5 above, which will equally require careful handling with the MOD not least in regard to presentation when it is first put to them.

Anthony Duff
3 August, 1977

cc PS/Mr. Judd (with attachments)
PS/PUS (with attachments)
Mr. Moberly
Defence Dept.
Planning Staff.

DOCUMENT 16

SIR JOHN HUNT

After leaving you yesterday afternoon I enquired and discovered that I was expected to see the Foreign Secretary, which I did at 7 p.m. Our talk focused on the note of my comments which you and I had discussed, and I told him that I had learnt from you that I had been wrong to attribute all the responsibility for GEN. 63(77) 1 to the Official Committee, since it had been endorsed by the Chiefs of Staff. He understood that, none-the-less, I did not withdraw my criticisms.

Fergusson was present, but no note was taken of our 'non-meeting'. At the Foreign Secretary's request I left behind copies of my two sets of notes, on the understanding that these were only for his eyes.

I am copying this note to Fergusson.

I shall be back next week, and Linda Brassington will no doubt arrange with Clive Rose.

S. ZUCKERMAN

5 May 1977
Z/0893

To: SIR JOHN HUNT
From: LORD ZUCKERMAN

NUCLEAR NON-PROLIFERATION
(Gen. 74)

1. I have few observations to make on the papers for the Ministerial/Official Group on Non-Proliferation, which I found most interesting. I shall side-line those of my comments which in effect are questions.

GEN.74(77) 1
   2. No comment.

GEN.74(77) 2
   3. No comment, except that it is clear that President Carter's statement was not affected by any observations we may have made to American officials.

GEN.74(77) 3
   4. No comment.

GEN.74(77) 4

5. Para.2b, Annex B, implies that we have rejected the contention in the Ford/Mitre report that reprocessing is uneconomic so long as uranium remains in international commerce – or if economic, only marginally so. Adelphi Paper 130 by Greenwood, Rathjens and Ruina, entitled 'Nuclear Power and Weapons Proliferation', argues the same point. Rathjens was a member of the Nuclear Energy Policy Study Group. They admit that the data are 'pretty uncertain', but conclude that "with or without reprocessing, the back end of the fuel cycle is unlikely to account for more than ten per cent of the fuel cycle costs and a few per cent of total electricity costs. Therefore the decision whether or not to include reprocessing in the LWR fuel cycle can and probably will be made primarily on non-economic grounds". Do our analyses lead to different conclusions? Are we assuming that any reprocessing we may do will be on a cost-plus basis? We could be undercut if the Americans were to give an undertaking to provide necessary fuel for reactors, and an assurance that they are prepared to dispose of spent fuel elements either for possible future retrieval or permanent burial.

6. The point made in Annex B of GEN.74(77) 4, para. 2(II)(a) is a useful one. I believe that the Americans would be all the readier to accept the proposal that a few commercial-sized demonstration breeder reactors should be built in Europe in the 80s and 90s 'to prove the practicability and acceptability of the system', if such a development were 'internationalised'.

7. In para.2(II)(c) it is said that the US proposals are based partly on the completely non-proven assumption that world uranium sources are significantly greater than those known at present. I shall take this point up later.

8. Para. 2(III)(b) & (c). These two paragraphs refer to the environmental consequences of storing spent fuel and the likelihood that American public opinion would be against the US becoming 'the world's nuclear dustbin'. I do not believe that the American proposal to do this was suggested lightly. The Ford/Mitre group included a very distinguished professor of genetics (Seymour Abrahamson) and also Gordon Macdonald, a geologist who was a member of the first triumvirate which ran the Environmental Protection Agency. Of course there would be hostility in some quarters, but equally, environmentalists would oppose any nuclear developments. A powerful political effort would be needed to educate the American public – and for that matter the world's public – about the consequences of deferring decisions in the nuclear field.

9. Para.2(IV). This paragraph proposes that the UK nuclear industry should have 'a fair share' of the enrichment services market. The same

point is made in para.4 of Annex C of Brief No.4B. We should bear in mind the possibility that the centrifuge systems which the Americans are now developing at vast cost are, according to my information, likely to be more economic than our own. The commercial prospects of our own project will depend upon its competitiveness.

GEN.74(77) 5

10. This is Bob Press's 'analysis' of the Ford/Mitre Study "Nuclear Power Issues and Choices". It is more a resumé than an analysis, which would have required far more than a reading of the published text, and access to expertise which Press does not possess. Ministers are told that 'twenty-one scientists and economists' were engaged in the study, but not who they were. I doubt if we could assemble in the UK a group which was as competent, sophisticated, knowledgable and authoritative about the subject. It is therefore worth noting that the group included *Harold Brown*, a nuclear technologist, ex-President of CalTech, and now the Secretary of State for Defense; *Joseph Nye*, a political scientist, who is now in charge of the non-proliferation desk in the State Department; *Kenneth Arrow*, a Nobel Laureate who is distinguished for his work on resource allocation; *Paul Doty*, the highly distinguished Harvard biochemist and also Director for the programme for Science and International Affairs at Harvard (Doty has for years been intimately concerned in secret bilateral talks with the Russians on behalf of successive US Administrations); *Philip Farley*, for years in the Disarmament Agency of the State Department; *Richard Garvin*, one of the cleverest men I know, and one who has never, to the best of my knowledge, been out of the confidence of the Pentagon; *Carl Kaysen* until recently President of the Institute for Advanced Study in Princeton, and before that Deputy to McGeorge Bundy when the latter was in charge of the National Security Council under President Kennedy; *Panovsky*, one of the best nuclear physicists in the United States, and in charge of the Linear Accelerator at Stanford. I also know some of the other members of the group, but without going into further detail, all I need add is that those of the Group who are not in Carter's Administration are almost certainly exercising considerable influence from the wings. It is also worth pointing out that the report was unanimous.

11. In para. 17 Press says that the report 'begs all the questions and judgments concerning the reprocessing of spent fuel from thermal reactors and continuing breeder development'. I do not understand what he means. To my mind that is the last thing which the report does. Everyone knows that US and other thermal reactors use far less of their fuel than can breeder reactors; but the Group's economic analysis nonetheless led to the conclusion that

given a free supply of uranium, breeders won't be as economic as thermal reactors, for years to come. The question is whether or not the far greater theoretical efficiency of breeders from this point of view is going to be significant before the turn of the century. The group argued that it won't. In para. 19 Press does put the right question – if work on breeder systems is to continue, then how and by whom. This is a matter for international negotiation.

GEN.74(77) 6

12. I have carefully studied this paper on world uranium supplies and compared it with recent issues of a Washington journal called 'Energy Daily' which have appeared since President Carter's announcement of his new policy. I have also had the opportunity of seeing in draft a recent report prepared by the Uranium interests.

13. The paper is excellent, but I myself would have been inclined to deal with the availability of uranium in a somewhat different way. First there is geological availability; second, commercial; and third, political. On the basis of what I know of non-ferrous metals, uranium ore will follow the same general history as most other minerals. Depending on advancing technology and changed economic conditions, I would be inclined to believe that it will be possible to exploit ores and reserves of lower and lower grade, and lesser accessibility. Once upon a time no-one would have touched copper below a yield of 20%. Today ½ per cent copper is economic in some parts of the world. In the latter half of the nineteenth century no-one would have touched the low-grade iron ore which we now mine in the UK. It would be flying in the face of mining history to suppose that uranium is going to prove different.

14. So far as commercial availability is concerned, the fact is that there was very little uranium when the price was fixed at 8 dollars. At 40 dollars there is almost too much in relation to demand. At 100 dollars uranium would be a totally different commodity.

15. Uranium miners and processors are worried about their prospects, and the scale of future exploration and exploitation will be dependent upon assurances about the market. It is paradoxical that while a part of the nuclear industry would like to proceed with the commercial development of the breeder, both it and uranium producers know full well that the breeder could reduce the demand for uranium.

16. The political aspects of uranium availability are perhaps the most important. It is not just a case of governments controlling both supply and demand. Some cannot control those environmental interests which are totally opposed to the exploitation of nuclear energy in any form. In

Australia, the unions are also a determining factor both in the economics of the industry and in the use of the product. Furthermore both in the United States and in Australia there is confusion about title to surface and mineral rights – which makes uranium producers wary of committing capital. The position would be different if surface and mineral rights were separated, as they are in some countries. Information that I have been given independently of the Ford/Mitre study is that, at projected rates of demand, there will be no difficulty about fulfilling world requirements for uranium up to the turn of the century. As I understand it, industry accepts the contention about supply of the Ford/Mitre study, given sufficient stimulus for exploration, and sufficient assurance that private investors will not be caught short by government regulations.

GEN.74(77) 7

17. The point about uranium supplies is referred to again in para.7 of this paper. I agree completely with the statement that it will be difficult to achieve international agreement on the matter of handling mined uranium deposits. Para.8 of this paper refers to the storage of unprocessed spent fuel elements. Obviously we would need to be convinced about this matter, but I would suggest that in asking questions on the subject, we do not indicate a scepticism which in my view is unjustified when one considers the quality and experience of the people who were involved in the Ford/Mitre study.

GEN.74(77) 9

18. I found this a good and interesting paper. There is one point on which, however, it did not touch, namely that American investment in centrifuge enrichment is following a somewhat different technological line from that of URENCO. On my recent visit I was told that the individual centrifuges were enormous compared to ours, and that they are going to be much more efficient both technically and in use of power. Over the years I have been disappointed so often in our confidence that we know best that I am not inclined to take the information I was given lightly.

GEN.74(77) 10

19. I do not understand the paragraph at the foot of page 1 of this paper. How does one compare the environmental implications of the permanent storage of spent fuel with the ('any') advantages of non-proliferation? The two seem to me to be two totally separate issues. If the Americans are fool enough to store spent fuel-rods at great depths in unstable geological formations, the disaster would be trivial compared with what might result from a nuclear war. I am assuming here of course that we all suppose that preventing non-proliferation will help deter a nuclear holocaust.

20. Most of the paper 'The Disposal of Irradiated Fuel – Reprocessing or Permanent Storage' is good stuff. But when I came to <u>para. 3.2.2</u> I found myself asking whether or not the financial considerations which are discussed under 3.2 really take into account the American contention that whatever financial advantages might come from reprocessing or from attempts to commercialise breeder reactors are incommensurate with the risks which would be associated with plutonium becoming freely available in the fuel cycle.

21. <u>Para.3. 3.2</u> worries me. Has any economist looked at the conclusions in this paragraph? The assumption seems to be that costs and prices would not be increasing evenly over the whole field. Why should one suppose that if uranium prices rise rapidly because of greater demand, reprocessing would necessarily become relatively cheaper. Why shouldn't the cost of reprocessing go up at the same rate? Maybe someone has done the necessary sums.

<u>GEN.74(77) 11</u>

22. <u>Para.2</u> of this paper states that the UK is more advanced than other countries in fast-reactor fuel cycle development. Whether or not we know for certain that this is so, it is certainly not the case that we will automatically maintain a lead if other countries, and in particular the United States, move onto the scene. Does this paragraph imply that because we may be ahead technically at the present moment that we will necessarily be ahead in the export market of the 1990's?

23. <u>Para.8c</u> in fact says that the Americans are not likely to be in a position to export fast reactors until well into the 1990s. Will we be? Furthermore according to 8f, the date could only be the early 1990s. I am suspicious. Furthermore, para.9 of the same paper states that exports of fast reactors are not likely to arise before we have demonstrated domestically the successful operation of such reactors in the 1990s! While para. 10 re-states the proposition – found in the Ford/Mitre report – that once they have been proved, fast reactors are not likely to have much of a market.

S. ZUCKERMAN

<u>3 May, 1977</u>
Z/0892

DOCUMENT 17

SECRET

To flash Washington Tel No 2649 of 29 September and to UKMIS New York

(personal for Fergusson or Wall).

Following personal for ambassador from private secretary No. 10.

The Prime Minister would be grateful if you would pass the following message to President Carter as soon as possible this morning.

Begins: Dear Jimmy,

I greatly appreciated the up to date account which Zbigniew Brzezinski was able to give me, when we met on 27 September, of the recent discussions with Gromyko on salt. I understand from what he told me that these discussions are proceeding quite rapidly.

David Owen who, as you know, has been attending the UN General Assembly and is speaking today to the council on foreign relations in Chicago, is due to return to London tonight and if any way could be found for CY Vance to brief him on the latest developments this would of course be very useful.

I have now put David in the picture about your recent letter to me and my response. He would be available to discuss these matters with you, or with anyone you would like to nominate, if this would be helpful. He would no doubt be ready to postpone his departure for London if necessary for this purpose: but I should much appreciate it if you would let me have your reaction during the course of today.

Warmest regards,

Jim Unquote. ENDS.

DOCUMENT 18

[Handwritten letter from Foreign Secretary]

Dear Prime Minister

    I entirely support your view this is a <u>dangerous</u> development, quite unnecessary – I would like to have been able to tell Cy my view but I respect your request to say <u>nothing</u>. I hope this initiative can be ditched and will <u>never</u> be revealed until the history books are opened – I think you are right to write in a low key way, but the impact of any such statement on the Germans will be <u>very</u> serious. If you wished I would fly back to Washington ostensibly to hear President Carter speak on the 4th but to reemphasize personally our concern. I may well arrive back in England before you read this, but in case not, I think you should have this comment in my own hand. I have <u>not</u> shown it to <u>any</u> of my private staff – I may send you a private message but since on present plans I will be back myself on Friday morning and will probably leave this and I suspect we may have to meet to discuss private conversation with Cy Vance and Henry Kissinger related to

> Enhanced Radiation Weapon)
> Non Circumvention   ) related to SALT
> Cruise Missile   )

    I hope my speech on Thursday in Chicago will help the President to see us as his <u>friends</u> and reinforce your warning.

Yours ever

David

DOCUMENT 19

TO IMMEDIATE FCO TEL NO. 4258 OF 30 SEPTEMBER.

FOR PS/PUS FROM PRIVATE SECRETARY.

1. Please transmit following message to Prime Minister from Secretary of State.

Begins:

I had an hour with Cy Vance in New York late last night and we both talked to Zbig Brzezinski on the telephone. I intend to do no more. I am however hopeful that there will be some new wording and clarification which will be helpful. If you receive any further communication, I think that we should talk before you reply. I can come to Brighton at any time. I currently plan to arrive on Sunday afternoon but can as easily come on Saturday. Perhaps No.10 could let me know as soon as they hear that any message is on the way. It may be that there will not be a message, or at least not until Sunday or Monday. I will brief you in detail when I see you.

David

ENDS.

2. The Secretary of State has discussed all this with PUS. Copies of this telegram should go to No.10, Sir A. Duff and Private Secretary only.

JAY

DOCUMENT 20

Foreign and Commonwealth Office
London SWIA 2AH
1 October 1977

Dear Jim,

I met Cy Vance at 10.30 pm on Thursday, 29 September. We talked alone for an hour.

I started by indicating your and my concern over the proposed UN statement. He told me Helmut Schmidt's reaction had been favourable as had been Valery Giscard d'Estaing's.

I said that I expected the French not to raise any objections and I doubted that their motives were wholly divorced from their own idiosyncratic attitude to nuclear weapons. Any European anxieties over the United States nuclear guarantee would only serve as the historic justification for the French decision, at a heavy price, to develop their own nuclear deterrent.

I queried Helmut's attitude in such detail, to ensure that they had interpreted it correctly, that Cy rang Zbig Brzezinski to confirm exactly what Helmut had agreed. Zbig said that Helmut had read the passage slowly two or three times and had commented , that he could "live with it". He attached a great deal of importance to informing the smaller countries. He had not been enthusiastic but did not raise any major problems.

I told Cy that your attitude would be strongly influenced by the Germans. If they were genuinely content, we would go along with less concern. Cy then told me that the Joint Chiefs had raised no objection, seeing it as no more than a statement of reality and making explicit the existing situation. He said that the Chinese Foreign Minister had not raised any objection when he had consulted him in New York. Confronted by this formidable line-up I started to probe the exact wording. I said that I felt that the danger of a misunderstanding was considerable as at present drafted. The Soviet Union saw their proposal for a Treaty preventing "first use of nuclear weapons" as being in the context of refusing ever to use nuclear weapons first. The proposed wording was clearly designed to allow the President to use nuclear weapons when faced by "first use" of conventional weapons in an overt attack, but this did not come out from the wording loud and clear. There was room for doubt, and I asked why conventional attack should not be mentioned explicitly and thereby make clear beyond doubt that the "first use" limitation *did not* apply to conventional attack and therefore did not challenge the whole

NATO nuclear strategy of flexible response. Cy agreed with this and thought that the language should be clearer. He promised to look into it again and we both discussed this possibility with Zbig on the telephone.

I touched on Third countries but I did not dwell on the Yugoslavian point as I did not find that very convincing myself. It can be argued that it is destabilising in that it removes a possible threat, but I thought that the possibility of its being used was always very slight.

I asked why there was a hurry. Cy said that the President had been considering this issue now for some time and that he had been finding it increasingly difficult to justify when challenged by the Soviets. They felt that the Soviet Union was about to launch a major propaganda campaign on this issue and they wanted to under-cut them now. On the short time for consultation, they felt that anything much longer than ten days for consultations meant the risk of a leak grew ever greater.

He was fulsome and genuine in his praise for the way in which you had defended the President to Helmut and Giscard and they looked on us as their firmest friends. The President would not want us of all people to be upset. I warned him that, if this step was taken, it was particularly important not to couple this with any weakening over non-circumvention, or commit themselves to SALT arrangements which would preclude us from having access to cruise missiles. With that combination what now might only be unease could easily escalate to alarm. Cy admitted to being worried about right wing opinion in the United States. He implied that this decision could tip them over into outright hostility on many fronts and this was a real concern. I was left, however, with the clear feeling that they would go ahead with the speech but that there was a definite chance of additional, helpful, clarifying language.

On SALT it appears that there will be a 600 kilometre limit for three years on cruise missile deployment, and it will only, I believe from what was said, be deployed in the air-borne mode. The sea-launched and ground-launched missiles could be tested in the three year period but only from the air. Testing, I understood, would not carry any restriction on range. In return for this, the Soviet Union have agreed not to deploy some weapons systems and to accept limitations on MIRVs in terms of number which they have hitherto resisted. I warned that if the three year initial period became permanent that would exclude us from sea-launched cruise missiles; also the 600 kilometre limit made sea-launched missiles valueless. Cy denied that the three years would become permanent. He thought that this would all come up in SALT 111, with Forward Based Systems included. He admitted that the main Soviet anxiety related to *land* based cruise missiles and he did not exclude a ban of them in SALT 111. The US Generals at present were very unhappy even to contemplate not deploying land-based cruise missiles in three years time and had been resistant to freezing deployment.

Cy was very confident on SALT. Overall he thinks that he has a good agreement. He confirmed that there would be no further ABM deployment. He confirmed that the Soviet Union had rejected very firmly their non-circumvention language. I said that I thought that they had tabled this too soon. I urged him to leave open the sea-launched cruise missile as being one way which we might be able to retain a nuclear capability and I left him in no uncertainty that we would be very bitter if this option was closed without the fullest consultation. He took the point but gave no commitment.

It was a worthwhile meeting with Cy, as usual, being extremely frank and open. The meeting finished with me far happier than when we started. But I still feel that it is an unnecessary gesture and would prefer him to have given up ERWs.

Yours ever,

David

(typed from manuscript)

DOCUMENT 21

CONFIDENTIAL

FROM BRYAN CARTLEDGE FOR PRIME MINISTER

The United States Embassy this morning delivered urgently to the FCO the following language on use of nuclear weapons, which will be included in President Carter's speech to the UN general Assembly to be delivered today at 1530 our time:

> "To reduce the reliance of nations on nuclear weaponry I hereby solemnly declare on behalf of the United States that we will not use nuclear weapons except in self-defence: That is, in circumstances of an actual nuclear or conventional attack on the United States, our territories or armed forces, or such an attack on our allies.

> "In addition, we hope that initiatives by the Western Nations to secure mutual and balanced force reductions in Europe will be met by equal response from the Warsaw pact countries."

The communication from the US Embassy explains that the President's statement is basically intended to make clear that the United States no less than the Soviet Union is interested in seeing that nuclear weapons never have to be used. The US commentary also makes the following points:

i) The statement has the additional advantage of giving the US and the allies firmer ground on which to stand if the Russians and East Eruopeans table their proposal for an agreement of no first use of nuclear A weapons in the CSCE meeting at Belgrade.
ii) The statement does not affect the current NATO strategy of flexible response including the role of nuclear weapons.
iii) It applies to self-defence against any attack on the US and allies, whether nuclear or conventional, and thus fully maintains NATO options to respond to attack.

OUR REACTION

FCO advice at official level is that the UK reaction to President Carter's declaration should be to welcome it as a constructive clarification of the US position, in the interests of peace and security for all. In answer to questions, we could draw on the points made in the US commentary above.

However, we shall also be faced with questions on the UK's own position on the use of nuclear weapons. On this, FCO advice, with which MOD concur at official level, is that we should say that President Carter's statement makes explicit the position which we for our part have always regarded as implicit in the possession of weapons of such destructive power as nuclear weapons. The alternative would be simply to state in terms that HMG's position is identical to that declared by President Carter (but my own view is that the first alternative is preferable in terms of UK relations with our European allies).

We are also likely to be asked whether we were consulted about President Carter's statement. FCO advice is that we should simply say that we were informed of the statement in advance.

You may wish to discuss the above this afternoon with the Foreign and Commonwealth Secretary and Defence Secretary.

It would be helpful to have very soon your decision on the line which the No 10 Press Office, FCO and MOD press offices and UK posts abroad should take. Questions are likely to start coming in by 1600 today.

MESSAGE ENDS

4 October 1977

[Postscript: On the telegram, Private Secretary Ewen Fergusson had marked in red for the Foreign Secretary the former text which had read "we will renounce the use of ..." instead of "we shall not use", "its territories" instead of "our territories" and "on the territory or forces of our allies" instead of "on our allies".

The Prime Minister's views had also been indicated by ticks on the first two paragraphs of Our Reaction and crossing out the last sentence of the second paragraph.]

DOCUMENT 22

FM BONN 071730Z

CONFIDENTIAL

TO PRIORITY FCO TELNO 914 OF 7 OCTOBER

INFO WASHINGTON, PARIS, MOSCOW, UKDEL NATO, UKMIS NEW YORK

WASHINGTON TELEGRAM NO 4324:
PRESIDENT CARTER'S SPEECH AT THE UN:
NUCLEAR WEAPONS AND ARMS CONTROL

1. In conversation today with Bullard the German Ministries of Foreign Affairs (Pfeffer and Ruth) and Defence (General Altenburg) took the line that we should all make allowances for Mr Carter's evident wish to create the maximum effect in the UN and at Belgrade, to seize the public relations initiative and to continue the impetus built up by his emphasis on the nuclear theme both before and since he became President. The trouble was that this method risked creating misunderstandings and doubts in the minds of the public and of America's allies which then required to be got out of the way.

2. The public relations aspect of President Carter's speech did indeed cause the German Government some trouble. At least one newspaper here presented the passage quoted in paragraph 6 of UKMIS New York Telegram No 1508 as if it had been a pledge on non-first-use of nuclear weapons. The government spokesman put out a corrective statement, welcoming President Carter's remarks and pointing out that they left open the option of defensive use of nuclear weapons in reply to either a nuclear or conventional attack. At the same time my American colleague was summoned by Genscher and asked for clarification of the White House press spokesman's comments on this passage, which was later provided.

3. In other words the Germans have once again been upset by the way the American administration has handled a military-political subject which vitally affects German interests. Officials here continue to express confidence that the American heart is in the right place, but Altenburg said on a personal basis that the strange remarks by Jody Powell, coming after the PRM 10 affair, provoked the question whether the White House (and he mentioned Brzezinksi) had some private ideas on nuclear policy which the state and defence departments might not endorse.

Wright

DOCUMENT 23

Private Secretary

THEATRE NUCLEAR WEAPONS

1. I attach a paper on theatre nuclear weapons policy, which is one of the subjects on which the Secretary of State has recently expressed an interest.

2. If Dr Owen thinks that the ideas in the final section of the paper are worth pursuing, then further work might perhaps be set in hand along the following lines:-

(i) The Joint Intelligence Committee could be asked to examine in a more detailed and specific way than it has done hitherto the particular circumstances in which an East/West war in Europe might break out. The examination should cover a range of different possible scenarios, including a small-scale local frontier incident; a major attack confined to a limited region; a full-scale conventional invasion; a full-scale invasion involving the immediate use of nuclear weapons against targets in Western Europe; and a full-scale strategic attack against both Western Europe and the United States. It should also consider under what circumstances a Warsaw Pact attack, of whatever kind, might be directed specifically against the United Kingdom. The JIC should be asked to offer some assessment of the relative likelihood of each of these possible scenarios (and of any others which it cares to examine). It should include if possible in each case, in addition to an account of the conditions which might cause the Russians to launch an attack, some assessment of the factors which would be most likely to deter them from doing so. A JIC paper of this kind would be useful not only for a review of theatre nuclear weapons policy but also in relation to the study on the Criteria for Deterrence which is being carried out under Sir A Duff's chairmanship as part of the planning for Britain's future strategic nuclear deterrent.

(ii) Defence Department could be asked to submit some illustrative options for arms control proposals whose effect would be to stabilise the theatre nuclear balance in a manner consistent with a deterrent policy on the part of NATO which placed a high value on longer range theatre nuclear systems and little or no value on short range systems. These options should be based on a willingness by NATO to renounce (on a basis of reciprocity) all nuclear systems with a range of less than 100 miles and to accept quite major reductions in its

194

holdings of warheads; little or no need by NATO for ballistic missiles other than those of strategic range; and as much freedom of action for NATO as possible over longer range theatre nuclear systems, particularly cruise missiles. The options should be geared to the concept of overall parity, as developed in SALT (ie not necessarily involving a numerically equal ceiling on all types of system straight away). They should be presented as options which could be regarded as equitable in their own right, irrespective of their likely negotiability with the Warsaw Pact.

3. I assume that, at this stage at any rate, Dr Owen would not want any approaches to be made to the Ministry of Defence on this subject.

18 April 1978   Paul Lever

THEATRE NUCLEAR WEAPONS

<u>Scope</u>

1. This paper describes briefly the development of NATO's doctrine on theatre nuclear weapons; and sets out some proposals for rationalising NATO's policy towards them.

<u>Definition</u>

2. For the purposes of this paper NATO's theatre nuclear weapons are defined as those weapons systems whose sole or primary role is for use within a limited theatre of military operations in Europe. Such use can range from close tactical support on the battlefield to long-range strikes against local military targets in the western part of the Soviet Union, though falling short of strikes against Soviet strategic targets such as cities or major military installations. (A few of the systems mentioned, eg Vulcan and F111 aircraft would be capable, in theory at any rate, of being used against such strategic targets as well. But they would only be marginally effective in this role and are therefore considered in relation to their primary, theatre-based function. Similarly, although reference is made in the paper to the possible use of certain strategic nuclear weapons such as Poseidon or Polaris for limited theatre strike purposes, these systems are not considered in themselves as part of the Alliance's theatre nuclear forces.)

3. The paper is concerned in the main with the land/air environment. Doctrine on the maritime use of nuclear weapons is only now being seriously examined within NATO and it is not possible at this stage to predict what the outcome of this examination will be.

Current Force levels

4. The theatre nuclear delivery systems now deployed by NATO are as follows:

(a) Short Range (up to 100 miles)

Type	Operated By (in nuclear role)	Total Number
Artillery (8" & 155 mm)	US, UK, FRG, ▮▮▮▮▮▮ ▮▮▮▮▮▮▮▮▮▮ ▮▮▮▮▮▮▮▮▮▮	about 1,000
Surface to Surface Missiles (LANCE & HONEST JOHN)	US, UK, FRG, ▮▮▮▮▮▮ ▮▮▮▮▮▮▮▮	about 200

(b) Medium Range (up to 1,000 miles)

Type	Operated By (in nuclear role)	Total Number
Surface to Surface Missiles (PERSHING)	US & FRG	135
Aircraft (F4, F104, Buccaneer, Jaguar)	US, UK, FRG, ▮▮▮▮▮▮ ▮▮▮▮▮▮▮▮▮▮	about 1,000

(c) Longer Range (over 1,000 miles)

Type	Operated By (in nuclear role)	Total Number
Aircraft (F111 & Vulcan)	US & UK	216

(d) Miscellaneous
   Surface to Air Missiles (NIKE HERCULES)
   Atomic Demolition Munitions (ADMs)
   Nuclear Depth Bombs (used from aircraft and helicopters)

(Of the above systems, the artillery and aircraft have an important conventional role: the others are wholly or primarily geared to nuclear delivery.) The United States maintains in Europe a stockpile of around 7,000 warheads (of which around 5,000 are in the FRG) for these forces. These warheads are available to the other members of the Alliance under "two key" arrangements. There are in addition a small number of British-made, and controlled, warheads for use as bombs from aircraft and as anti-submarine depth bombs from helicopters.

5. The bulk of NATO's stockpile is thus taken up with short or medium range systems. It has been estimated that some 70% of the warheads are associated with delivery systems of less than 100 miles range. Future equipment replacement plans suggest that this emphasis on shorter range systems will continue. LANCE, which replaces the old SERGEANT and HONEST JOHN systems, is still coming into service and will on present plans be deployed throughout the 1980s. Work is going ahead on a Mark II version of the PERSHING and on improvements to the 8" and 155mm nuclear artillery shells which, if continued, will mean the maintenance in service of these systems for another decade or so. As regards aircraft the trend is away from a long range strike capability. The British Vulcans and Buccaneers will be replaced by the Tornado, which has a range of well under 1,000 miles, ie not sufficient to strike Soviet territory, even from the FRG; and the F16, which will be the only other new nuclear-capable aircraft to come into service during the 1980s, will have a range shorter than the F104s and F4s which it will replace. The only potential improvement to NATO's long-range theatre nuclear capability currently in prospect is the cruise missile. The Americans however have not yet given any clear. indication of whether they intend to introduce it into the Alliance's armoury or, if so, in what types or numbers.

6. France also has theatre nuclear forces: current holdings are 25 Pluton missile launchers and around 60 nuclear-capable Mirage Fl and Jaguar ground attack aircraft. (The 32 French Mirage IV A bombers and the 18 French Intermediate Range Ballistic Missiles are thought to be targetted primarily against strategic targets, although they could also be used for theatre strike.)

Warsaw Pact Theatre Nuclear Systems

7. The Warsaw Pact has a similarly wide range of theatre nuclear capability (though probably without some of NATO's refinements such as ADMs or nuclear air defence systems). Warsaw Pact holdings of short range battlefield systems are similar in numbers to those of NATO; and the numbers of its medium-range nuclear capable aircraft (though not of its total holdings of medium range aircraft) and missiles are broadly similar to those of NATO. But the Warsaw Pact has a marked superiority in longer-range systems and it is in this area that it is currently placing the greatest emphasis, with major new systems, such as the SS20 MIRVed and mobile missile and the Backfire bomber, now coming into service. These two systems will probably be targetted indiscriminately on local military targets in Western Europe, on major cities and on major military installations. All the nuclear systems with the Warsaw Pact's forces are supplied by the Soviet Union and the vast

majority are operated by Soviet forces. The other Warsaw Pact countries operate a small number of nuclear-capable systems but it is not known what arrangements they may have for access to Soviet warheads. There are thought to be around 3–4,000 such warheads deployed in Eastern Europe outside the Soviet Union.

Development of NATO's Doctrine

8. NATO's current stockpile of theatre nuclear weapons is a hang-over from the 1950s and 1960s. Such weapons were introduced into Europe originally as part of the American proclivity to exploit nuclear weapons technology in every available direction and to develop any kind of nuclear weapons system which seemed to be of possible military use. Little or no attention was paid at the time of their introduction to the particular politico/military scenarios under which they might be used: the overwhelming nuclear superiority enjoyed by the US over the Soviet Union, and the reliance by NATO on a strategy of massive nuclear retaliation in response to any kind of attack, tended to discourage too rigorous an examination by the Allies of what exactly the consequences of using nuclear weapons in various ways might be.

9. The abandonment by NATO, largely under the influence of the then US Secretary of Defense Mr Macnamara, of the doctrine of massive nuclear retaliation and the adoption instead of the strategy of flexible response led to a recognition by the Allies of the need for a systematic review of their nuclear policies. The Nuclear Planning Group was set up specifically for this purpose in 1967 and since then has done a good deal of work in examining the role of nuclear weapons in the Alliance's overall strategy, concentrating in the main on theatre nuclear weapons since it is tacitly recognised that the characteristics, targetting and numbers of strategic weapons are for the Americans alone to decide, whereas planning on theatre nuclear policy is a collective matter. In the course of its studies the NPG has examined both general policy issues and the role of individual weapons.

10. A common assumption in all the NPG's studies – which has come to be regarded as almost axiomatic to the whole doctrine of flexible response itself – has been that if war were to break out in Europe it would most likely take the form of a major Warsaw Pact conventional attack; that the Alliance's conventional forces would be unable to sustain a viable defence against such an attack for more than a limited period of time; and that therefore NATO would be obliged to take the initiative in escalating the conflict, at a time and in a manner of its own choosing, to the nuclear level. The NPG has never examined in any depth the possibility of a Warsaw Pact attack

which employed theatre nuclear weapons from the outset and hence has not considered what type of theatre nuclear forces would be best suited to countering such an attack. Nor has it considered what the role, if any, of theatre nuclear weapons might be in the context of a more "accidental" conflict in Europe where Soviet motives in committing aggression against NATO territory were less clearcut.

Initial Use

11. The principal studies which the NPG has done on the general role of nuclear weapons are the Provisional Political Guidelines for the Initial Defensive Tactical Use of nuclear weapons by NATO and the Phase I and Phase 2 studies on Follow-On Use. The Pro-visional Political Guidelines, adopted by the NPG at its meeting in Athens in 1969 and by the Defence Planning Committee in 1970, set out in general terms the various ways in which NATO might deliberately escalate the level of a conflict. These range from, on the one hand, the purely demonstrative use of nuclear weapon not aimed at any military target at all (which Dr Owen has at times referred to as the "Gobi Desert" option) to the use of a number of weapons against a range of military targets in an extended geographical area. But the guidelines do not really do more than set out a number of options and/or make a number of fairly obvious, even banale, observations. For example, on the crucial question of when exactly NATO would resort to the initial use of nuclear weapons, they do no more than say, in effect, that this should be neither too early on in a conflict nor too late. And on the question of the scale of initial use they say merely that the more limited the scale, the lesser the danger of an over-escalatory Warsaw Pact reaction, while the more unrestrained the scale the greater the psychological and political effect would be likely to be. As a guide to practical policy, therefore, the Provisional Political Guidelines for Initial Use are of little value. There was, however, an implicit inference in them that NATO would not be likely to take the crucial decision to use nuclear weapons until its conventional forces were near to defeat, i.e., when Warsaw Pact forces had already penetrated some way into NATO territory; and that the scale of initial use would be likely to be limited and of short range. In practice this would mean that NATO would probably start off by using nuclear weapons on its own territory.

Follow-On Use

12. The NPG's studies on the follow-on use of theatre nuclear weapons started where the Provisional Political Guidelines left off. It was assumed that NATO's initial use of nuclear weapons had failed to cause the Warsaw

Pact to call off its attack and withdraw from NATO territory; and that the Warsaw Pact's response to employ its own theatre nuclear forces. (It was considered inconceivable that the Warsaw Pact, if it was going to continue fighting after NATO had introduced nuclear weapons, would not go nuclear as well.) The follow-on studies were conducted over a period of 5 to 6 years in two phases. In the first phase the NPG examined in detail a number of possible war scenarios in Europe on the Central Front, on the northern and southern flanks and in the Baltic approaches. The starting point in each case was a Warsaw Pact conventional attack which NATO's conventional defences had failed to withstand; a decision by NATO before its forces were utterly exhausted to introduce nuclear weapons in one or other of the ways set out in the Provisional Policy Guidelines and in a manner consistent with SACEUR's employment constraints (eg on collateral damage); and a nuclear response by the Warsaw Pact at least equal in scope and kind to NATO's initial use. The scenarios varied from the use of a mere handful of nuclear weapons on each side to the` exchange of several hundred; and from their use in a very limited battlefield area to their use over almost the entire theatre of operations in Europe, though stopping short of attacks on cities and on major strategic military installations.

13. The results of the studies were remarkably consistent. They showed, other than in one or two very specialised instances, that the effect of an exchange of theatre nuclear weapons in Europe, at virtually any level, would be an accentuation and acceleration of the trend of the preceding conventional battle. They showed also that it would require the use of only a very few nuclear weapons on either side to inflict a massive degree of physical devastation and human losses, even if the kilotonnage of the weapons used was kept to the minimum necessary to achieve the required military effect. In other words, if NATO were already failing to withstand a Warsaw Pact conventional attack and was sustaining unacceptable losses in terms of troops and/or territory, the result of introducing nuclear weapons (assuming that the Warsaw Pact responded in kind) would be to increase drastically the attitrition and devastation rate and ensure that NATO in effect lost even faster than it was already doing. Victory in such a war (if it could be called victory) would accrue eventually to the side with the largest number of available reserves, and this would inevitably be the Warsaw Pact.

14. In the second phase of the studies the results of the examinations of these scenarios were collated and some general conclusions for NATO's policy on the use of theatre nuclear weapons were set out. The main conclusions to emerge were:–

(a) The use of such weapons could not help the Alliance to "win" a war which was not winnable by conventional means and that therefore they could not be considered as any kind of substitute for conventional weapons.

(b) The main value of such weapons was political: they served as a necessary link between the Alliance's conventional forces and its strategic nuclear forces, in that without them as an intermediate step on the ladder of escalation the deterrent threat to employ strategic nuclear weapons would not be credible.

The Phase II report did not however attempt to extrapolate from these conclusions any blueprint for precisely what types of theatre nuclear weapons and in what numbers the Alliance required for this latter purpose. It talked merely of the need for a "wide and full range". But the scale of devastation which could be caused by even a small number of nuclear weapons suggested that there were no conceivable circumstances in which more than a tiny fraction of NATO's theatre nuclear armoury could ever be used. And even allowing the need for SACEUR to cater for a variety of potential military contingencies, a figure of 7,000 warheads and associated delivery systems looked, in the light of the NPG's studies, significantly over-generous.

15. The conclusions of these studies were something of a disappointment to the enthusiasts for theatre nuclear warfare, of whom there were many around at the time, who had tended to view such weapons as warfighting tools which could help NATO to compensate for its conventional military inadequacies. Certain sections of the nuclear weapons community in the US Department of Defense, were, and still are, reluctant to accept that NATO has nothing to gain, and everything to lose, militarily by a theatre nuclear exchange. Nonetheless, the Follow-On Studies were accepted by NPG Ministers and they constitute the Alliance's formal doctrinal position on the subject. The NPG has undertaken further work in the field in more recent years, and has in particular examined the implications for the Alliance's theatre nuclear doctrine of certain new technological developments such as improvements in accuracy of guidance systems and the introduction of specialised forms of warhead such as ERWs. (It was of interest that during the NPG's study of new weapons technology the ERW was presented by the American military community as a fairly minor and specialised new technique whose military significance was regarded as much less than the improvements in target acquisition capability and the accuracy of delivery systems being studied at the same time.) These studies showed that, although it would be possible in future to use nuclear weapons against targets which had not previously been thought suitable for nuclear attack, nonetheless the

overall effect of the new technological developments would not be such as to change the basic conclusions of the Alliance's earlier studies, namely that they could not be regarded as war-fighting tools, and that their main value was primarily political.

Recent Attempts to Change the Stockpile

16. NATO thus has a large stockpile of theatre nuclear weapons systems which grew up almost by accident; and a doctrine for their use which bears little or no relation to the actual stockpile. But, although it is generally recognised in the Alliance that the present stockpile is unsatisfactory, no attempt has been made to construct from scratch a different one which would be based on NATO's own conceptual studies. Instead the Allies have simply relied on the Americans to come up with proposals for change and have reacted, often somewhat grudgingly, to them.

17. The first such proposal was for the inclusion of the Option III package (removal of 1,000 American warheads, 54 F4 aircraft and 36 Pershing Missiles from the FRG) in MBFR, the acceptance of which by the Allies in 1973 was tantamount to a recognition that NATO had more theatre nuclear systems in Germany than it really needed. Since then the Americans have urged the need for further changes. They have done so partly as a result of Congressional pressure (Senator Nunn introduced an amendment to the 1975 Defense Appropriation Bill which required the Administration to submit proposals for rationalising the theatre nuclear stockpile) and partly as a result from pressure from the nuclear technologists themselves. The Americans have argued that the Allies should concentrate on theatre nuclear systems which are responsive to political direction, which are geared especially to producing certain specific politico-military effects such as shock and surprise and which are survivable themselves in a nuclear environment. In practical terms this would mean a greater concentration on the more longer range theatre nuclear systems, a lesser need for the shorter range battlefield ones and probably little or no need at all for nuclear air defence systems or ADMs, and a greater degree of reliance on SSBNs for certain long range theatre strike missions.

18. These proposals have however not got very far. NATO's military authorities have been reluctant to contemplate the reduction or abolition of any elements in the present stockpile (though they readily agree to any proposed additions); and the Germans have shown great sensitivity to the removal of any nuclear systems from the territory of the FRG, even when, as is the case of the NIKE HERCULES Surface to Air Missile, there is little or no military case for its retention. The Ministry of Defence has been somewhat

more forthcoming. The Chiefs of Staff accepted in 1975 that the Alliance's stockpile of theatre nuclear warheads in Europe could be reduced by 2,000 without damage to NATO's security (ie by 1,000 more than the offer which had been already made in MBFR); and it is generally accepted in MOD that NATO has unnecessarily high holdings of nuclear capable artillery, nuclear capable surface to air missiles and ADMs. But it is still impossible to get the MOD to study in any serious way what would be an "ideal" mix of theatre nuclear weapons, derived logically from NATO's agreed doctrines for their use. There is an in-built tendency on the military side of the MOD to feel that any radical change would somehow jeopardise deterrence and that things are best left as they are.

The Need for a New Policy on Theatre Nuclear Weapons

19. The failure of the Alliance to draw any practical conclusions from its own conceptual studies is damaging on four counts:-

(i)   Proposals are still made for introducing, improving or increasing theatre nuclear hardware which bear no relation at all to the Alliance's real political or military needs. For example, SACEUR has just submitted proposals for a set of short term measures to improve NATO's theatre nuclear forces (as part of the overall programme of short term measures commissioned by last year's NATO Summit meeting) which, if implemented, would almost double the numbers of nuclear capable artillery pieces available to NATO and would make significantly more aircraft nuclear-capable. Yet there are no conceivable military circumstances in which NATO could employ greater numbers of such systems than it already has. Nor is there any reason to suppose that the overall political credibility of NATO's deterrent would be enhanced either. Similarly, moves are afoot within the Ministry of Defence to consider the replacement of theatre nuclear warheads which are manufactured nationally by the UK and whose life-expectancy will expire towards the middle of the 1980s: on present form it will simply be assumed that the general requirement for such weapons will remain more or less unchanged.

(ii) The Alliance devotes significant resources, in terms of research and development, procurement costs, running costs, personnel, storage and training, to its theatre nuclear forces. (It has been estimated that in manpower alone the cost of maintaining the 50 or so nuclear storage sites in Europe is equivalent to that of maintaining a full US division.) These resources are not at present being deployed in a cost effective way.

(iii) It is bad for the general credibility and public acceptability of the Alliance's deterrent posture for NATO to maintain theatre nuclear forces without having coherent or intelligible philosophy for their use. The present doctrine has been summarised, not unreasonably, by one of Dr Kissinger's former assistants as "to fight a conventional war until we lose; to fight a theatre nuclear war until we lose; and then to commit suicide". It will not be easy in the long run to sustain public support for a policy of this kind.

(iv) Possible opportunities for stabilising the East/West theatre nuclear balance in a satisfactory way through an arms control regime are being missed or misused. NATO is at present hanging on unnecessarily to large numbers of nuclear capable systems which it does not need and which could, without damage to the Alliance's security, be bargained away on a reciprocal basis with the Warsaw Pact. At the same time it is allowing other systems, particularly cruise missiles, to slip into the orbit of arms control discussions without ever having properly studied their importance to the Alliance.

20. In order to rationalise its policy on theatre nuclear weapons the Alliance probably needs to take the following steps:-

(i) To develop a doctrine for the use of such weapons which is geared more directly towards deterring those forms of East/West conflict of which there is the greatest danger and which reflects their real military capabilities and limitations.

(ii) To re-structure the stockpile so that it matches the doctrine and to ensure that future changes in the stockpile are consistent with the doctrine. This will be particularly relevant in considering options for the development of those nuclear forces under British national command and control.

(iii) To consider possible aims control approaches to the whole area of theatre nuclear weapons or to certain parts of it which might help stabilise the East/West balance in a way which would not jeopardise the Alliance's deterrent requirements.

In practical terms this might mean the following.

Doctrine

21. NATO should moderate its obsession with the idea of a massive Warsaw Pact conventional attack. Of all the possible scenarios for a conflict in Europe this is perhaps the least likely. If a war breaks out at all it will most probably be the result of confusion, miscalculation or mismanagement rather

than as the result of a deliberate conscious decision by the Soviet leadership to launch a full scale all-out invasion. If the Russians were to contemplate such an invasion (and all the current intelligence estimates suggest that they have no intention at all of doing so), it would probably be either because they feared in some way that the West was about to attack them; or because they calculated that the United States would not be prepared to use its strategic nuclear forces, and thus risk the destruction of its own territory, in defence of Western Europe. In either case the Russians would be most likely to use theatre nuclear forces themselves from the outset rather than limit themselves simply to a conventional attack. Warsaw Pact forces are trained and equipped to fight in a combined nuclear and conventional environment (indeed, to some extent in a chemical/biological/radiological environment as well); and Soviet military doctrine, tactics and published strategy clearly envisage the prospect of a prolonged nuclear battle. Moreover, NATO's present conventional and theatre nuclear force posture presents particularly inviting targets for theatre nuclear strike. Road and rail facilities within the Central Region and the ports of entry to it for reinforcement forces are easily interdictable; airforces are concentrated on a limited number of fairly vulnerable airfields; and many of NATO's own theatre nuclear forces, and its nuclear storage sites, as well as critical headquarters and command control and communications centres are unhardened and vulnerable. If therefore the Russians, for what ever reason, had decided upon a full scale invasion, there would be every military motive for them to start off with theatre nuclear strikes on a massive scale just as their tanks began to roll.

22. In order to deter such an invasion, remote though the possibility of it may be, the Alliance needs to demonstrate, both by its avowed doctrines and by the posture of its forces, that a theatre nuclear attack would be met by the use by the Allies of nuclear forces, which were themselves invulnerable to first strike, on an equally massive scale and in a way which would involve not only Soviet forces but Soviet territory (albeit not necessarily Soviet strategic installation or major cities) from the outset. Similar considerations would in any event apply, albeit on a somewhat lesser scale, to the deterrence of a full scale conventional attack. If the Russians had decided to launch such an attack they would hardly be deterred from pressing it home by the prospect of NATO exploding a few nuclear shells or short range nuclear missiles or bombs on its own territory (which is where, according to present doctrine, any initial use of such weapons would be almost bound to take place). They would only be deterred by the prospect of suffering major losses on their own territory. In either case, the ultimate deterrent would be the threat of US strategic nuclear forces being brought into play. The more, therefore,

that NATO's theatre nuclear forces are meshed in, both doctrinally and in terms of hardware, with its strategic nuclear forces, the greater their deterrent value is likely to be.

23. There is therefore no political requirement for the Allies to go through the kind of stately nuclear gavotte which is currently envisaged in escalating the level of a theatre nuclear conflict – starting off, for example, with the explosion of a nuclear shell on NATO's own territory, followed by a somewhat deeper, second echelon surface-to-surface missile or air-delivered strike against Warsaw Pact forces on Warsaw Pact territory, followed in turn by a deep interdiction strike on military installations in the rearward areas of Poland, followed eventually by strikes against the territory of the Soviet Union itself. And, as the NPG's own studies have shown, there is no military utility to the Alliance in going through this whole process either. Of course, so long as the Warsaw Pact maintains its own holdings of short range nuclear systems, NATO can hardly give them up altogether. But it should be accepted as part of the Alliance's theatre nuclear doctrine that NATO has no military or political requirement for such systems, and that the Alliance's own deterrent posture should be based on the threat of using straight away the longer range weapons.

24. The Stockpile

The sort of weapons which NATO would most require under such a doctrine would be those systems which are themselves invulnerable to pre-emptive strike and which are capable of inflicting major damage against military targets deep in Warsaw Pact territory and in the western military districts of the Soviet Union itself. For the purposes of invulnerability, the choices lie between the hardening of installations or mobility. Hardening is difficult and expensive. The French have invested in it for their MRBM systems in the Plateau d'Albion (though it is not clear how effective this would be) but it is probably not a viable option for all the systems which the Alliance will require. Airfields, for example, can be protected, but they will always be tempting targets even with the system of Quick Reaction Alert such as NATO already has. Moreover, given the vulnerability of aircraft themselves in the deep strike role, it would be unwise to rely on them alone for theatre nuclear deterrence. The addition of Air Launched Cruise missiles will almost certainly be required if manned aircraft are to have much chance in the 1980s of hitting targets on Soviet territory. Mobility on land is probably not possible in the Central Region: although it would in theory be possible to develop a road – or rail – mobile longer range version of Pershing along the lines of the Soviet SS20, it is not realistic to think in terms of deploying such a system in the tightly crowded conditions which obtain in most Western European countries. The most attractive option, in terms of mobility, is therefore submarines. At present some of the United States' Polaris and Poseidon SSBNs are assigned to SACEUR and are targetted for strike against high value, non-strategic targets in Eastern Europe and the Soviet Union. The declared use of SSBNs for this purpose helps reinforce the link between theatre nuclear and strategic nuclear systems. But it would probably be unwise for the Allies to rely wholly or even crucially on SSBNs for the theatre nuclear strike task. An attractive alternative, or complementary, option might therefore be to develop a force of cruise missile carrying submarines geared specifically to the theatre strike role.

25. By contrast NATO's holdings of shorter range systems could be run down to a minimum level required to demonstrate a capability parallel, but not necessarily equal or similar, to that of the Warsaw Pact in this area. Some systems, for example ADMs and Nike Hercules surface-to-air missiles (which are both nuclear capable only, and to which there are no comparable Soviet systems) could be got rid of straightaway. Others, for example Lance and Pershing, which have no useful conventional application, could be reduced in numbers. Artillery and aircraft are required, of course, in themselves for conventional purposes, but the Alliance could consider reducing the numbers of them which are configured for nuclear delivery. Corresponding changes could be made in the numbers and types of warheads stockpiled by NATO. Given the large percentage of NATO's 7,000 warheads which is at present tied to short range delivery systems, there would clearly be scope for a very considerable reduction in the theatre nuclear warheads stockpile, even if there were to be increases in the numbers of longer range systems. There would probably also be savings in terms of training, manpower and running costs associated with the present high holdings of short-range systems.

26. Arms Control Implications

The Alliance clearly has a good deal of scope for using its existing holdings of short-range nuclear-only delivery systems as bargaining counters in arms control negotiations and has little to fear from an arms control regime which imposes reciprocal limitations between East and West in short-range nuclear capability. As regards dual-capable systems (artillery and aircraft) the position is more complex, since they are required in their conventional mode as part of the Alliance's conventional defence capability. Nevertheless there may be scope for renouncing the nuclear capability of some of them (though this would pose considerable problems of verification) as part of some kind of wider arms control arrangement.

27. In the case of the longer-range systems, the Alliance has a clear need not to allow arms control arrangements to jeopardise its future requirement for an adequate long-range theatre nuclear capability. This is particularly important in the case of cruise missiles, where there is a potential requirement for both air-launched and submarine-launched systems (and just possibly, though less probably, ground-launched as well). On the other hand, the Alliance would benefit militarily from a reduction in Soviet longer-range nuclear systems targetted on Europe, particularly the SS20 and the Backfire bomber. And there would be a major political benefit in complementing the present strategic regime of SALT with an arrangement which stabilised the balance at the theatre nuclear level as well. (It will look increasingly anomalous if the Allies continue to support SALT, to press for progress in MBFR but show no interest at all in constraining nuclear systems which fall into the grey area between the two sets of negotiations.)

28. The kinds of arms control approaches which might be worth pursuing in the field of theatre nuclear weapons will need careful study. It might be feasible to develop further the Option III package in MBFR by adding to it certain short-range systems; or to propose as an ancillary measure to a conventional MBFR agreement some kind of mutual renunciation or reduction of certain types of short-range nuclear system – for example a declaration by both sides that after a certain date none of their artillery pieces would be nuclear capable. Alternatively it might be possible to devise a wholly separate negotiation covering all theatre nuclear systems; or to include some of the longer-range ones in the SALT III negotiations in some way.

29. Some of the considerations involved in an arms control approach to theatre nuclear systems were set out in a recent minute from Sir J Hunt to the Prime Minister. There is no doubt that it is an extremely complex area with no immediately obvious or attractive line of approach for the Alliance. Nonetheless discussions in Whitehall hitherto have been based in part on the erroneous premises

  (a) that NATO has a valid military need for all the theatre systems which it now has (whereas in practice a good many of them are militarily valueless), and
  (b) that the alternative to some kind of negotiation on grey area systems is unfettered freedom on NATO's side to do what it likes: in fact the most likely alternative is that the United States' ability to deploy certain types of modern theatre nuclear forces in support of NATO, particularly cruise missiles, will be circumscribed through the bilateral SALT process in return for restrictions on Soviet strategic systems targetted on the United States.

30. The Alliance, and particularly its European members, ought therefore to be studying urgently possible arms control approaches to the theatre nuclear balance which avoid the latter danger. One possibility might be the acceptance of some kind of common numerical ceiling on nuclear or nuclear-capable delivery systems with ranges of over 1000 miles (excluding those systems already dealt with definitively in SALT) which would allow freedom to mix between ballistic missiles, cruise missiles and aircraft but which would, as in the case of SALT II, involve overall some reduction in the total number of delivery systems which might otherwise have been introduced into service. A common ceiling of this kind would not be easy to define or negotiate. But it would have the additional advantage of promoting the concept of military parity between East and West which has already been achieved in SALT and which the Alliance is seeking to capitalise on in MBFR as well.

DOCUMENT 24

PM/78/47
PRIME MINISTER

NATO'S THEATRE NUCLEAR FORCES

1. I was interested by read Fred Mulley's account, in his minute to you of 15 May, of NATO thinking on theatre nuclear forces. I very much endorse Fred Mulley's view that the UK should take an active part in future work within the alliance in this field, which is of increasing relevance to our arms control strategy.

2. What disturbs me, however, is the lack of a coherent doctrine for the use of NATO's theatre nuclear weapons. For example, it has long been accepted that their use on the battle field could not help to "win" a war for the allies on the ground. The introduction of such weapons into the battle by NATO could evoke a response in kind by the Warsaw Pact, thus intensifying the conflict and causing massive physical and human losses. Despite this, NATO has invested extensively in short range battle field nuclear systems, as Fred Mulley recognises in his minute. Nearly three-quarters of NATO's nuclear warheads in Europe are, I believe, associated with systems with a range of 100 miles or less. This implies a commitment to fighting a protracted short range theatre nuclear war.

3. I am glad, therefore, that the Alliance is coming to realise that this investment is not the most cost-effective, and I share Fred Mulley's view that there is room for a substantial reduction in some of NATO's weapons of this type, without any harm to our security. Reductions would not only result in the savings in storage and material costs, to which Fred Mulley refers in paragraph 4 of his minute; but could also give the West a bargaining counter in future arms control negotiations with the Soviet Union.

4. This arms control aspect applies to longer range theatre systems as well. I accept the case for NATO improving its capability in this area. But I believe it would be a mistake to think in purely military terms. The political and practical problems of some of the options mentioned by Fred Mulley are considerable. Which European members of the Alliance, for example, would be prepared to have a new generation of IR/MRBMs based on their territory? A weapon of this kind could be justified as a direct parallel to the Soviet SS2O. But the long term implications of introducing it into NATO's armoury would be considerable. We should think very carefully before engaging in competition with the Russians in this field. On the other hand, we should not close the option entirely. One hope is that the Russians may be suffi-

ciently concerned at the prospect of NATO improving its long range theatre nuclear capability in this or other ways to agree to discuss some form of arms control regime involving both Eastern and Western intermediate range nuclear capabilities in Europe. Some of Helmut Schmidt's recent remarks suggest that the Germans are thinking along these lines, and are anxious to bring eg the Soviet SS20 and Backfire into arms control discussions. We too should be prepared to consider this possibility.

5. Finally, I was struck by the assumption in Fred Mulley's minute that an improved longer range NATO capability against targets in Eastern Europe and the Soviet Union must be based on European soil. I imagine that this does not imply that such weapons ought necessarily to be ground launched, rather than based on aircraft, surface ships or submarines? I can see the argument for not relying wholly on United States SSBNs assigned to SACEUR for this purpose. But submarines have the advantage of being much less vulnerable; and it is not inconceivable that a submarine based cruise missile force might prove an attractive option for this as well as for other roles.

6. I am sending copies of this minute to the Defence Secretary, the Chancellor of the Exchequer and Sir John Hunt.

DAVID OWEN

Foreign and Commonwealth Office
30 May 1978

DOCUMENT 25

MINISTRY OF DEFENCE WHITEHALL LONDON SW1A 2HB

<u>SECRET</u>
MO 13/1/34

PRIME MINISTER

NATO'S THEATRE NUCLEAR FORCES

Having read David Owen's minute to you of 30th May, I believe that there is broad agreement between us. But there are some points in his minute on which I must comment.

2. David suggests that NATO's prevailing doctrine for the use of theatre nuclear weapons implies a commitment to fighting a protracted short-range theatre nuclear war. This is not so. The purpose of theatre nuclear weapons is not to fight battles but to contribute to deterrence, and thus to reduce the risk of any conflict in Europe. To fulfil this purpose under the Alliance's flexible response strategy, they must be seen to enhance the defensive effect of NATO's conventional forces, to counterbalance the Warsaw Pact's equally numerous theatre nuclear weapons and to provide a source of options short of the use of strategic forces but signalling a willingness to use these forces rather than sacrifice vital interests; and for this variety of functions a wide range of weapons systems and warheads, widely deployed and capable of flexible employment, is needed.

3. I agree with David Owen, however, that the Alliance has not yet fully developed its guidelines for the actual employment of these systems in accordance with this doctrine. This is obviously an area where precision is neither possible nor desirable. But at the last Ministerial meeting of the Nuclear Planning Group I urged the need for progress. This is now being made, and I believe that a consensus is emerging, despite some hesitation on the part of the USA, that theatre nuclear forces achieve their deterrent effect not through a potential to win any nuclear wars in the classic military sense but by expressing the strength of the Alliance's political will and signalling the risk of deliberate escalation to unacceptably high levels of conflict.

4. The increasing emphasis being placed in NATO on long-range systems is, of course, consistent with this approach. But it does not mean that there is any easy option of bargaining away large numbers of short-range theatre nuclear forces in arms control negotiations. A further offer of reductions in these systems may be an option for the longer term but, unless and until there is a favourable Soviet response to the West's existing 'nuclear' offer of 1000 warheads and certain US delivery systems in Option III of MBFR,

I doubt whether there will be enthusiasm in NATO for pursuing more than the modest possibilities outlined in paragraph 4 of my minute of 15th May.

5. As regards the longer range systems, I agree with David Owen that it is as yet unclear whether in the longer term the balance of security advantage will lie in deploying new NATO systems or in limiting their deployment in arms control negotiations in return for restraint of Soviet long-range systems which cause concern in the West. But given the existing asymmetries, it is difficult to see how a "grey area" negotiation could help us unless we first take steps to develop and acquire the counters with which to bargain. We did, of course, go through these arguments when we decided recently that in present circumstances the widening of the SALT process to include these systems was unlikely to be to our advantage. Although Chancellor Schmidt's recent remarks make it necessary for us to review the position in conjunction with our allies, I should be most reluctant to engage in negotiations with the Russians until NATO has built up its hand with cruise missiles or equivalent systems.

6. Finally, to clarify the position on what NATO means by improving its longer range European-based capability, it does not mean ballistic missile submarines, for the reasons given in paragraph 3 of the Annex to my earlier minute. From the point of view of the United Kingdom, I would agree with David Owen that a submarine-based cruise missile force could represent an attractive option. But given the importance which the Germans and others attach to being able to participate in nuclear actions and to the "visibility" of the United States nuclear commitment to Europe, I would not rule out the other options of ground or air-launched systems.

7. I am sending copies of this minute to the Chancellor of the Exchequer and the Foreign and Commonwealth Secretary and to Sir John Hunt.

Fred Mulley

9th June 1978

DOCUMENT 26

Private Secretary

NATO'S THEATRE NUCLEAR FORCES

1. Mr Mulley's comment on Dr Owen's minute of 30 May to the Prime Minister about NATO's theatre nuclear forces reflects in part the predictably cautious attitude of MOD officials. If the purpose of theatre nuclear weapons is "not to fight battles but to contribute to deterrence" by "expressing the strength of the Alliance's political will and signalling the risk of deliberate escalation to unacceptably high levels of conflict", then why has NATO invested so heavily in systems whose only military effect would be to devastate large areas of West and East Germany; and so inadequately in systems (other than primarily strategic systems) capable of hitting targets in the Soviet Union? The present NATO stockpile is open to criticism precisely because it fails to meet the political requirements of deterrence to which Mr Mulley's minute alludes.

2. On the arms control aspect the key question is, as Mr Moberly points out in his minute of 12 June to Mr Wilberforce, whether it is necessary to wait until a weapons system has actually been deployed before it can profitably be the subject of arms control negotiation. The MOD view seems to be that we first introduce cruise missiles on the Western side in whatever numbers and types we think desirable and then we offer to negotiate some of them away again. This seems to me to be naive. Of course the Russians will only negotiate seriously if they are convinced that the things being negotiated about are really going to be deployed. But it would be quite feasible for Western countries to indicate a general willingness to discuss theatre arms limitation before the full shape and size of their weapons programmes had finally been decided. This is what the Americans and Russians are already doing in SALT: the limitations on, for example, MIRVs and heavy missiles were introduced into the discussion long before the systems themselves had been fully deployed. Whether it will, in the event, prove possible to negotiate an attractive theatre nuclear/grey area balance is of course another matter: but there would be some advantage in trying to do so before the programmes of the countries concerned became irreversibly set in concrete.

3. I assume that Dr Owen would not want to take up these, or any other, points in further Ministerial correspondence at the stage. There will no doubt be plenty of future opportunities to do so.

13 June 1978   P Lever

3

The Comprehensive Test Ban Treaty

There is renewed interest, in 2009, in the US and China ratifying the Comprehensive Test Ban Treaty (CTBT) in 2010–11. It is therefore relevant to look back on the debate over this question in 1977–79.

On 1 December 1977, the Prime Minister, James Callaghan, called a meeting with the ministers who managed policy on nuclear weapons. I attended as Foreign and Commonwealth Secretary along with the Chancellor of the Exchequer, Denis Healey, and the Secretary of State for Defence, Fred Mulley. We discussed whether the UK should be associated with the US and the USSR in the proposed separate agreement on verification, the so-called Inner Track. This was to be in addition to the UK's participation in the multilateral arrangements which would apply to all the parties to a CTBT. It was decided to seek more information about the costs and other implications and meet in the New Year. I was in favour of participating.

Following a memo from the Cabinet Secretary, Sir John Hunt, dated 20 March 1978 (Document 27), we agreed, in principle, that the UK would participate, a decision helped by the Americans telling the UK government that they would not expect the UK to contribute to the capital or overhead costs in connection with the separate agreement. The UK would only meet its own personnel costs and the cost of modifying our own teleseismic stations (the costs were estimated at £1 million capital costs and a little under £0.75 million annually). This arrangement was facilitated by Cy Vance. Our intention was to have a reasonably independent capability for assessing compliance with the Treaty.

By 1978 it had been agreed that Lord Zuckerman would formally become, though on a personal basis, my adviser on nuclear matters, while retaining his links with the Cabinet Secretary. For many years after leaving the MOD, Lord Zuckerman had continued to play a key role as an informal adviser to the Cabinet Office and, using his influence – a powerful influence even in retirement – with the US Admiral Rickover, on the US side of Anglo-American cooperation over the Polaris programme.

On 23 March, Lord Zuckerman sent me one of his many fascinating and

often herctical contributions, a 'think-piece' (as he called it) titled 'Comprehensive Test Ban' (Document 28). He stated that 'another spoke has been
put in the wheel of negotiation', prompting me to write a letter to Peter Jay,
the UK's ambassador to Washington, who replied on 28 March and 21 April
(Documents 29 and 31). Zuckerman followed up with comments to me
on 30 March on the papers previously circulated by the Cabinet Secretary
(Document 30) in which he asked, on the last page, very pertinently, 'How
is it that no tests for reliability and safety of the kind now proposed were
carried out before talk of a CTB became the issue as it now is? [...] How is
it that if tests are not started now, guarantees of reliability and safety cannot
be given for more than 3–5 years?'

The other papers included here also demonstrate the power of the nuclear
scientists working closely together on both sides of the Atlantic to scupper
progress towards a meaningful CTB. They emphasize the need for politicians to understand the technicalities and to put themselves in a position,
by means of independent advice, to stand up to the vested interests of those
whose job it is to produce ever more sophisticated nuclear devices. Some of
these people, for understandable reasons, not all of which are selfish, have
little time for the political wish to control, reduce and eventually end the
nuclear arms race. Particularly at that time, the two superpowers were locked
in a deep ideological conflict and suspicion of Soviet motives held sway over
trust in their declarations. Sadly, that suspicion of Russia continues in 2009.

FCO Telegram 1015 records a note from me to Peter Jay:

> You will have seen a telegram on cut off in production of fissionable material
> asking you to do nothing further. Whitehall is up to its old tricks without ever
> consulting me. They have been telling the Americans that we could not possibly
> accept this. The political facts of life are that every American Administration
> since Eisenhower has been committed to this, so there is very little chance of
> them not going ahead. Meanwhile, we appear once again as reactionary and
> foot dragging. I am examining the whole issue [...]

I go on to state my belief that we (the UK) should accept a cut-off.

A memo from Lord Zuckerman to me dated 3 October 1978 (Document
37) also illustrates the UK's absurd predilection for secrecy, which still
continues in the twenty-first century. In paragraph 11 he writes:

> The paper on which you have asked me to comment is given the highest
> security classification in the UK, yet – and this is of critical importance –
> the whole argument, in every detail, is in the public domain in the United
> States. It is there, printed in the Congressional Record, for all to read. No-one
> supposes that the Russians are not devious and suspicious, and we have solid
> reasons for our mistrust. But they must surely be laughing now when they
> see the 'nuclear testing boffs' being controverted publicly on technical issues

by people who know every bit as much as they do, and who can speak with even greater scientific and engineering authority. Who, they might well ask, is cheating now?

In paragraph 13 he continues: 'But in this respect the UK is not an open society. There is no meaningful public debate on any of these matters. What can be read about the CTBT in the daily newspapers of the USA we guard as TOP SECRET.'

Zuckerman also sent me a powerful paper (Document 41) which I sent the Prime Minister prior to his trip to Guadeloupe on 3 January 1979. It contains many wise words and it includes a chilling reminder of the suicidal battle of determination that would follow if first use of nuclear weapons, having failed to deter, was followed by a nuclear exchange. Written by a man who was scientific adviser to Lord Mountbatten in South East Asia at the end of the war and knew first-hand of the destruction of Hiroshima and Nagasaki, it represents a view that it was right the Prime Minister should see.

> The fact is that no-one has ever suggested a convincing scenario in which nuclear weapons – whatever their category or yield – are used which does not get out of control. A few tactical 'interdiction' strikes in some NATO war game played on a map by eager members of a 'Defence Studies' course might, in theory, hold up a Russian threat. But if the 'interdiction strikes' were on Belgian soil they could mean the strategic end of that country. We used to hear about warning nuclear shots 'across their bows'. These now seem to be out of fashion. We hear today of mythical tactical nuclear battles, presumably presided over by some Marquis of Queensbury whose job it is to see that neither side contravenes some set of rules relating to yield and range of weapons and to numbers of civilians killed. But there are no such rules. We have Sir John Hackett's picture of a Third World War ending when just one city in the USSR and one in the UK had been 'taken out' by nuclear fire. Like most who have devoted real thought to the subject, and as a member of the fast declining body of men who had to study the process and nature of destruction at first hand, all this leaves me totally sceptical. Once nuclear weapons cease to have a deterrent effect, there would be no decoupling barriers to the progress of their use. The outcome would not depend on some pre-arranged scenario, but on factors which could not be gauged in advance; on, for example, the stability of political control, on the strength of the political control of the military machine, on military discipline – on any number of acts which rarely, if ever, are taken into account in abstract war-games. And we also need to remind ourselves that were nuclear weapons ever to be used, only a trivial percentage of the stockpile on either side would be required to bring about irrevocable destruction and chaos. Nuclear arsenals overflow, and against such weapons there are no realistic defensive systems – either passive or active. Nuclear weapons have no function other than to deter – for the good reason that once they fail to deter, and their use becomes a suicidal battle of determination, no-one knows

how the process would end, or were it to end, what political goals would have been attained.

One of the pressures to introduce a CTBT came from the discovery of an underground nuclear testing facility in the Kalahari desert about 100 km south of Botswana and 145 km east of Namibia. This development was brought to the attention of President Carter and Prime Minister Callaghan by the President of the USSR, Leonid Brezhnev, on 4 March 1978. President Nelson Mandela gave up South Africa's nuclear weapons.

Another pressure was the continued evidence that Pakistan was building a nuclear weapon, and this was frequently discussed in terms of blocking measures by the Cabinet Committee on Nuclear Proliferation, established early in 1977 after the Prime Minister and I had visited Washington. Nevertheless, Pakistan acquired nuclear weapons and sold the technology to North Korea, Iran and Libya.

POSTSCRIPT

A CTBT, originally envisaged in 1954, was eventually negotiated and signed in 1996. Unfortunately it was defeated in the US Senate in 1999 and it has still not come into force. President Obama, however, supports the ratification of the CTBT and Senator McCain, during the 2008 presidential campaign, pledged to have another look at the Treaty. It has also been publicly supported by the four US elder statesmen, George Schulz, William Perry, Henry Kissinger and Sam Nunn.[1] There are 179 signatory states, of which 144 (including the UK, France, and the Russian Federation) have ratified, and 16 non-signatory states. China has yet to ratify. The CTBT's global alarm system is constantly expanding its monitoring facilities, and once installed – the number has tripled since 2004 – all transmit data to Vienna. The first ever on-site inspection field exercise is being conducted in Kazakhstan.

By 2009 the US Congress had stopped funding research into the Reliable Replacement Warhead (RRW), not wanting it to delay the ratification of a CTBT. Yet it is clear from an interview with John Harvey, the policy and planning director at the US National Nuclear Security Administration during George W. Bush's presidency, that a new deal had been struck with the UK by amending the Mutual Defence Agreement 'to allow for a broader extent of cooperation than in the past, and this has to do with the RRW effort'. The RRW is being developed at the UK Atomic Weapons Establishment (AWE)

---

1 *Wall Street Journal*, 4 January 2007.

near Aldermaston. No policy decisions will be made for the foreseeable future, but options include a life extension programme and Robust Nuclear Earth Penetration (RNEP), a technique allowing a warhead to penetrate reinforced concrete underground shelters.

On 9 February 2009, under the headline 'US using British atomic weapons factory for its nuclear programme', the *Guardian* raised concerns about joint warhead research being carried out at Aldermaston. The MOD admitted in the article that the two countries were working together 'on examining the optimum life of the UK's existing nuclear warhead stockpile and the range of replacement options that might be available to inform decisions on whether and how we may need to refurbish or replace the existing warheads, likely to be necessary in the next Parliament'. This is meant to be done within the constraints of a CTBT. Yet nuclear scientists on both sides of the Atlantic delayed the implementation of such a treaty thirty years ago. I hope history is not repeating itself in the twenty-first century.

DOCUMENT 27

Re. A06916

PRIME MINISTER

Comprehensive Test Ban: Verification

At the meeting on 1st December, you discussed with the Chancellor of the Exchequer, the Foreign and Commonwealth Secretary and the Secretary of State for Defence whether the United Kingdom should be associated with the United States and Soviet Union in the proposed separate agreement on verification (the "Inner Track") in addition to our participation in the multi-lateral arrangements which will apply to all parties to a Comprehensive Test Ban Treaty. The meeting concluded that a decision should be deferred until we had more information about the costs and other implications of possible United Kingdom association in the separate agreement.

2. This information has now been obtained and is recorded in the attached note which has been agreed in the Official Group (GEN 63). American officials have told us that they will not expect us to contribute to these capital or overhead costs in connection with the separate agreement. Thus the only expenditure which would fall to us to meet would be our personnel costs and the cost of certain modifications to our own teleseismic stations. Total United Kingdom expenditure is estimated at just over £1 million capital costs and a little under £¾ million annually.

3. The Official Group concluded that only by being associated with the separate agreement could we achieve our objectives of having a reasonably independent capability for assessing compliance with the Treaty and playing a role in verification which accords with the prominent part we have played in disarmament since the war. The Group therefore recommends that we should confirm to the Americans that we wish to participate in the agreement. The Group's full recommendations are contained in paragraph 14 of the note.

4. The total cost involved is relatively small when measured against the political advantage of association and the benefits in terms of access to detailed United States data. I believe it would be consistent with the views expressed at meeting on 1st December for Ministers to agree to the Official Group's recommendations.

5. The Chancellor of the Exchequer made clear at the 1st December meeting that he would expect any costs to be met within existing estimates.

The Secretary of State for Defence reserved his position. I suggest that, in view of the need to give an early indication of our views to the Americans, this point might be reserved for discussion at a later meeting and that a decision in principle on participation should be taken now. We shall also need to inform the Russians, who have been making enquiries about our position on the American proposals.

6. I am sending copies of this minute and the enclosure to the Chancellor of the Exchequer, the Foreign and Commonwealth Secretary and the Secretary of State for Defence. If you agree with the recommendations of the Official Group, I suggest you should ask your Private Secretary to confirm that they are also acceptable to the other recipients.

John Hunt

20th March, 1978

DOCUMENT 28

CABINET OFFICE
70 WHITEHALL
LONDON SW1A 2AS

PERSONAL
D/0913

SECRETARY OF STATE FOR FOREIGN AND COMMONWEALTH AFFAIRS

I shall do as you ask, but I realise that the Easter break being only a day away I shall not have time to let you have my commentary on GEN. 63(78) 4 before sometime next week.

I am, however, enclosing what the Americans call a "think piece", which I did to clear my own mind on the report which was circulated to the GEN. 63 group reporting on the visit of Dr. Press, Mr. Macklen and Mr. Moberly to Washington in February.

I am copying this to Sir John Hunt.

S. ZUCKERMAN

23 March 1978

COMPREHENSIVE TEST BAN

Two major issues provided the momentum in the late 1950s and early 1960s in the effort to secure international agreement to ban nuclear tests. The first was to put an end to radioactive fallout from atmospheric tests; the second, to decelerate the nuclear arms race. The three parties to the 1963 Treaty were at one about the first objective; only the UK, in the person of Harold Macmillan, was committed to the second. Mutual hostility and suspicion between the USA and the USSR, coupled with a belief that more and more sophisticated nuclear warheads enhanced national security, were the reasons why both major parties to the Partial Treaty wanted to embark on programmes of underground tests. The Americans justified their stand by arguing that if there were either a complete ban on nuclear testing, or an agreement to a limited quota of underground tests, the Russians would be bound to cheat. They would, for example, test in vast caverns in the earth's crust, thus 'decoupling' the shock of the explosion, or in outer space behind the moon. Since teleseismic techniques were insufficiently sensitive to detect and discriminate between earthquakes and underground explosions, the Russians, if a CTB was to be negotiated, would therefore have to permit the on-site inspection of suspicious events, a condition which it was soon clear they would not agree in any circumstances. At the time the Americans not the Russians – were also concerned not to foreclose the option of using nuclear explosions for peaceful purposes (it was the reverse position which prevailed at the start of the present round of CTB talks).

In the end the UK had to rest satisfied with a Partial Treaty, at the same time as we made repeated efforts to persuade both the Russians and the Americans that seismic techniques were improving so fast as to be adequate to detect and discriminate underground disturbances above any threshold level which had meaningful military significance. We failed. Then came the Non-Proliferation Treaty of 1966. Later came other agreements, including the bilateral one between the USA and USSR not to test underground above a threshold of 150 Kt.

Once the Russians ceased insisting on keeping open the option of PNEs, the present round of talks for a CTB seemed to be well set on a successful course. But now another spoke has been put into the wheel of negotiation – given that we are really after a CTB – by the Americans raising, and the Russians apparently welcoming, the suggestion that while underground tests should in general be prohibited, some should be permitted. In effect we want a CTB but the big 'C' should be a little 'c'. The non-nuclear states are bound to see in this the catch they found in the NPT. The big powers want to prevent the spread of nuclear weapons, i.e. prevent 'horizontal proliferation', as the Indians put it, but they want to go on with 'vertical proliferation', i.e. improve their own vast nuclear armouries.

The arguments that have been put forward belong to the same genre as those which all but tripped us up in the negotiation of the 1963 Partial Test-Ban Treaty. Essentially, the major nuclear powers have to reassure themselves from time to time that their own stockpiles are not deteriorating, the justification being that if anyone were to believe that the weapons were becoming ineffective, nuclear arsenals would no longer be credible. The second main argument is that unless there is some testing, it won't be possible to improve warheads. The fact that the Russians accepted the introduction of the issue by the US side should come as no surprise. The US nuclear enthusiasts and their opposite numbers in the USSR are interchangeable. What strategic advantage doubt about this new variety of credibility will impart to either side is certainly not clear to me. I cannot see any political leaders taking the risk that over the next ten years, or even twenty years, if nuclear armaments still exist, they won't go off if used.

No doubt the political determination of Mr. Carter (and presumably Mr. Brezhnev) to bring about a CTB, is as strong as was the political determination on the two sides in the negotiations leading up to the 1963 agreement. In the fifteen years that have since elapsed, however, the opposition to any nuclear cutback within both countries is far stronger and better organised than it was when fallout was the major issue. On the other hand, the opposition seems less intelligent when it comes to weighing the political advantages of a CTB from the point of view of non-proliferation – for which it is critical.

Harold Macmillan was the main driving force in the negotiations leading up to the 1963 agreement. He wanted a CTB, and in preparing his case he neither sought, nor if he did, did he heed the views of our Chiefs of Staff. On the other hand, both the American and the Russian military were anything but silent, and President Kennedy was at times shaken in his resolve. At the Birch Grove meeting on his last visit to the UK before his assassination, he gave Harold Macmillan a paper which set out the American Chiefs' objections to any agreement. There arguments were the usual ones, and of the same kind as is now being deployed. In spite of this hiccup, an agreement was reached in Moscow a couple of months later – but not the agreement which we had been seeking. The nuclear arms race has gone on, and uninterrupted underground testing since then has made the situation even more perilous than it was in 1963. What has either side gained in security in the years that have passed – nothing. What has the world gained – greater insecurity.

My guess is that President Carter's preoccupation with other matters may for the moment have dulled his appreciation of the implications of introducing the issue of prohibited and permitted explosions into the present round of negotiations. Surely we have an opportunity to help him here. What have we to lose from a CTB? The basic and essentially simple significance of terms like 'strategic nuclear systems', or 'theatre nuclear weapons', has become deadened with time. Today otherwise sane men talk of field warfare in which such weapons are used. This, and the fact that the nuclear arms race – in spite of SALT – goes on, increases the possibility, however remote it may be, of the destruction of Western civilisation. Whatever the outcome of the SALT talks, the nuclear armouries which would remain would still be more than enough, several times more, to bring this about. The Middle East, the Horn of Africa, Africa south of the Equator; these are immediate and dangerous issues. But they have to be seen in the perspective of the whole of Europe – and possibly the USSR and America – blowing up. Outside the field of deterrence there is no military significance to nuclear weapons. And whatever else, nuclear deterrence does not prevent turmoil and non-nuclear war.

Even if the broad lines of CTB are now agreed in Geneva, President Carter is likely to run into difficulties with Congress. But I cannot but feel dismayed that some of the difficulties on both sides of the negotiating table are now being generated not by the political leaders concerned, but by technical people whose business it is to devise nuclear weapons and who have an understandably professional interest in the continuation of their weapons establishments. Disarmament is surely a political, not a military, determination.

What conceivable political benefit will accrue to the Great Powers if the rest of the world sees them bent on maintaining, even improving, their nuclear armaments at the same time as the virtues of non-proliferation and SALT are being proclaimed?

S. ZUCKERMAN
21.3.78

DOCUMENT 29

SECRET
TO FLASH FCO TELNO 1288 OF 28 MARCH 1978

Personal for SOFS
CTB

1. In the light of your private letter I had a word with Cy Vance Monday evening about CTB prospects, mentioning that your anxieties about foot-dragging on both sides of the Atlantic had increased since you last spoke with him on this topic.

2. He told me to tell you that, with the full support of the President, he now planned to sidestep all the problems about stockpile testing by going for a five-year comprehensive ban without exceptions, thresholds etc. He believed that this would be enough to outflank Congressional opposition.

3. You should be aware that Carter has written to the PM personally about the Indian dimension of all this. He will be taking this up with you on his return.

4. Stowe agrees.

Jay

DOCUMENT 30

To: FOREIGN SECRETARY
From: LORD ZUCKERMAN

COMMENTS ON GEN. 63(78) 4

I have now studied GEN. 63(78) 4 carefully, and have also re-read GEN.63(78) 2. Here, as requested, are my observations.

1. What the new paper implicitly says is that a CTB would not be in our interest if it meant that we could not continue to carry out nuclear tests up to a limit of 3 Kt. The implication is that the Americans are in the same boat, but that the Russians would not have the same need to test. On the other hand they might well cheat, and carry out clandestine explosions up to a threshold of 10 Kt, although 'some Americans' – not defined – believe that were the Russians to do so, they would in due course be caught out by teleseismic and other Intelligence which would be sensitive down to 3 Kt (para.9 of GEN.63(78) 4).

2. The main reasons given for our need to test is to prevent any erosion of the credibility of our weapons. This, it is said, could only be done by assuring their safety and reliability. Other reasons for testing are the need to keep open the option of improving the designs of low yield warheads (para.3 of Annex), and to assure recruitment of personnel to our weapons laboratory, the staff of which is getting 'long in the tooth' (para.11 of GEN.63(78) 2).

3. It was neither the USA nor the USSR but the UK which first suggested that a CTB would be detrimental to the maintenance of weapon stocks (GEN.63(77) 1). In response to a question which we put, the State Department then provided us in September 1977 with an official 'assessment' which in effect said that Washington did not share our worries. Para.2 of GEN. 63(78) 4, in which we are reminded of this exchange, ends with the sentence that the conclusion stated in the American paper "purported to represent an agreed United States Administration position". The word 'purported' is somewhat curious.

4. Dissatisfied with this answer, our technical people approached their opposite numbers in the US weapons laboratories, from whom they elicited an echo of their own doubts. This is hardly surprising. Further contacts between weapons people on the two sides resulted in the visit in February paid to Washington by Dr. Press, Mr. Macklen, and Mr. Moberly.

5. Para.5 of GEN, 63(78) 4 states that any doubt about the reliability presumably of any of the US and UK warheads will not only undermine

Western confidence but also the policy of deterrence on which Western security depends. The paper then goes on to consider possible solutions (including one which implies our 'cheating', given that a CTB is negotiated) to what is seen as a major dilemma, But the paper also recognises that every one of the proposals it puts forward would raise suspicions about our good faith in relation to the objective of non-proliferation.

6. There are many questions which Ministers might ask before they face the problem of deciding which is the more critical political goal – that of arresting the spread of nuclear weapons, or agreeing (whether overtly or tacitly hardly matters) to breaching the idea of a CTB – for that in effect is what is being proposed. Here are some questions which I would want answered if I had to share any part of the responsibility of deciding so momentous an issue:

(a) Unless a CTB provided for "a small quota of low yield tests" (para.15) we are told (para.11) that "the best guess of British experts" is that the safety and reliability of our stockpile of warheads might under normal conditions be 3–5 years –

   (i) Is it supposed that <u>all</u> our warheads should be regarded as unreliable and unsafe at the end of such a term? Is the parallel with, say, the shelf-life of some unstable vaccine or antibiotic?

   (ii) If this is so, why is it not necessary to test <u>every</u> warhead to see if it is becoming unsafe or unreliable? If the answer is that it is not necessary, how do a few tests guarantee the reliability and safety of all our stockpile?

(b) What tests are in fact proposed for these two characteristics? If they are not carried out on existing warheads, how would the results of experimental tests give the political authority an assurance of the safety and reliability for <u>all</u> our own stockpile or the vastly bigger US stockpile?

(c) If reliability and safety cannot be guaranteed for every nuclear warhead (as in all logic would seem to be the case), are the technical experts in effect advising their political masters to play 'Russian roulette' with nuclear weapons? Would a potential aggressor be less deterred if he believed that there was a 10% or 20% risk of his opponent's nuclear weapons not working? (A gourmet with a passion, say, for oysters, would certainly be deterred from eating a plateful if he was told that all were infected with botulinus toxin. Would he be any the less deterred if he was told that only one in three or one in four was infected, and that it was impossible to tell which were the dangerous ones?)

(d) If 'a small quota of low yield tests' cannot guarantee the reliability and safety of every single warhead, does it mean that credibility and confidence in our stockpile will become eroded whatever we do?

(e) Were our experts worried on this score before the Carter proposals surfaced? If not, why not? If they were, why did they not relay their fears to the Cabinet five, ten, years ago?

(f) The Annex to GEN. 63(78) 4 is a report on the Washington visit made by Dr. Press and his two colleagues in February of this year. It is an abridged version of GEN.63(78) 2, but it curiously omits the statement that all our present warheads were fashioned in the period 1965 to 1968 i.e. all of them are already 10 to 12 years old (para.10 of GEN.63(78) 2).

(i) How is it that no tests for reliability and safety of the kind now proposed were carried out before talk of a CTB became the issue it now is?

(ii) How is it that if tests are not started now, guarantees of reliability and safety cannot be given for more than 3 to 5 years?

(iii) GEN. 63(78) 2 also says (para. 11) that assurances on safety, reliability and credibility (credible to whom is not indicated) "would not be valid for more than about five years" if tests were limited to yields below 100 tons. What exactly does this mean? What proportion of our present stockpile cannot be guaranteed now? What were the corresponding figures 5 years ago and 10 years ago?

I have focussed these suggested questions on the technical arguments set out in the paper, and have intentionally avoided any discussion of the relevance of a CTB to the major issues of security, deterrent policy, and the belief – not shared, so far as I know, by the Russians – that a distinction can be made between so-called strategic and so-called theatre nuclear weapons.

I am copying this to Sir John Hunt, even though I have marked it 'Personal'.

S. ZUCKERMAN

30 March 1978
Z/0914

DOCUMENT 31

British Embassy,
Washington, D.C.

21 April 1978

The Rt Hon David Owen MP
Foreign and Commonwealth Office

Dear David,

You will recall that I visited the Massachusetts Institute of Technology last January. I sent you at the time a note on the discussion I had on CTB with a group of distinguished academics whose interest is in nuclear weapons, nuclear energy and arms control. During that meeting they also took the initiative in raising the future of the British strategic deterrent, on which discussion I am enclosing the record. Dick Garwin mentioned that he did not believe that the deterioration of the submarine hulls was a factor which would dictate the lifespan of the present Polaris boats.

2. I have since dropped the subject here; but Garwin has now written me a letter on this subject; and I think you may like to have it. As you will see, he has been in correspondence with the Pentagon about the hull life of the Poseidon submarines and has been told that, as a result of extensive research, the Americans are satisfied that "hull corrosion and fatigue are not limiting considerations for extending the life of Poseidon SSBNs". The same conclusions would apply to the Polaris boats.

3. As the Assistant Secretary of the Navy points out, the major consideration determining the life of these submarines is that the technology contained in the Poseidon design is now over 20 years old and that replacing the technology would be as expensive as building new boats.

4. Garwin is a very able roving ambassador for IBM. His credentials are impressive. I attach a copy of his biographical note.

Peter Jay

PS: I had breakfast with Solly today. He has been seeing Harold Brown, Frank Press and others who are solid. Harold Brown is going to be crucial in selling CTB and SALT on the Hill. The next two weeks are going to be decisive here on the stockpile issue, I think.

Ambassador

COMPREHENSIVE TEST BAN

1. You asked me to record the points I made to you recently about my conversation with Mr Marcum (Office of Science and Technology Policy).

2. Mr Marcum said that he had been struck, during the recent meetings in Washington and Aldermaston, and in other US/UK contacts over the CTB, by the fact that concern in the UK about the disadvantages of a CTB seemed to predominate over support for the treaty. Marcum said that the Foreign Office line appeared to him to be virtually neutral, whereas the line of the MOD and the Cabinet Office was clearly hostile. There seemed to be no one who was prepared to stand up and support the line which had been publicly taken by Mr Callaghan.

3. I said that this was hardly a fair description of the Foreign Office position. The Foreign Secretary had certainly spoken out in public in favour of a CTB. Speaking personally, I could understand why officials tended to be a little hesitant at the present time. Until we were certain that the Administration were not going to change their public policy of supporting a truly comprehensive ban we probably felt that it would be prudent to keep a relatively low profile.

4. Marcum said that this was precisely the point he was concerned about. The Administration were shaping up to take a decision on the question of permitted nuclear experiments in the course of the next few weeks. If, as this decision was approached, the signals from London were all strongly suggesting doubt and concern about the wisdom of a CTB, it might be much more difficult for the supporters of a comprehensive ban to win the day. He was not suggesting that the permitted nuclear experiments issue was not a serious matter, but he nevertheless thought that if the Prime Minister and Foreign Secretary were indeed committed to seeking a CTB, this view should be reflected more strongly in dealings between our respective officials.

A Reeve

20 March 1978

DOCUMENT 32

Private Secretary

CUT-OFF IN PRODUCTION OF FISSIONABLE MATERIAL FOR WEAPONS PURPOSES

1. With reference to your two minutes of today, I attach the correspondence this year between the Department and the MOD, including Mr Johnston's letter of 9 March to Mr Burns.

2. I summarised certain considerations about the cut-off idea in my submission of 15 December 1977 about policy for UNSSD. In February and March the Department spoke to First Secretaries in the US Embassy and Canadian High Commission, making basically two points:

(a) that the UK, unlike the US and USSR had limited stocks of fissionable material.

(b) that a cut-off would require verification by extremely intensive inspection, which the Russians would not consider.

At the suggestion of the US Embassy, Mr Moberly mentioned the matter briefly to Mr Gelb at the end of a meeting in February about Conventional Arms Transfers. The approaches to the Americans and Canadians were reflected in telegrams which were distributed to the Private Office on 16 February and 2 March. The Private Office also saw a telegram of 20 February instructing our delegation at the UNSSD Preparatory Committee to point out, if the cut-off idea was included in any drafts for the Special Session, that verification would be an important problem.

3. Subsequently the Department made to the US Embassy some additional points suggested by the MOD (Mr Johnston's letter of 9 March) and Washington, when they heard that the US Administration was about to study the subject, repeated these points at working level (Washington tel No 1626).

4. With reference to point (a) in your longer minute, the MOD say that our current stocks of fissionable material are just enough to continue until the mid-1980s the current level of work in maintaining the effectiveness of our warheads; but that any need to increase that level of work or to add to our numbers or types of warheads, would require more fissionable material than we have in stock.

C L G Mallaby
Arms Control and Disarmament Dept

24 April 1978
cc. PS/PUS, Sir A Duff, Mr Moberly, Defence Dept: Mr Lever, Planning Staff

[The Foreign Secretary made the following handwritten comment on this memo: 'In the light of the full information I would like a proper submission putting the case for and against going to the US with a recommendation coming to me through Sir A Duff. Private Secretary to send out a message that policy decisions are to come to Ministers. This is the second case involving the Arms Control and Disarmament Department, CTB being the first, and I hope that this will not happen again. The 15th December can in no sense be taken as a submission on this important subject. Washington should say nothing further at all on this subject.']

DOCUMENT 33

TO IMMEDIATE WASHINGTON TELNO 1015 OF 26 APR 78
INFO UKMIS NEW YORK, UKDEL NATO, UKIS GENEVA, MODUK
(DS11, DSC6)
YOUR TELNO 1626.

CUT-OFF IN PRODUCTION OF FISSIONABLE MATERIAL.

1. PLEASE SAY NOTHING FURTHER TO THE AMERICANS UNTIL
INSTRUCTED OTHERWISE.

OWEN.

[handwritten annotation by the Foreign Secretary to be sent to Peter Jay]

You will have seen a telegram on cut off in production of fissionable material asking you to do nothing further. Whitehall is up to its old tricks without ever consulting me. They have been telling the Americans that we could not possibly accept this. The political facts of life are that every American Administration since Eisenhower has been committed to this, so there is very little chance of them not going ahead. Meanwhile, we appear once again as reactionary and foot dragging. I am examining the whole issue and will keep you informed. My belief is that we should accept a cut-off.

DOCUMENT 34

Foreign and Commonwealth Office
London SW1A 2AH

4 May 1978

Dear Peter

Many thanks for your letter of 21 April enclosing the correspondence between Dick Garwin and the Assistant Secretary of the Navy. I found it very interesting. I now have a bright person called Paul Lever working direct to me on Defence policy and so we can absorb and process any material you like to send totally confidentially and feed it in as we like.

The Americans' evident confidence that deterioration of submarine hulls of SSBNs is not a serious problem is interesting and important. Hitherto, as you know, our own MOD experts have insisted that hull life is the main reason why our Polaris boats will not constitute an effective deterrent force after the early 1990s. It is not, of course, the only consideration: their vulnerability to detention and tracking is another important factor and there would no doubt be a problem in ensuring an adequate supply of spare parts and replacements for the missiles if we were to want to keep in service a lot longer than is currently planned. But if hull life is not per se a problem, then clearly we shall need to reassess carefully the current conventional wisdom among British experts that the Polaris force will not remain viable for more than another 15 years or so. Your exchange will be useful background for this. The longer we can extend Polaris' life the more time we have to consider other options and other technologies. I will keep you in touch and please continue to do the same for me.

One small point: do not neglect Cy at the expense of the White House. I think he counts for more than anyone else with the President; not because he is intellectually exciting, but because he has a very solid record of being right on issues. I suspect that Tony Lake has Cy's ear more than most; and he is very much his new man.

Yours ever
David
(DAVID OWEN)

DOCUMENT 35

MINISTRY OF DEFENCE WHITEHALL LONDON SW1A 2HB

TOP SECRET
UK EYES ONLY
M0 14/2

PRIME MINISTER

You should know that some new information, given to us in the greatest confidence by a recent United States' visitor, has shed more light on a particular US nuclear warhead stockpile maintenance problem. Apparently the Americans discovered a few months ago serious corrosion faults in their Poseidon warheads. We have no precise details as the US has not released the design of this warhead to us, but the indications are that the fault is so bad that the functioning of these corroded warheads is very doubtful. We do not know the extent of the problem except that it was not an isolated occurrence, nor how or if the US has solved it. But if this fault had been found during a test ban it is the type of fault that would demand a low yield nuclear test to discover if the corroded warhead would function. If the solution to the problem required a change in material or design this too would require a low yield nuclear proving test. The information correlates with a less specific statement made to us in our bilateral talks earlier this year with the Americans on the Comprehensive Test Ban. The problem does not affect our own Polaris warheads.

2. If this type of problem is really extensive in the US Poseidon warheads the President would have very serious worries on US national security grounds in relation to CTB duration. We do know that in late July he had a long discussion with Mr Schlesinger and the US Weapon Laboratory Directors. It was after this meeting that the President began to change his mind on duration and become more positive about an announcement about resumption of tests. The appropriate US Congressional Committees will have all the detailed information on US stockpile problems given to them in closed executive session and there is no way that this problem can be kept from them.

3. I am sending copies of this minute to David Owen and Sir John Hunt.

Fred Mulley

29th September 1978

DOCUMENT 36

Private Secretary

Mr Mulley's minute raises the following questions:

(i)   How convenient for the US nuclear scientists to have "discovered" a corrosion problem just at the time when President Carter seemed likely to opt for a more constringent CTB. It's reminiscent of the way our own MOD happened to discover a new assessment of Soviet tank capability just at the time when British Ministers were considering what to do about replacing Chieftain. But why, in the case of the Poseidon warheads, was the fault not discovered earlier? Has it only just occurred or is it thought to have been present throughout most or all of the warheads' life?

(ii) How widespread is the fault? Is it likely to affect all Poseidon warheads or only those of a certain batch or type? If the latter, would it not be possible simply to replace all the warheads of that batch or type by others which have shown no propensity to corrode or to remanufacture to a proven design?

(iii) If testing was definitively precluded, what degree of confidence could be placed in the use of non-fissile chemical or engineering techniques to monitor or correct this kind of material or design fault? After all, even a nuclear test only shows that one particular nuclear warhead works: it does not prove that all other similar ones will necessarily do so as well.

2. Without much more information about the circumstances of this particular US problem and without the assistance of a qualified and objective expert as nuclear warhead design, it is impossible to judge how much credence should be placed in this incident. On the face of it it sounds like the transatlantic nuclear scientific Mafia at work again – no names given, nor any factually challengeable details. I doubt though whether it is worth Dr Owen commenting specifically on Mr Mulley's minute. Lord Zuckerman is about to offer comments on the general problem of stockpile maintenance; and Dr Owen could perhaps discuss it further with Dr Garwin if he sees him later this month.

3. The draft telegram to UKMIS Geneva on CTB duration seems to me to protect Dr Owen's, and the Prime Minister's, position satisfactorily.

Paul Lever

3 October 1978

DOCUMENT 37

To: SECRETARY OF STATE FOR FOREIGN AND COMMONWEALTH
AFFAIRS
From: LORD ZUCKERMAN

1. I have thought hard about the statements set out in the document which you showed me, but shall confine my comments mainly to the question of the effect of a CTBT on stockpile reliability. (There is little point in discussing the matter of new warheads, which most designers – whatever their nationality – would probably want to test). You asked me to say without reserve what I think, and that I have done.

2. Unless I have misread the document, its general slant accords closely with views that started to be canvassed publicly in the USA when President Carter let it be known, even before his election, that he was determined to reach a SALT agreement and a CTB. The opposition was led by men such as Harold Agnew, the Director of the Los Alamos Weapons Laboratory, the US Chiefs of Staff (who are briefed mainly by Agnew and his people), and officials in that section of the Department of Energy which deals with nuclear weapons.

3. What the paper says is that stockpiled weapons are subject to ageing problems which could at any moment, and without notice, become serious, and which would call for nuclear testing in their correction. Reference is made to "two or three" such incidents over the past fifteen years. I could not make out from the paper whether these were problems that had affected our own stockpile or the American one. I assume the former since I can hardly imagine that the Americans keep us informed about their warhead problems – they certainly did not over the years when I was – at least nominally – at the apex of the pyramid of technical exchanges on these matters. Since fifteen years is mentioned, at least one of these incidents must have occurred during the period I was in charge. I can in fact recall one piece of trouble, but I am quite certain that it was put right without testing. I am therefore puzzled.

4. The paper then says, in a statement hedged with conditional 'ifs' and 'coulds' and 'mights', that if tests were not allowed to cure defects, a large part of the United States nuclear armoury, and all of ours, might have to be taken out of service. This observation closely echoes what Donald Kerr, an Assistant Secretary in the US Department of Energy, said in Washington in August 1978 in open testimony that was immediately challenged by Senator Edward Kennedy, who then put in evidence a letter sent to the President on August 15, 1978 by three nuclear warhead specialists.

5. This letter is crucial to the whole argument. It was signed by Norris Bradbury, for 25 years Director of the Los Alamos Weapon Laboratory until succeeded by Agnew in 1970; Carson Mark, a top physicist who was a key figure in nuclear warhead design for more than 25 years; and Richard Garwin, a consultant in the nuclear field ever since 1950. Hans Bethe, a Physics Nobel Laureate and consultant to the Weapons Labs, later added his name to the submission. It needs to be said that there is no one in our own weapons laboratory who can hold a candle to these men, either in scientific eminence of in breadth of experience of nuclear weapons technology.

6. What the letter says is in stark contrast to the drift of the paper you gave me to read. The Americans have practically never resorted to nuclear testing in order to assure the operability of stockpiled nuclear weapons ... "it has been exceedingly rare for a weapon to be taken from a stockpile and fired for assurance ... it has also been rare to the point of non-existence for a problem revealed by the sampling and inspection programme to *require* a nuclear test for its resolution". If improvements in performance, reductions in maintenance costs, and the like, are neither attempted nor allowed, we have it from Bradbury and his colleagues, speaking on the basis of fact and not of 'ifs' and 'buts', that the reliability of stockpiled weapons can be assured without any testing.

7. In short a CTBT need not affect stockpile reliability. But it could affect changes in design, which would have to be forbidden. Who forbids the people in weapon laboratories and who monitors the forbidding is another matter. The trouble is that the basic drive in the arms race is with the designers of weapons not with military people stating some specific requirement in a kind of vacuum.

8. I do not want to speculate about the motivation of the US officials who are campaigning to defeat a CTB: nor would it be useful to discuss the why's and wherefores of the opposition of politicians like Scoop Jackson, with whom I discussed the matter in some depth last April. But it is worth noting that Harold Agnew, a leader of what Senator Kennedy calls the 'nuclear testing buffs', who is openly opposing the President's policy, is also on record that 'he could live' with a test ban that lasted longer than five years. I have a recent letter in which he is quoted as saying that he had not changed his views 'on the narrow question of stockpile integrity' i.e. that the latter could be maintained indefinitely given that the people in Los Alamos were provided with enough money to carry out as many non-nuclear tests as Agnew felt were necessary. Harold Brown, the Secretary of Defense, with whom I also discussed Agnew's views, took the line that one could not expect any other stand from the Head of a Weapons Laboratory. He, Brown,

would probably have argued the same way (he in fact did at the time of the Partial Treaty in 1963) when he was Head of Livermore! Today, however, he is strongly in favour of a CTBT.

9. My own view is that the conclusion of a CTBT will in the end depend on political determination and decision, not on the resolution of technical obfuscations. Were I a politician I would therefore be seeking answers to questions such as these:

(i) Will the world be a safer place than it now is if nuclear testing continued?

I suppose there may be some people who would answer 'Yes'. I can only say that over the many years in which I have been involved in the nuclear debate, the world has become decidedly more perilous with the multiplication and elaboration of nuclear arsenals.

(ii) How can I, a politician, assure myself that the technical advice I am given is dispassionate and devoid of vested interests or political intent?

This means that it would be necessary to decide between Bradbury *et al* speaking on the basis of fact, and Harold Agnew, who while on record that a CTB need not affect the stockpile for 5 years plus, nonetheless now takes it as his responsibility to foster the contrary view in order to keep Los Alamos alive in the nuclear warhead business, regardless of any defined strategic necessity and contrary to the policies of the Administration. [Both Los Alamos and Livermore, the second nuclear weapons laboratory, are technically part of the University of California. Agnew uses this fact as justification to speak out publicly against White House policy when it so pleases him. When the OPEC crisis broke a few years ago he published a piece in the Los Angeles Times in which he proposed that the US should move in and occupy Saudi Arabia! I was his guest at Los Alamos at the time.]

(iii) Is it conceivable that Norris Bradbury, who directed the Los Alamos establishment over the years in which America built up her vast nuclear arsenal, and who, at the time of the Partial Test Ban Treaty in the early 1960's, was opposed, like Harold Brown, to a complete ban on testing, could be lying when he now says that testing was never necessary to assure the viability of a nuclear stockpile?

10. This brings me to the question of cheating. Right from the start of negotiations in the late 1950's, test-ban discussions have been bedevilled by the belief that if a treaty were concluded the Russians would be bound to

cheat. Hence the need to monitor a ban by on-site inspections, or by means of black-boxes, and at least by a world-wide network of seismic stations, etc. etc. We have the same arguments, the identical arguments today. Nuclear explosions can be decoupled in large holes, or masked by conventional explosions, or carried out in earthquake areas. The ultimate absurdity in this *genre* of arguments used to be the belief that it would never be possible to monitor nuclear explosions of a magnitude no greater than big dynamite bangs in quarries, and that such explosions "might" have a military significance.

11. The paper on which you have asked me to comment is given the highest security classification in the UK, yet – and this is of critical importance – the whole argument, in every detail, is in the public domain in the United States. It is there, printed in the Congressional Record, for all to read. No-one supposes that the Russians are not devious, and suspicious, and we have solid reasons for our mistrust. But they must surely be laughing now when they see the 'nuclear testing buffs' being controverted publicly on technical issues by people who know every bit as much as they do, and who can speak with even greater scientific and engineering authority. Who they might well ask, is cheating now?

12. We are reminded that the USA unlike the USSR, is an open society. The debate on the pros and cons of a CTBT or of a SALT agreement – lies and all – takes place in public. I have heard it said that there is no merit in this, since the military/industrial/scientific complex of the USA is too powerful to be moved by arguments which counter its purposes. I myself do not share this view. The open ABM debate certainly played a part in leading to SALT 1, and exposed the fact that neither the Russian nor the American system was either feasible technically or strategically of any major significance.

13. But in this respect the UK is not an open society. There is no meaningful public debate on any of these matters. What can be read about the CTBT in the daily newspapers of the USA we guard as TOP SECRET. Even so, the technical people, amongst whom I still count myself, present to Ministers and senior civil servants only one side of the picture. Over the years and with scarcely any exception this side has usually reflected the views of the directors of the US weapons laboratories.

14. I have said enough for you to see that I regard the paper on which you have asked me to comment as a document which gives a distorted view of the technical issues which it discusses. I take it that the paper is based on technical advice. It lacks even the redeeming quality of saying anything novel as compared with what was argued twenty years ago. Secrecy is vital in certain

fields, but in these matters it can sustain technical mediocrity, and prevent any challenge to dubious assertions. I have focussed on the implicit distortion of fact about the need for nuclear tests in order to assure the viability of stock-piled warheads. But what about the bland assertion that because they might be more crudely designed and constructed, Russian warheads could be expected not to degrade as frequently or as fast as our own. To me this sounds, *a priori*, like nonsense. The whole trend of technology has been to make things smaller, more precise and more, not less, reliable. But the contrary view is implicitly stated as if it were a kind of gospel. The reverse proposition makes far greater sense. Because they are cruder, with poorer tolerances etc. Russian warheads in stockpile would need to be tested.

15. I have done as you asked and not pulled any punches in stating these views. I believe that we should continue as a nuclear power, both from a narrow national point of view and from that of NATO. But in the pursuit of spurious claims in the nuclear field we have already wasted so much money to the detriment of urgent defence needs that I can only hope that there will be a SALT agreement followed – if it cannot be preceded – by a CTBT. We certainly cannot afford to engage in a nuclear arms race with the Americans and Russians. And if we are to have any military security we cannot afford that ultimate nonsense, an arms race with ourselves. A CTBT and a slowing-down of the further elaboration of nuclear arsenals should help obviate that.

ZUCKERMAN

3 October 1978
Z/0917

SECRET & PERSONAL

PS/PUS

I attach a summary record of the discussion this morning between Dr Owen and Mr Mulley, at which Sir Michael Palliser and Sir A Duff were also present. In view of the sensitivity of this subject, I am not distributing this note further at present.

P. Ramsey
pp (G G H Walden)

Defence and Disarmament

In the course of a private discussion this morning with Mr Mulley, the Secretary of State discussed a number of defence and disarmament issues.

On nuclear tests, Dr Owen said that he had been disturbed by the assumption in Mr Mulley's recent minute to the Prime Minister that testing would automatically resume after a three-year CTB. Mr Mulley expressed doubt about the possibility of signing a CTB before next July. Dr Owen insisted that pressures for a voluntary moratorium were growing, and repeated his serious doubts about the view of MOD officials on the reliability of stockpiled nuclear warheads. The PUS pointed out that this problem was endemic; it had existed ten years ago though Lord Zuckerman had taken a different line at the time.

After further discussion, Mr Mulley offered to send a careful letter in reply to Dr Owen's request for further information on proposed tests, making it clear that the MOD favoured an effective CTB. The truth was however that slots for tests had to be booked in advance. Such bookings did not constitute a commitment. This commitment was reached by stages, and not all the £10 million involved would be spent at once. If a CTB Treaty prevented a planned test from taking place, the loss would only be around £3 million.

Dr Owen then turned to the NATO Council meeting on 8 December. He would like to make a major statement there, which he would clear with Mr Mulley. As a preliminary to this he would be talking to the French Foreign Minister on disarmament tomorrow. He thought that the present situation, especially over MBFR, was farcical and that some of the French proposals could be helpful. There might be a case for wrapping up stages 1 and 2 of MBFR and starting in parallel the European Defence Conference proposed by the French. Even the Germans were indicating greater support for an EDC. The PUS pointed out that this might be their way of getting out of MBFR. Dr Owen said that he was thinking of withdrawing from MBFR altogether.

The Germans were being obstructionist and were not prepared to face up to the reality of reductions. Grey areas were also a problem: the only other place they could be discussed if not in SALT would be in the MBFR forum. Mr Mulley thought that this would merely transfer all the MBFR papers and arguments from one discussion to another. The PUS thought that the French might use such a move to get into the disarmament game without any commitment to force reductions.

Dr Owen still favoured abandoning MBFR. In his view we should decide our future defence policy without reference to it. He thought there were too many troops committed in Central Europe. Mr Mulley said that to withdraw them would be to break the Brussels Treaty unilaterally. Dr Owen said that we could surely consult our allies about how to deploy our forces. There was also the question of the proposed amendment to the Protocol of the Brussels Treaty to ease restrictions on German construction of naval vessels and submarines. Dr Owen and Mr Mulley agreed that we may have to give in to German pressure over this in the end; but the Germans would have to obtain our agreement as well as that of the French, and we should be in no hurry to acquiesce. Mr Mulley pointed out that German motives were probably largely commercial: they wanted to sell warships to South America. They were also becoming interested in manufacturing nuclear-powered submarines.

Dr Owen said that he was growing increasingly concerned about the distortion in our defence spending, and our whole defence stance. The PUS said that he thought it right to probe the French position during the Anglo-French Summit, but thought it might be dangerous to go too far in agreeing to their proposals. Our real priority should be to sort out our own ideas first, and then talk to the Germans. The NATO Council meeting on 8 December would enable us to concentrate our minds on the major issues.

Mr Mulley wondered whether this was a good moment to promote a debate on UK defence policy, given that the election manifesto was under discussion. The PUS said that we were coming under increasing pressure to sort out our ideas and that the Germans and the French were moving.

Dr Owen said that he saw the intellectual force of the French arguments against MBFR The terms of reference were too narrow. It had become a block on serious thinking and we should recognise that our attempts to give it impetus had failed. Mr Mulley thought that we could not simply put conventional arms control proposals on the sidelines and concentrate on nuclear matters. We should look for reductions in both areas. Dr Owen thought that we might get the Germans to agree to Stage 1 reductions in MBFR. He thought the whole subject needed shaking up.

On British nuclear defence policy, Dr Owen thought that we were entering a phase in which we might have a rare opportunity to pull off a Nassau-type agreement with the Americans. In his view, this had been one of the best deals we had ever done. Relations between the President and the Prime Minister were extremely good, and the process of SALT ratification would soon begin, which would make it difficult for the Americans to be helpful to us. We should therefore move quickly to obtain a straight transfer of cruise missile technology from them. He was not however in favour of mobile land-based cruise missiles. Mr Mulley said that the Americans were giving priority to airborne cruise missiles. The PUS said that the German position seemed to be that they were reluctant to have missiles on German soil unless we accepted them too. The Dutch and the Belgians might take a similar position. Dr Owen said that he would prefer SLCMs on our existing submarines.

Mr Mulley said that it was important to recognise that cruise missiles could not be fired out of Polaris tubes. Cruise missiles were based on the saturation philosophy: out of 20 or 30 only one would get through to the Soviet Union. It was not simply a question of replacing 16 Polaris missiles by 16 cruise missiles. Sir Neil Cameron pointed out that cruise missiles were also vulnerable because of their 4–5 hours flight time.

G G H Walden

23 November 1978

DOCUMENT 39

SECRET

RECORD OF A TALK BETWEEN THE SECRETARY OF STATE FOR FOREIGN & COMMONWEALTH AFFAIRS AND MR CYRUS VANCE AT WINFIELD HOUSE AT 14.30 HRS ON 9 DECEMBER 1978

Those present:

The Rt Hon Dr David Owen MP	Mr Cyrus Vance
Mr G G H Walden	Mr Brewster
	Mr Tony Lake

ARMS SALES TO CHINA/SALT/CTB/MBFR

Dr Owen said he was worried about the general lack of progress on disarmament. Mr Vance agreed: there was too much talk and not enough action. He was also worried about arms sales, but had made it clear in reply to questions after his speech that morning that each country must make its own choices. Dr Owen asked whether this reflected Mr Vance's attitude to the sale of Harriers to China. The Americans had no need to worry about Taiwan; Harriers could not get there and back with a full payload. Mr Vance asked which version we were contemplating selling the Chinese. Dr Owen said that it was the present military version, and not the one we were working on with the Americans. He himself had hesitated on this issue. But Brezhnev's message had made it more difficult for us not to sell. Mr Vance commented that Brezhnev's' tactics had been stupid.

Dr Owen said that we expected a pretty aggressive response from the Russians. Much, however, depended on the whole package, and particularly the civilian element in any increased sales to China. If the Russians had played the game on detente, he might have taken their representations more seriously. One advantage of selling some arms to China was to show the Russians that they could not run detente entirely on their own terms. Moreover, Harrier was really a cross between a helicopter and an attack aircraft. We would not be hurried into taking a decision, although the Chinese had now made specific requests. The Chinese were talking to everyone about large purchases – there must be some limit on their foreign exchange resources.

Mr Vance said that the Chinese must simply be shopping and comparing prices. On Harriers, he knew that Dr Owen was aware of his private reservations. But if we had reached the point where we would like him to see what the differences were between one type of Harrier and another, he would be prepared to talk to the President about it. Dr Owen said that we had got different noises from the American Administration, and although Harold Brown had said that he shared Mr Vance's attitude, the Press had attributed a different line to him. Mr Callaghan was extremely cautious on the issue, and no final decision was likely to be taken before the Guadeloupe meeting. If a SALT and CTB Agreement were signed soon, however, we might look at the issue differently. Mr Vance said that we would know whether or not there would be a SALT Agreement by the time of the Guadeloupe meeting. Dr Owen said that he did not expect a decision on Harriers before February. Mr Vance said that he ought to make it clear that if a SALT Agreement were followed by a Brezhnev/Carter meeting, the Communique would not be confined to SALT, but would almost certainly contain language urging very early progress of CTB and movement on MBFR. Dr Owen said that he was fed up with the lack of progress on MBFR, and had done his best to push it along. A few months ago he had sensed that the Germans and French were doing a deal on the issue. Herr Genscher did not want an MBFR Agreement and German officials took a right-wing stand on the negotiations. The only French interest was to obstruct them. Mr Vance said that he thought Chancellor Schmidt did not agree with Herr Genscher on MBFR. Moreover, Mr Trudeau had told him that he would soon "blow his stack" on the negotiations.

Dr Owen said that the Canadians had been quite helpful in drafting the NATO communique. This had included useful references to approximate parity; the movement in the negotiations since April; the possibility of a meeting at Foreign Minister level; and the need for a political presence at the CSCE meeting in Madrid. It was worth paying a price to get the French involved in disarmament, but they must not be allowed to obstruct MBFR. Their proposal to include all CSCE countries plus Albania in their European Disarmament Conference (EDC) was not serious. The EDC would also exclude nuclear weapons. He would like to get agreement on some MBFR reductions, if only limited, and had considered if we ought to widen the terms of reference. He was prepared to meet Herr Genscher to some extent on national forces levels, and agreed that more movement was needed from the East.

Mr Vance agreed. He had recently changed his mind on MBFR, especially since the Russians had told him that they were ready to make another major move in the negotiations. Brezhnev had apparently cancelled the order to make this move, but if the West was ready to breathe more life into the negotiations the Russians would probably respond. Dr Owen said that the question was whether we could develop a new negotiating forum which would include the French, but not all the CSCE countries. The present participants of MBFR plus a few extra countries could help to save the French face. New movement in MBFR, together with a serious attitude to confidence building measures in Madrid, could add up to significant progress. Mr Vance agreed. Dr Owen said that he was encouraged by his remarks. The Americans were clearly not entirely preoccupied with SALT. Mr Vance said that he was very serious on MBFR, and thought the President would be too after a SALT Agreement. Mr Trudeau had subjected Mr Jamieson and himself to a fierce attack over the lack of movement on MBFR. Movement must be injected into negotiations either through a Foreign Ministers' Meeting, or by direct instructions from Heads of Government.

Dr Owen said that a French-style EDC in parallel with MBFR was a recipe for stagnation. He was prepared to meet French anxieties about a bloc-to-bloc approach; but we could not have people like Dom Mintoff holding up a consensus. Mr Vance said he would urge the President to raise MBFR at Guadeloupe. He thought Mr Carter would be prepared to do this. He himself was not at all enthusiastic about French proposals, and could not see how the Russians could be brought to agree with them. He was sure Mr Gromyko would accept an MBFR meeting at Foreign Minister level. Dr Owen said that he had found Gromyko slightly more positive about this when he had last seen him in September.

Foreign & Commonwealth Office
11 December 1978

[Postscript: We made no progress on MBFR and by 1979 had to stop pressurizing Hans Dietrich Genscher because it was affecting relations with Helmut Schmidt. I took a great interest in the wording of the briefing notes prior to Guadeloupe before they were sent by the FCO over to No. 10, going over every word. Fortunately CTB was an issue that Jim Callaghan concerned himself about when he was Foreign Secretary and he was knowledgeable on the subject (see Document 40).]

DOCUMENT 40

THIS DOCUMENT IS THE PROPERTY OF HER BRITANNIC MAJESTY'S GOVERNMENT

PMVP (79) 3
18 December 1978

Quadripartite Meeting, Guadeloupe
5–6 January 1979

COMPREHENSIVE TEST BAN

Brief by Foreign and Commonwealth Office for bilateral use with President Carter

SUMMARY OF ESSENTIAL FACTS AND OF POINTS TO MAKE

1. I favour a major bid for tripartite agreement as soon as' possible, followed by a period of consultations with other states which could be extended somewhat if SALT ratification in Washington required it.

2. Specific decisions on the Soviet proposals for 10 National Seismic Stations (NSS) in the UK and Dependent Territories must await our detailed analysis but we are willing in principle to accept at least one NSS in the UK and probably some also in dependent territories.

3. The non-proliferation value of the Treaty is particularly important. The US and UK should propose language that would allow the Review Conference to consider all options on what might happen after the Treaty period. This should encourage adherence by non-nuclear weapon states.

4. I also hope that any statement on resumption of US testing after the Treaty period will not be in categorical terms.

5. "Permitted experiments" should be handled as informally as possible in the negotiations.

Line to Take

6. In your message of 25 September you said that tri-lateral agreement on CTB should not be concluded before a SALT II agreement. How do you see prospects for CTB? I should like to see a major drive to reach tripartite agreement as soon as possible, followed by consultations with other states which if necessary could be extended in time if the situation on SALT ratification in Washington required it.

7. It is good that the Russians have made a move on National Seismic Stations (NSS). Their acceptance in principle of 10 stations in the Soviet

Union is welcome but their position remains unclear on other important aspects of the issue.

8. We are studying carefully the Soviet proposals for 10 NSS in the UK and dependent territories, a bid which seems based more on political than technical considerations. "We are concerned about the cost of these proposals; and in dependent territories we must take local views into account. But we have already decided not to object in principle to at least one NSS in the UK and probably some also in dependent territories, although not necessarily a total of 10."

We will not allow this issue to impede the negotiations.

9. As you know, because of expectation in Britain and abroad, the UK reserved its position on three year duration until the outline of the whole treaty package could be seen more clearly. The other aspects of particular concern to me in relation to our non-proliferation aims (here I have India particularly in mind) remain much as they were when we corresponded in September. One is the role of the Review Conference. I believe we shall need to offer the Russians new treaty language on this before they will be more forthcoming on verification. My officials have suggested to yours that the role of the Review Conference should be "to review the operation of the treaty and to consider the question of any future treaty arrangements". This is a neutral formula which neither closes any options for the future nor leans in the direction of any particular option. It might help to meet the Soviet objections to the current US formula about a replacement treaty. It might also help to persuade key non-nuclear weapon states to adhere to a fixed duration treaty, by giving them a say at the Review Conference on what arrangements should follow. It would not prejudice US or UK security, since nuclear weapon states would have a veto on decisions at the Review Conference. I hope US and UK can agree soon on our formula or something similar to put forward when the negotiations resume.

10. You wrote in September that you would keep in mind the points I had put to you on the assurances you planned to give the Senate about resumption of US testing after the Treaty period. I remain convinced that a virtual undertaking to resume testing would seriously undermine our chances of persuading many non-nuclear weapon states to adhere to the CTB. If a statement has to be made something less categorical would be highly desirable, in my view, for non-proliferation reasons. Have you had further thoughts on this?

11. We agreed in September that the yield limit of any programme of "permitted experiments" that may be conducted during a CTB should be 100 lbs or less. Of course any such programme is a sensitive issue since it could

have a negative effect on the attitude of non-nuclear powers to the Treaty, above all if they thought it could be used to start a design programme for new warheads. I believe that any understanding on "permitted experiments" between the three negotiating parties should be as informal as possible and not figure in the Treaty. This is a subject I hope will be discussed in Anglo–US official talks on CTB in January.

Background
The Timescale

12. There is a general assumption in the US Administration that a CTB treaty should not go to the Senate for ratification until SALT II has been ratified. However, we take the view that this consideration need not mean that the tripartite negotiations should proceed slowly if, as we and the Americans intend, they are followed by discussions with other states before any treaty is signed. We believe that a realistic forecast for a conclusion to the negotiations would be May–July 1979 although if the other two negotiating partners were to agree to negotiate intensively this could be advanced to the end of March 1979.

13. Once tripartite agreement has been reached, the Russians would like the treaty to be signed by the three negotiating partners and opened for signature by other states. The UK favours an American idea of a pattern of direct consultations with key non-nuclear weapon states, after which a decision would be taken on whether to submit the treaty to the Committee on Disarmament (CD) in Geneva or adopt the Russian approach.

National Seismic Stations (NSS)

14. On 27 November the Soviet Union presented proposals for 10 NSS in specified locations in the US and 10 in the UK and its dependent territories. The Russians said they could accept 10 NSS in the Soviet Union, as earlier proposed by the US with UK support, only on the basis of "equal obligations". They have not indicated whether they will accept the quality of equipment or the locations or the timetable for installation proposed by the US.

15. The US have accepted in the negotiations that there should be 10 NSS in the US and that the general locations proposed by the Soviet Union were appropriate. But the proposal for one NSS in the UK itself and 9 in British dependent territories is open to objection. For-example, four of the locations are in territories which are already, or soon will be, independent. The list also includes the politically objectionable idea of an NSS in Hong Kong, which the Russians presumably hope would monitor Chinese testing. More generally, the Soviet call for "equal obligations" can be challenged because the UK

has not sought an independent and equal role under the tripartite Separate Verification Agreement but has proposed to act only in association with the US in relation to NSS in the Soviet Union. On the technical side there is the fact that NSS on most small islands would not be able to monitor seismic activity beyond the island itself.

16. Nonetheless a constructive British response may well prove to be the necessary political price for securing an adequate system of NSS in the Soviet Union, which would be a notable gain for the West for verifying a CTB as well as a precedent for future arms control agreements. In view of that possibility the Americans have asked us to be open-minded. Officials are assessing the complex political, financial, technical and security implications of the Soviet proposals with the aim of putting recommendations to Ministers early in the New Year. (The reference in the Line to Take to our deciding not to object in principle to NSS in the UK and dependent territories is subject to the agreement of the Prime Minister and other Ministers to a proposal to this effect which is being put forward by the Foreign end Commonwealth Secretary).

Review Conference

17. The UK/US formula for the role of the Review Conference that is at present on the table in the negotiations is to "consider the question of whether there should be a replacement treaty". The Russians have never accepted this and on 27 November reiterated their view that the treaty must provide for its possible extension, which would depend on whether non-parties were conducting tests. The tabled formula is also open to criticism on non-proliferation grounds, since it could be held to exclude the option of extending the CTB treaty. We have ourselves never been entirely happy with the US/UK formula which was based on US language and we have therefore proposed to the US the alternative formula in para 9 above.

"Permitted Experiments"

18. President Carter decided in May 1978 that during a CTB the US should conduct a programme of nuclear weapons experiments at minimal yield levels, which he confirmed in a letter to the Prime Minister in September as meaning up to 100 lbs. The US had already referred in the negotiations to a need to reach "mutually acceptable understandings" on this question. The Russians, who can conduct experiments far in excess of 100 lbs in yield without risk of detection, have made negative comments on the need to consider this issue.

19. The case for a programme of "permitted experiments" is largely based

on the need to retain the skills of weapons design staff under a CTB, so as to remain capable of dealing with any problems that might arise in the nuclear stockpile. It would also be important that a CTB should not inhibit civil nuclear energy research, where some processes could be said to involve nuclear micro-explosions. The Americans will be obliged to announce their programme of experiments when presenting the CTB to Congress and this is virtually certain to attract criticism from some non-nuclear weapon states. We have still not received any clear ideas on how the Americans want the question to be handled in the tripartite negotiations or publicly. In accordance with Ministers' instructions we have proposed to the Americans a bilateral official consultation in Washington in January, to discuss "permitted experiments" and other issues outstanding in the negotiations.

Foreign and Commonwealth Office
18 December 1978

DOCUMENT 41

PM/1/79

<u>PRIME MINISTER</u>

1. I hesitate to burden you with more paper prior to Guadeloupe, but if you have time on the plane you might consider it worth reading this paper by Lord Zuckerman which he recently sent to me.

2. His views are always worth considering seriously because he represents the rare combination of a highly knowledgeable scientific background in nuclear weapons and also a firm commitment to nuclear disarmament. This combination is very rare in the United Kingdom but is quite common in the United States and many of the questions which he poses represent the viewpoint of a number of President Carter's senior policy advisers.

DAVID OWEN

Foreign and Commonwealth Office
3 January 1979

THE SHOOTING BOX,
BURNHAM THORPE,
KINGS LYNN,
NORFOLK,
PE31 8HW.

2nd January, 1979

<u>Foreign Secretary</u>

I wrote the attached piece before Christmas, in an effort to clear my own mind about the issues you have discussed with me in recent months. In the light of the message I had this morning, you might find it useful.

All good wishes
Solly Zuckerman

The UK in the Nuclear Debate

The support which we have given President Carter's initiatives in the field of disarmament, and particularly of nuclear disarmament, has been somewhat mixed. First, our decision to expand Windscale was no help to his particular concept of a 'non-plutonium economy'. Second, while we have publicly prayed for the success of the SALT II talks, we have, at the same time, been concerned lest the non-circumvention clause will be neither in our own nor in the Nato interest. Our worries on this score – as indicated to American officials by our own – have not helped an Administration which is more preoccupied with the question of assuring that a SALT II agreement is ratified in treaty form by the Senate, than it is with our problems. Third, while we have made it plain that we recognise the reasons why the President has been driven to the idea of a CTB Treaty limited to three years, we have also indicated that we would find it difficult to support an arrangement which presupposed that at the end of a three-year term tests above a threshold of 100 lb yield would be automatically resumed. Our view is that such a treaty would be no better than a limited moratorium and could hardly help discourage would-be nuclear powers from the pursuit of their ambitions.

Our position is, in short, ambiguous. On the one hand we want to see an end to the nuclear arms race – for that matter, any arms race – and we are all for 'non-proliferation'. On the other we are a nuclear power, and with international relations such as they are, we want to remain one. The fact that in the totally unreal numerical scale that rules in this field we are a relatively weak nuclear power is neither here nor there. The pressures are for us to continue. No doubt it was in part because of our dependence on the USA that Giscard d'Estaing recently declared that we are a 'weaker' nuclear power than France. Whatever his views, our technical and military advisers are determined to cling to our 'special' relationship, to our dependence on America, regardless of the way this relationship is viewed from the other side of the Atlantic, and regardless of our long-term European aspirations.

Our immediate concerns are, first, with the CTBT, in which we are one of the three parties directly involved, and, second, with the question of what successor system there is to be to Polaris – given there is any. The answer to the latter question partly depends – both directly and via Nato – on the success or failure of the SALT negotiations. If we opt for a new system, will the non-circumvention clause in the draft SALT II treaty legally deter the Americans from helping if we want help? And if the answer is 'no', would the Americans anyhow want to help us? Since SALT II, if concluded, inevitably and as intended moves into SALT III, would they indeed deem it wise for them to do so? Unless we take a fresh look at the whole problem; unless in doing so we stand right back so as to see the wood as well as the trees, we are going to be confounded by our past patterns of behaviour. We are inevitably blinkered as we peer at the future.

C.T.B.T.

First, the CTBT. A month ago Harold Brown asked me if I believed that a 3-year CTB treaty would discourage potential nuclear states from going ahead with their plans. The obvious answer was that no-one could tell, but that at least a CTBT would not be an encouragement – unless it had the looks of a shaky moratorium, like that of 1958–1961, might be broken without notice by one of the main parties. (We need to remember that the Russians did the breaking in 1961, but that in the autumn of 1960 General Eisenhower had already given notice that the Americans might well resume testing – a declaration which was an open invitation to the Russians to begin.)

Among other steps which he has felt he should take in order to secure the necessary support for SALT, to which he accords a higher priority, President Carter has whittled down the terms of a CTBT which he can get agreed domestically. At the political extreme there are those, like Senator 'Scoop' Jackson, who genuinely believe that a CTBT is irrelevant. He and those who think like him are determined that there is not going to be a second SALT agreement; and if there is to be no end to the nuclear arms race, testing will be necessary. At the technical extreme, the people in the weapons laboratories, as in the days before the partial test-ban treaty of 1963, have shown that there is no argument, valid or invalid, that they are not prepared to deploy to 'prove' that a CTBT is against the U.S. national interest. This time they have focused their arguments on the need to carry out nuclear tests in order to assure the reliability of stockpiled weapons. In doing so, their spokesman in the Department of Energy – Dr. Donald Kerr – declared in open congressional testimony that the technical views of those whom he represented were shared by U.K. nuclear weapons experts who, indeed, in one of their Washington meetings early in 1978 went even further than the American test enthusiasts by introducing to the argument the irrelevant issue of testing in order to assure the safety – as opposed to reliability – of stockpiled warheads. The Prime Minister and other Ministers concerned were apparently under the impression that there was only one technical view on this issue, until they were made aware that a distinguished group of U.S. scientists with intimate and lengthy experience of warhead design and maintenance, had openly rejected as gross exaggeration the arguments of the weapons laboratory people. The emptiness of the technical case for testing has since been fully exposed. Dr. Harold Agnew, the retiring head of Los Alamos, and the most eminent protagonist of the view that it is necessary to test to assure stockpile reliability, has allowed himself to be cited, in a report that is now being circulated in draft in the USA, as not differing significantly from those who do not believe that there are fundamental technical reasons which call for testing to assure stockpile reliability. In doing so, Agnew has reaffirmed a view which he stated in writing in April 1977, and which, with his permission, has now appeared in print in a Congressional Record dated October 13, 1978 (H.A.S.C. No. 95–90). The only argument of possible substance by the laboratory people – and then one not related directly to the issue of stockpile reliability – is that unless testing is allowed (or, in lieu of testing, resources for extensive new non-nuclear experiments), the weapons laboratories will not be able to hang on to their good people or recruit new ones. Even this view is contested by certain of those who are experienced in the warhead field.

It is not difficult to sympathise with the views of those who speak for the nuclear weapons laboratories. If nuclear disarmament becomes a reality, the laboratories would lose their basic raison d'etre. Those whose first loyalty is to their work in the weapons establishments must ipso facto be opposed to nuclear disarmament. They represent the nearest one can think of to a secret society which practises some mysterious cult that is accepted without argument as essential to national well-being. If the weapons laboratory people say that a nuclear test is necessary, who is to deny them? When a test is completed, who is there to say that it was justified by the results obtained – surely not their political masters, nor the military who deploy the weapons once they are produced, On the basis of what experience can they validate or challenge the claims of the nuclear priesthood? In an authoritative paper which has, I believe, just gone up to Harold Brown, Herbert York, once head of the Livermore weapons laboratory, and then Director of Defense Research and Engineering in the Pentagon (a post in which he preceded Harold Brown) has written that

"In fact, the weapons laboratories have made no significant breakthroughs since Teller and other scientists-experts put forth their claims in the early 1960s that new advances were just around the corner. Even the "neutron bomb" – a highly controversial political issue in 1978 – is a creature of the late 1950s and early 1960s. Moreover, it provides only marginal advantages over the weapons it aspires to replace. Of course, substantial improvement in the physical characteristics of nuclear bombs have been made in the past twenty years, and more evidently are in store, including the possible extension of the clean bomb idea to very small yields. Indeed, Livermore and Los Alamos now focus much of their attention on what were considered earlier to be peripheral issues: making bombs safe and secure against accidents, misuse, tampering, and robbery, and modifying existing designs so that they better fit new delivery systems. Many of these improvements involve very consid-erable technological cleverness and expertise, but they have done relatively little to shift the nuclear balance – whether strategic, tactical or naval."

This is a general view which I would strongly support. But so far as the CTBT is concerned, it matters little at the moment. Whatever the reasons, the CTBT will be on the back-burner until SALT II is out of the way, or at any rate before the Senate.

Successor Systems?

The USA and the USSR have been on the verge of agreeing a SALT II agreement for so long that outside the USA the subject arouses little, if any, public interest. The nature of the terms of the agreement under negotiation is no secret – particularly in the USA – and it is months since those who were interested knew that only a few, relatively insignificant, items still had to be settled. Up till mid-November, many 'in the picture' but on the sidelines were declaring that all would be ready for signature before the end of the year. A new round of talks is to begin this week, and even though there are only a few more days to go before what was assumed to be the deadline, all might still be well. But equally there might be a new delay because of the transformation of the political scene brought about by the USA/China rapprochement, by the continuing unrest in Iran, and by the tardy progress of the Israeli/Egyptian peace-talks. Yet, by all accounts, a SALT agreement is a very high priority for both the USA and the USSR; the greater the delay, the greater the peril for all, both direct and indirect. But even if an agreement is initialled soon, President Carter will still have to contend with opposition in the Senate and in the American electorate. Mr. Vance and Dr. Harold Brown, who will have to bear the brunt of this attack, have a tough fight on their hands if ratification is not to be unduly delayed.

What is known publicly about the terms that have been provisionally agreed provides a useful picture of the relative size, as of today and projected to 1985, of the strategic nuclear armouries of both the USA and the USSR (as measured in numbers of launchers and deliverable warheads). The estimates may turn out to be wrong by a large margin either way, but in terms of the reality of potential destruction, whatever error there may be is totally irrelevant. The phrase 'enough is enough' still has meaning in a world of nuclear weapons, even though its significance may have long been drowned in the noise of an arms-race in which the public at large has long lost interest.

For purposes of comparison, the nuclear armaments of the Western and Warsaw Pact powers may be separated into three main categories: 'central strategic' weapons, 'grey-area' or 'eurostrategic' weapons, and 'theatre' weapons. The central strategic armoury is the one that is being negotiated in SALT II. It comprises the weapons-systems (land-, sea- or air-launched) with which the USA and USSR could hurl nuclear-warheads at targets in each other's homelands. Eurostrategic or grey-area nuclear weapons comprise our own and the French nuclear missile submarines (as well as an unknown number of assigned US boats), aircraft (land-or carrier-based), and intermediate or medium range ballistic missiles. Their numbers are not subject to negotiation either in SALT or in MBFR, and while accounting for fewer warheads today, they could, given no restraint in their multiplication, soon outclass the central strategic nuclear armouries in destructive power. Then comes the third category consisting of thousands of what are now fashionably called 'theatre' nuclear weapons, previously known as tactical nuclear weapons – free-falling bombs, artillery shells, short-range launchers, etc. Their number is not known publicly. More than ten years ago Mr. McNamara, then Secretary of Defense, disclosed a figure of 7,000, a number which is still bandied around.

Assuming that SALT II is agreed, and using the best known figures for deliverable warheads that have been either directly or indirectly revealed or 'leaked' (including multiple warheads, MIRV'd or not), the balance in the central strategic equation has recently been given in the States as:

Deliverable Warheads

1978		1985			
		Moderate *Estimate*		*High* *Estimate*	
USA	USSR	USA	USSR	USA	USSR
9,500	4,900	13,100	8,300	15,600	14,100

The Russians are obviously aware of these and other 1985 projections, and presumably accept them as meaningful in assessing the numerical and essentially 'static balance' of strategic nuclear forces.

But whether 'static balances' have any real meaning is another matter. Two to three strikes on London with war-heads of, say, the average yield of the weapons in the central strategic stockpiles would wreak more destruction and kill more people than the total for all the second world war air-raids in Europe. A detailed analysis carried out nearly twenty years ago by methods more precise and sophisticated than the sketchy ones now regarded as adequate by today's nuclear theorists indicated that a single megaton strike on Birmingham could kill one-third of its (then) a million inhabitants and transform the city into a waste fit only for bulldozers. It was presumably this particular study which provided General Sir John Hackett with the material for the vivid picture he painted in his recent book The Third World War of Birmingham destroyed by one 'shot' from a Russian SS20 missile (not a weapon counted as part of the central armoury) – and then the retaliatory elimination of Minsk (by two Polaris missiles). Even if SALT II puts a stop to the elaboration and multiplication of strategic missiles, enough will still remain on both sides to efface all the cities and most of the towns of the northern hemisphere – together with their populations.

The Eurostrategic or 'grey-area' weapon systems may not have the range but are every bit as destructive as their central strategic counterparts. The estimates of numbers of Western power warheads are:

Range in Excess of 1000 n.m

1978	1985	
	Moderate Estimate	*High Estimate*
2,100	1,800	3,200

Range between 500 and 1000 n.m.

1,600	3,400	3,600

Three-quarters of the total of 1000 n.m.÷, separately deliverable, warheads estimated for 1985 will be American, the remainder British and French, with the French, according to these estimates, controlling the greater number. The ratios for the 500–1000 n.m. range show the Americans still the 'national' owners of three-quarters of the total armoury, with the British ahead of the French in their share of the rest. The Western grey-area weapons are by definition directed at targets on USSR soil. They include our 64 Polaris missiles as well as free-falling bombs at present carried on our current aircraft (e.g. Vulcan and Buccaneer), and to be carried on the Tornado, when it comes into service. The numbers of Russian warheads that correspond to these figures are about 4,100 for 1978 and between 5,300 and 6,700 by 1985. Whatever the degree of their uncertainty, the figures imply a slight preponderance of Russian weapons in the 'grey-area'.

According to some US scholars of the present military scene, it was mainly a UK insistence to keep 'forward-based' systems out of SALT II that now makes them an obvious part of SALT III, that is to say 'grey-area', negotiations (given, of course, that SALT II is consummated). This is where the totally fictional nature of the numbers and categorisation 'game' of nuclear weapons becomes immediately apparent. From the point of view of the USSR it makes no difference were Moscow and its environs to disappear from the face of the globe as a result of a salvo of American central strategic missiles, or of a salvo of weapons drawn from the eurostrategic or grey-area stockpile. But some of the latter are also notionally NATO 'theatre' weapons – so-called tactical or battlefield weapons. Were any of these weapons ever to be used, it would make no difference whether some future historian were to call the weapons with which the Russians responded tactical or strategic. Nor would it make any difference which way one diagnosed a weapon which had, say, totally eliminated Liege or Cologne. They could be called central strategic, eurostrategic or theatre; the result would be the same.

The fact is that no-one has ever suggested a convincing scenario in which nuclear weapons – whatever their category or yield – are used which does not get out of control. A few tactical 'interdiction' strikes in some NATO war game played on a map by eager members of a 'Defence Studies' course might, in theory, hold up a Russian thrust. But if the 'interdiction strikes' were on Belgian soil they could mean the strategic end of that country. We used to hear about warning nuclear shots 'across their bows'. These now seem to be out of fashion. We hear today of mythical tactical nuclear battles, presumably presided over by some Marquis of Queensbury whose job it is to see that neither side contravenes some set of rules relating to yield and range of weapons and to numbers of civilians killed. But there are no such rules. We have Sir John Hackett's picture of a Third World War ending when just one city in the USSR and one in the UK had been 'taken out' by nuclear fire. Like most who have devoted real thought to the subject, and as a member of the fast declining body of men who had to study the process and nature of destruction at first hand, all this leaves me totally sceptical. Once nuclear weapons cease to have a deterrent effect, there would be no decoupling barriers to the progress of their use. The outcome would not depend on some pre-arranged scenario, but on factors which could not be gauged in advance; on, for example, the stability of political control, on the strength of the political control of the military machine, on military discipline – on any number of facts which rarely, if ever, are taken into account in abstract war-games. And we also need to remind ourselves that were nuclear weapons ever to be used, only a trivial percentage of the stockpile on either side would be required to bring about irrevocable destruction and chaos. Nuclear arsenals overflow, and against such weapons there are no realistic defensive systems – either passive or active. Nuclear weapons have no function other than to deter – for the good reason that once they fail to deter, and their use becomes a suicidal battle of determination, no-one knows how the process would end, or were it to end, what political goal would have been attained. And even if nuclear weapons did have some useful military function, there are certainly twenty, fifty times more of them in the nuclear arsenals of the NATO and Warsaw Pact sides than would be needed for the discharge of whatever function it is assumed they did have other than to deter. I am fully aware of the proposition that one cannot deploy weapons to deter aggression if one is unprepared to use them. What I am also aware of, and what seems to me more important, is that no country that disposes of nuclear weapons is prepared to face the reality of the consequences of their use.

Yet the nuclear arms race continues. For years we in NATO have deluded ourselves that we are able to compensate for numerical inferiority in manpower by resorting to nuclear weapons. This is not a proposition to which it would seem the Russians subscribe. When we threaten to strengthen the NATO nuclear shield – for example, when it is proposed that NATO should be equipped with neutron bombs or cruise missiles – the Russians do not offer to reduce the number of their troops that face the West; they take a reciprocal nuclear step. Here the MBFR negotiations exercise no restraint.

Sheer numbers of nuclear warheads, as opposed to a sophisticated view of what measure of destructive power is consistent with any political or military purpose, seem to have become the operative reality on both sides. There was a time when an arms race was pursued in the hope that, given a resort to arms, one of the sides engaged would succeed in imposing its will on the other. Today we in the West are engaged in an arms race which were it ever to end in nuclear conflict could only mean the destruction of both the NATO and Warsaw Pact powers. This is widely recognised in Europe, the USA and, no doubt, the USSR. But the fact that the race nonetheless goes on imparts to nuclear weapons a glamour which is irresistable to sophisticated or unsophisticated leaders of certain non-nuclear states. There is bound to be proliferation if the major nuclear powers do not call a halt to the arms race in which they are engaged.

The UK played a central and almost critical part in the initial development of nuclear weapons. That, essentially, is why we still try to impart some kind of reality to the belief that we remain an 'independent nuclear power'. To the world at large we have tied ourselves to the Americans, and like the rest of Western Europe have at the same time become captive to the nuclear arms race between them and the USSR. France has tried to break away, both by leaving NATO and by fashioning its own nuclear armoury. But we remain tied, at the same time as we are so conditioned by our past decisions and actions in the nuclear field, and so innured to the international failure to arrest the nuclear arms-race after decades of talk, that we are driven on, panting, way behind the leaders, in a race for which there can be no prize.

What options then are open to us now in our consideration of what we do as a 'follow-on' to Polaris? I propose first to consider the matter in the form of a series of questions.

1. Given that the state of deterrance breaks down, are there any conceivable circumstances in which we would, independently of the USA or of the other members of NATO, launch a nuclear strike against the USSR, short of what Harold Macmillan, if I remember correctly, once called 'posthumous revenge'?

2. Can we conceive of any political changes in the years ahead which could generate circumstances in which we would launch such a strike against one of our current allies on the Continent?

3. Is there any other power in the world against which we would ever direct nuclear weapons on our own?

4. If the answer to these questions is 'yes', then we could argue that it is worth paying a price to continue as an 'independent' nuclear power. If the answer is 'no', is there any reason to regard our nuclear forces as more than a small fraction of the present eurostrategic and theatre nuclear arsenal?

5. Is it the Government's view that tactical (so-called theatre) nuclear weapons are weapons of war which could be used on NATO soil to withstand a thrust by Warsaw Pact forces (or against targets on Warsaw Pact soil) without opening up an exchange of the eurostrategic nuclear forces – i.e. to attacks against Russian targets and to nuclear attacks on targets in the UK?

6. According to current doctrine we would retaliate in kind if targets in the UK were attacked with Russian nuclear weapons. Do we suppose that the West Germans or the Dutch would not expect a corresponding response (regardless of the consequences) if Russian nuclear weapons were used against them in a 'theatre' war, i.e. a so-called tactical exchange?

7. Is it the official U.K. view that the chances are that a nuclear exchange on NATO territory would not lead to an exchange between the eurostrategic forces (with nuclear attacks on Russian targets and with Russian nuclear strikes on targets in the UK as well as the U.S.A.)? Is this the official American view? The French act as though they do not believe that it is, and that the Americans would not risk the destruction of their homeland to save Europe. Is the logic underlying their policy of nuclear independence faulty or sound?

8. What benefits do we derive from our dependence on (i.e. special relationship with) the Americans which we would not get if we were merely part of the NATO line-up? What political benefits are we sacrificing in the European context in order to secure our special American benefits?

9. Setting aside these basic issues, what options are open to us if we continue on the assumption that every nuclear weapon system we now deploy will have to be replaced.

(a) First, can we continue with Polaris as it is or, as has been suggested, will the hulls of our boats wear out? Have the Americans enough spare parts in their moth-balled Polaris and A3 armoury to keep us going till the circumstances of the present world line-up of nuclear forces change?

I believe that here the answer to the central question is that technically we could carry on. The 'bits and pieces' are there, and there is nothing in the non-circumvention clause of SALT II to inhibit the Americans from helping us.

(b) Would the Americans help us to a new missile – for example, the Trident C4?

The answer is probably 'no' because of the non-circumvention clause.

(c) Could we – both in terms of technological know-how and the resources it would take – try to make a 'Chinese copy' of C4, with its longer range, and suitable to our boats?

My belief is that the realistic answer would be 'no' on both counts – as it would be to the suggestion that we build a newer class of boats. The last would obviously be within our technical and industrial competence, but the cost in resources (taken no doubt from other parts of the public expenditure budget) would be out of all proportion to the possible political disadvantages as compared with the strategic benefits of so doing.

Could we, or should we, opt for a different nuclear system – for example, the cruise missile? If we did, would we require American help? What would it cost in resources? Would such missiles be launched from land (which would resurrect the old Blue Streak debate), air (the old Blue Steel debate), or from naval platforms?

(e) Would a cruise missile be our 'independent strategic deterrent', or a theatre weapon? Would the same weapon do for either role? Would there be much point to our adding a relatively small number of warheads – a very small percentage – to an already overstocked alliance armoury?

10. Supposing we do none of these things:

(a) What international benefits could we derive world-wide from making it apparent that while we remain a nuclear power, we are dropping out of the nuclear arms-race?

(b) Is there any possibility of a sensible get-together with the French on all these matters? And with the West Germans? Should we start enquiring seriously how to reconcile our defence interests with those of our membership of the EEC?

(c) Since saturation point has long been passed in the build-up of all three nuclear categories, should NATO policy – as has long been urged – not be to strengthen the conventional arms of the Alliance in response to the presumed superiority of the Warsaw Pact countries in man-power as opposed to spending resources on further nuclear systems?

Having set out these various questions and observations, I should like to repeat what I said at the start – that unless we take a fresh look at the whole nuclear problem, and in particular reach a clear view on the points I have numbered 1 to 8 (pp 9 and 10), we are more than likely just to blunder on, as we have in the past.

S. Zuckerman

18th December, 1978

DOCUMENT 42

THE SHOOTING BOX
BURNHAM THORPE,
KINGS LYNN,
NORFOLK.

22 January, 1979

In the aide memoire that I wrote just before Christmas about the way I saw our military nuclear problems, I used some figures from an American draft paper, of which a copy had been sent to me, about the numbers of warheads now and projected on to 1985. I have now had the final version and I thought you ought to know that some of the figures have changed, although not to any extent which affects my argument. The main effects of the changes are:

1. to reduce the high estimates for the USA and the USSR for 1985 by a thousand apiece (head of page 6.);

2. to reduce the numbers of Western warheads in the grey-area (eurostrategic) by between 500 and a thousand;

3. according to the new tables which I have it would be necessary to say (first paragraph of my page 7, third line) that the U.K. will be controlling more warheads than the French in 1985;

4. (foot of same paragraph) New figures credit the USSR with more warheads for 1985.

But, as I have said, these changes do not make any difference to the argument.

Another paper which I have been sent, and which was commissioned by and has now been submitted to the State Department (dated December 1978), deals with the question of civil defence in nuclear war. I wrote in my aide memoire that if Salt II were negotiated both sides would have enough left in their nuclear armouries for reciprocal obliteration. You may have seen the phrase, with reference to 'theatre nuclear weapons' that in West Germany no village or town is more than 2 kt away from another. This new study shows that after what is assumed to be a successful Soviet first strike against the American central strategic forces, the US would still have enough left for a retaliatory attack to cause the total destruction of the USSR, e.g. the destruction of 80 percent of all Soviet cities with populations above 25,000; the massive destruction by fires that could not be fought due to radiation and lack of water; the immediate death of at least a hundred million Russians in spite of civil defence measures that they might be taking.

S. Zuckerman

4

Enhanced Radiation Weapons

In 1978 I wrote in *Human Rights*[1] that the decision by President Carter to postpone production of the enhanced radiation warhead or neutron bomb was, in the circumstances, absolutely right and thoroughly praise-worthy. Whatever the military attractions of a weapon of this kind, it was portrayed in the press as a weapon to hold up a massive Soviet tank incursion, encouraging the view that it was possible to have a limited battlefield nuclear exchange. It could in fact be represented not unfairly as a relatively minor piece of technological innovation in the nuclear weapons field, but there were obvious political dangers in introducing it into Europe at that time, when the fear that nuclear weapons might be used on German territory was starting to build up among Europeans.

It was right then that the leaders of the two superpowers should think very carefully before introducing qualitative or quantitative changes to their nuclear forces. President Carter had shown considerable courage already on the decision to cancel the B1 bomber programme. In the case of the neutron bomb, it would have been better if it had never been developed. The onus was being placed on the Soviet leaders to show restraint over those elements of their own forces, both nuclear and conventional, which caused apprehension in the minds of other countries. The neutron bomb was not a weapons system which came into the orbit of the then SALT talks. Nor did some of the other nuclear weapons – for example, the new Soviet SS-20 missile, which was arousing public concern. The debate about SS-20s broke out in 1977 and raised the whole question of a battlefield nuclear weapons strategy such as the neutron bomb programme.

It was Chancellor Schmidt, a genuine social democrat and a politician I much admire, who first raised the question of the so-called Euro-strategic balance in 1977. As the West German leader he argued strongly that the SS-20s should be discussed in future SALT negotiations. He believed that relying on a global balance of ballistic missiles fired from sea or from land silos in the Soviet Union and US was an insufficient safeguard for West

---

1 David Owen, *Human Rights* (London: Jonathan Cape, 1978), pp. 136–37.

Germany. The Soviet Union deploying SS-20s with a range capable of hitting any West German city from Warsaw Pact countries was, he felt, likely to change the balance in Europe and needed matching by an equivalent deployment in NATO countries in Europe. Once Schmidt had raised the issue it had to be grappled with by the Americans. It was true that new intercontinental nuclear missiles had an incredible accuracy and this new accuracy did challenge all previous strategic thinking. It questioned the vulnerability of second-strike land-based nuclear forces and emphasized once again the superiority of the submarine platform for a second-strike strategy. It also made it possible to target these ballistic missile weapon systems as part of a theatre strike strategy. The distinction between strategic weapons and theatre weapons had, therefore, become increasingly blurred. Yet although, in theory, the so-called theatre balance or Euro-strategic balance should have begun to lose its salience, European public opinion saw only the deployment of new Soviet missiles on European territory. Europeans were worried and therefore – not unreasonably – so was Helmut Schmidt.

Some idea of the contrast in thinking on these issues at this time can be seen by comparing the publicly stated views of three former recent British Chiefs of the Defence Staff. I had known all of them in the Ministry of Defence when I was dealing with Polaris in 1968–70 and as Foreign Secretary. I described their views in a book written in 1981 entitled *Face The Future*.[2]

Field Marshal Lord Carver, who argued publicly against a Trident system when he retired, wrote an article in the *New Statesman* on 15 August 1980, saying, 'We should take our share, as we do, of manning theatre nuclear weapon delivery systems, including those which use American warheads, so that the allies are seen to share the responsibility, the odium and the determination to use them if need be'. He warned against believing that even if the Soviets could be persuaded to disband their tactical or theatre nuclear armoury and retain only a strategic force directed at the USA and China, we should think of conventional warfare as being a comparatively harmless affair: 'The Yom Kippur War of 1973 reminded us of the purely military effects of modern warfare. In a contest that lasted less than three weeks, with limited forces in a limited area, both sides lost about half of their tanks and a quarter of their aircraft. To provide sufficient material to last out a prolonged major conventional war demands immensely expensive industrial effort, and its use would bring about a devastation in the area of operations.'

Admiral Lord Hill-Norton, a former Chairman of the Military Committee of NATO, who wanted Britain to buy Trident, thought it idle to suppose for

---

2 David Owen, *Face the Future* (London: Jonathan Cape, 1981), pp. 464–68.

a second that we could fight a battlefield nuclear war. He wrote in *The Times* on 18 August 1980, 'I believe with Hermann Kahn, that once you cross the nuclear threshold you have taken an irreversible step which is almost bound to lead to a strategic nuclear exchange, which in turn is almost bound to lead to the end of civilization [...] I will go to my grave being certain that if you let off a neutron bomb anywhere in Europe you have gone 90 per cent of the way to triggering a strategic nuclear exchange.' The real as opposed to the propagandist argument against the neutron bomb is that it does make it more likely that a battlefield nuclear exchange will be started.

Air Marshal Sir Neil Cameron, in a lecture to the Royal Society of Arts on 30 April 1980, also criticized the concept of limited nuclear war when he said that 'so-called battlefield or nuclear weapons are not means of winning military victories. That is a conclusion to which NATO has inevitably come, through the work of its Nuclear Planning Group over a dozen years or more ago [...] The warfighting school of nuclear theorists has lost the argument in the West. The role of nuclear weapons is to deter war – all war – not just nuclear war, between East and West.'

Scepticism towards the current British nuclear strategy, which they were expected to carry out, has been present among officers in the armed forces, quite apart from scientists such as Lord Zuckerman, for three decades. Furthermore, a number of very senior British political leaders have held the private belief that it was never credible to expect them as political leaders to actually authorize a battlefield, theatre or even strategic nuclear exchange, although they have been prepared to give the impression that, if forced by an overwhelming threat, they would have authorized the use of nuclear weapons.

The theory of nuclear deterrence still remains, on the face of it, widely held, but fewer people now believe that we could survive a nuclear exchange, and the UK no longer builds its defence strategy on the possibility of a limited nuclear war. In the 1970s and 1980s, as part of a tactical nuclear weapon strategy, some strategists both wanted the neutron bomb and accepted the concept of the Euro-strategic balance, advocating land-based cruise and Pershing missiles in Europe. Nevertheless it was accepted that there was a need for arms control negotiation and that it could not be perfectly balanced and symmetrical at all stages. President Carter's decision ensured that the neutron bomb was never deployed. Theatre and battlefield nuclear weapons began to be withdrawn and the Euro-strategic nuclear balance is long forgotten. President Reagan and President Gorbachev achieved very satisfactory arms control agreements.

Perhaps the debate I championed inside government in 1977–79 helped to bring about the situation that exists today in the UK, where there are no longer any battlefield or purely theatre nuclear weapons.

The papers included here are also important in showing the extent of the dissent within governments pledged to act together in NATO. The then US Secretary of State believed that we needed ERWs 'like a hole in the head'. Few wanted them in Europe, particularly in Germany, from whose territory they would probably have been fired. In the UK the government only went along with deployment because of solidarity with the US. Yet for a time it looked as if we might have to agree deployment against our wishes and accept ERWs as part of the NATO armoury. Then, just as the German government, and particularly Chancellor Schmidt, began to try to convince the public of the need to deploy them, President Carter changed his position and decided to cancel. Apart from the slight embarrassment, most politicians were delighted and few in the military shed any tears.

This little vignette of NATO in practice represents another example of how weapons system deployment can be driven by scientists and a relatively small number of military leaders, who are instinctively ready to endorse the most up-to-date and sophisticated technology, irrespective of its likely impact on public opinion, or even its military relevance.

Denis Healey has spelt out some of the political complexities: 'This is not, after all, to do with technology; this is to do with how likely you think a certain contingency, how you think the other side will react to their knowledge that you have certain capabilities. That's what it's all about. It's nothing whatever to do with scientists or, with respect, with generals.'[3]

We need to remember that the Soviet Sputnik in 1957 launched the era of the Intercontinental Ballistic Missile (ICBM), and that the development of Multiple Independently Targetable Re-Entry Vehicles (MIRVs) forced the pace of Anti-Ballistic Missile (ABM) defence networks, feeding the concept that we did not have to accept Mutual Assured Destruction (MAD) and that a nuclear war-fighting strategy could 'prevail'. This was replaced for a while by the belief that MAD would ensure 'survival'.

The lesson from the ERW episode of 30 years ago – yet, I fear, to be fully learnt – is that political leaders must now do everything in their power to get rid of all nuclear weapons, through step-by-step negotiations.

---

3 Quoted in Peter Hennessy, *Muddling Through: Power, Politics and the Quality of Government in Post-War Britain* (London: Indigo, 1997), p. 124.

DOCUMENT 43

TO IMMEDIATE FCO TEL NO 1456 OF 29 SEPTEMBER 1977

FOLLOWING FOR THE PRIME MINISTER FROM SECRETARY OF STATE (TO BE TAKEN BY PS/NO 10 ONLY AND WITH ALL COPIES)

NUCLEAR MATTERS

1. I have had two absolutely private talks, the first yesterday with Cy Vance and the second today with Henry Kissinger, which I am reporting immediately because I thought that you would like to know in particular about Henry Kissinger's thinking. This is obviously a very sensitive area and is relevant to other matters on which I agree totally with your views.

ENHANCED RADIATION WEAPONS (ERWS)

2. Cy said that we needed ERWs 'like a hole in the head'. It was not worth taking on a major public dispute over this. The President was getting fed up with appearing 'aggressive' and his personal inclination was not to take the lead in pressing for ERWs though he would agree if the NATO allies openly asked for ERWs. Speaking entirely personally, I said that if the Alliance decided that it did not want ERWs we might all the same get a quid pro quo from the Russians or contemplate using it for the proposed treaty banning new nuclear weapons. Gromyko had a tough denunciation in his UN speech on the 'neutron bomb'. Cy too thought this could be part of a trade-off, and is clearly considering using it in the context of MBFR. I said that I thought that the Germans might well be under-estimating the effects on German public opinion of a decision by the Alliance in favour and I mentioned Egon Bahr's views. Cy said to me that he thought that Brzezinski took a rather harder line and you may have found this during your talks with him. Cy also said that Simonet had expressed some anxiety to him here about the 'neutron bomb'. Max van der Stoel is opposed as is K. B. Anderson; both of them raised the issue with me.

3. Somewhat to my surprise Henry Kissinger also took the same line in opposing ERWs. He commented that even though he was not normally thought of as a moralist he blanched at the prospect of having to defend them publicly as a theatre weapon and they were not necessary anyhow. This is the sort of area the President could make a gesture at little cost.

SALT.

4. Cy Vance confirmed that, in the negotiations, they were close to agreeing that a range limit of 600kms should be put on cruise missiles, for

an introductory period of three years. The Soviet Union's prime concern was the risk of allowing cruise missiles to get into the hands of the Germans. I mentioned my wish not to close the option on submarine launched cruise missiles which, since they can be fixed with adaptations from existing torpedo tubes, is an option worth considering for all our nuclear submarines. I asked why we could not keep this option open, while possibly closing the option on land based cruise missiles if they were vital for SALT. Cy Vance said that he thought that the whole concept of cruise missiles needed a fundamental rethink but every time that one asked the question the military insisted vociferously on being allowed to continue to test and that the 600 kilometer limit was as much as they would accept. We touched on the question of the maintenance of our own deterrent capacity in the context of no transfer and I said that my private view was that so long as France retained a nuclear deterrent we needed to keep ours but I said that no decisions were yet needed on any sort of replacement for Polaris.

5. Henry Kissinger was clearly well informed on SALT and the Administration want his support. He was seeing Cy Vance on Friday. He warned that there were influential people in the Administration who would like us to cease to be a nuclear power. He personally did not hold this view, both because of the French and because he is genuinely convinced of the value of having multiple strategic decision-making centres. In respect of SALT his earnest advice is that we should assume realistically that any temporary agreement will end up by being permanent and this applies in particular to the idea of a three year limitation on cruise to 600 kms range. Exclusion from cruise missile technology would, in his view, be a very heavy price for us to pay.

Henry is also convinced that the main anxiety of the Soviet Union is the possible transfer of land-based cruise missile technology into German hands. He commented that this was a 'central gut issue' for the Soviet Union. I floated on him the possibility of our aiming to keep open the option that sea launched cruise missile technology might be restricted to the UK and France: he thought that this might be saleable with the Soviet Union. Restriction on land based cruise missiles for three years would be giving the Soviets enough as it was. We tossed around a formula on the lines that the ban would 'not exclude the transfer of technology relating to cruise missiles for submarine launch to the two existing nuclear weapon states with which the United States already has technology exchange agreements and which currently operate nuclear submarines in a strategic role'.

6. My personal belief is that we could if necessary make a deal on these lines more attractive by considering some limitations on the total number of submarines.

7. Incidentally, in more general discussion over lunch, Henry also made the somewhat contradictory point that range limitations on cruise would be extremely difficult to monitor.

8. I know that we are due to discuss these nuclear issues with you on 24 October but things may move faster here than we expect. I would be prepared to stay to talk to anyone in the US Administration while I am in the United States if this were to be helpful. But this will mean delaying my departure from Chicago. I am due to leave Chicago at 2050 hrs local time (29 September).

DOCUMENT 44

Summary Record of a discussion between the Foreign and Commonwealth Secretary and the Secretary of State for Defence at the Foreign and Commonwealth Office on Thursday, 2 March 1978 at 9.15 a.m.

Those present:

The Rt Hon Dr David Owen MP   The Rt Hon Fred Mulley MP
Sir M Palliser   Sir Neil Cameron
Sir A Duff   Sir F Cooper
Mr E A J Fergusson   Mr R L L Facer

Nuclear Test

Mr Mulley mentioned his minute to the Prime Minister of 1 March. Dr Owen said that he was content with the proposal but he wondered whether, if there were to be a meeting of Cabinet on 23 March, it would not be better to defer telling them till then [I have spoken to the Cabinet Office: it is. by no means certain that there will be a meeting of Cabinet on 23 March; this is the day on which the House is likely to go into recess with Question Time between 11.00 and 12.00 and, possibly, the Prime Minister answering questions at 11.45].

ERWs

Concern was expressed about the timing of a decision on ERWs, though it looked as though the Americans felt that they could go ahead with decisions on production without putting at risk the SALT and CTB negotiations. There was however a danger that with SALT in trouble a decision on ERWs might be seen as a withdrawal from the general dialogue on disarmament. German attitudes were important but Herr Apel had not yet had time to establish his own firm views. Sir N Cameron referred to information that Chancellor Schmidt had recently written to the US President giving a qualified approval to a decision on production. Dr Owen said that in New York Mr Vance, who was no enthusiast for ERWs, was prepared to go along with a decision to produce them. There was likely to be trouble with the Senate Armed Services Committee and a hawkish line on ERWs might allow the US Administration to be more dove-like over SALT and CTB. Above all Dr Owen felt that the decision should be got out of the way before the UN Special Session on Disarmament in May, though a decision in favour of ERW production could be used by the Soviet Union as an excuse for getting out of negotiations on other aspects of arms control.

There was general agreement that a decision in favour of the production

274

of ERWs should be defended on the basis that NATO would go ahead only if it could not get measures of global disarmament. Moreover (Dr Owen having expressed his serious concern at the build-up of Soviet tank forces), the quid pro quo in any bargaining with the Soviet Union over the deployment of ERWs should not just be the SS-20 but should be widened to cover tanks and, what followed logically, elements of the MBFR negotiations (though Mr Mulley was concerned that we should not make further unrequited concessions).

The immediate timing was difficult, with the joint meeting of Cabinet and NEC on 13 March, the Defence Debate probably on 13 and 14 March and the Prime Minister's restricted meeting of Ministers on 17 March, followed by a NATO Meeting on 22 March. It was agreed that it would be appropriate for a shorter version of the paper prepared by the Ministry of Defence to go forward to the Prime Minister as a joint paper by the Foreign and Commonwealth Secretary and the Secretary of State for Defence. The paper should indicate our preparedness to go along with a production decision in favour of ERW provided that the possible quid pro quo for foregoing deployment could be widened, as indicated above. Talks at official level should take place urgently with the FRG on a bilateral basis so that a line could be agreed before a further bilateral meeting with the United States permitting the FRG, US and UK to hold to a coordinated view in NATO. There was no doubt that a decision in favour could create domestic political problems and this was why it was so important to set a decision on ERWs in the context of our overall disarmament posture in the run-up to UNSSD. <u>Dr Owen</u> commented that, in the light of his earlier discussions with Mr Secretary Vance he would be prepared to set out our views in a message to him.

The Horn of Africa

There was a general discussion of the situation in the Horn with particular emphasis on the sensitivities of the Kenyan Government to any supply of arms to Somalia. Reference was made to our security understandings with the Kenyans (Dr Owen said that he expected Vice President Moi to raise this with the Prime Minister) and to possible Kenyan requests for military supplies, whether or not they had the capacity to absorb them (Mr Mulley said that he would be seeing the Kenyan Permanent Secretary of Defence on Wednesday 8 March). The visit was a useful opportunity to steady the Kenyans down. There was agreement that our present stance vis-a-vis the United States over a naval presence in the Indian Ocean (both in terms of naval units and of Diego Garcia) was the right one. <u>Dr Owen</u> said that he was thinking of getting one of the Conservative MPs who had questioned him at the IPU Meeting about Kenya and Somalia to put down an Early Day Motion in the House of Commons on the Kenyan dimension to the Horn of Africa problem.

DOP

There was an inconclusive discussion about the role of DOP, particularly its role over major defence equipment programmes and the opportunity which Ministers should have to consider them at the conceptual stage before operational requirements were developed and commitments entered into (this came up in the context of the Harrier/Jaguar replacement aircraft). There was a general feeling (though not firm agreement) that questions of this kind needed serious ministerial discussion at an early stage; DOP might be one forum; alternatively such questions might be discussed in the small group of Ministers under the Prime Minister's Chairmanship which discussed nuclear issues. Mr Mulley said that he would be glad at any stage to arrange a presentation on the Harrier/Jaguar replacement before decisions had been taken about the available options.

Arms Sales

Mr Mulley raised the question of the possible Vosper Thornycroft contract to supply a frigate to Argentina. In discussion it was recognised that no-one could be enthusiastic about such a prospective contract, for instance, because of the improved military capability which it would give the Argentines, but on the other hand, if the United Kingdom did not supply vessels of this kind they were readily available to the Argentines from other NATO allies such as the Germans, French or Italians, who would be glad to reap the commercial benefits. Dr Owen said that despite his lack of enthusiasm he would not fight against the proposal.

General

There was brief reference to the UK proposals for UNSSD and to the Secretary of State's paper for DOP on Belize.

As the meeting broke up Dr Owen asked Mr Mulley how he would feel about a suggestion that, in the context of a comprehensive settlement to the Arab/Israel dispute Jordan, Israel and Egypt might be brought within NATO. This was, he said, one of his maverick ideas. There was no discussion of this point.

DOCUMENT 45

10 DOWNING STREET

From the Private Secretary   30 March 1978

Dear Ewen

As the Prime Minister has asked Dr Owen to see Mr Warren Christopher, President Carter's Special Emissary, on Saturday, you should have some account of what happened in Washington on the subject of ER/RBWs.

This subject was discussed at a meeting the Prime Minister had with Vice President Mondale and others at 1130 on Tuesday 28 March at the White House, following a private briefing of the Prime Minister by Secretary Vance. At this meeting the Prime Minister had been informed of a negative decision by the President on ER/RBWs. The Prime Minister had told Secretary Vance that he wondered very much whether Mr Christopher should be instructed to tell Chancellor Schmidt that the President was "leaning" to the abandonment of ER/RBWs in view of the high probability that this would leak in Bonn. The Prime Minister had said it would be better to tell Chancellor Schmidt the decision straight out. Mr Vance had said he would talk again to the President and give him the Prime Minister's advice.

It was suggested on the American side that the intention had been to give Chancellor Schmidt the feeling that he was being genuinely consulted and also to leave some flexibility in case Chancellor Schmidt had fundamental objections to the President's decision. The Prime Minister said that the Americans were covered against this since Chancellor Schmidt had always said that the United States must itself decide about production of ER/RBWs. He said that Herr Genscher would be difficult but that Chancellor Schmidt would be relieved by a negative decision. It was important that the Americans presented their decision in such a way that it was clear that they knew their own minds and did not appear to be yielding to Soviet pressure.

The discussion of this topic concluded with a decision to obtain further instructions from the President and a request from the Prime Minister to be informed in advance if the Americans decided to make an announcement.

Copies of this letter go to Roger Facer (Ministry of Defence) and Martin Vile (Cabinet Office). It is strictly for the personal information of the Secretaries of State and Permanent Secretaries concerned.

Yours sincerely
JOHN MEADWAY

DOCUMENT 46

TOP SECRET

PRIME MINISTER
PM/78/33

1. Warren Christopher conveyed to me privately this morning the message from the President about ERW. Initially only the US Ambassador (at Christopher's request) was with us but I asked Sir Michael Palliser to join us after the first ten minutes.

2. Christopher said that he was telling us the same as he had told Schmidt and Genscher: namely that the President, after careful consideration of all the arguments, was "leaning towards" a decision not to proceed with ERW production. Although that was the way Christopher put it, the rest of our conversation was based on the clear assumption by Christopher not only that the President had decided against production but that this decision would be made public on 5/6 April.

3. Christopher said that there were four main reasons for what represented a very personal decision by President Carter:

(1) There was still substantial disagreement within the Alliance. In particular ERW were opposed by four countries, in descending order of strength of view: Netherlands, Norway, Denmark, Belgium;

(2) The US military establishment did not regard this as a make or break issue. The weapon only added marginal improvement to NATO defence;

(3) That sector of public opinion which, though sceptical, could usually be brought to accept the need for the alliance defence effort would not be convinced of the need for ERW: such potential benefit as ERW might produce would therefore be offset by loss of support in this sector of public opinion;

(4) The notion of an ERW/SS20 trade off would carry no conviction, since it was clear that the Russians would not agree to it.

There was also in the President's judgement the general feeling that the present psychological climate including the state of the SALT negotiations, the approach of UNSSOD etc was fundamentally wrong for the taking of a decision to go ahead.

4. German reactions. Genscher had received the decision coolly and had indeed said remarkably little. (I commented that this was typical Genscher and too much should not be read into it.) He had referred to the work the

Germans had done to prepare their opinion for the opposite decision. He had urged that no decision should be announced before he himself had been able to visit Washington; and he proposed accordingly to bring forward his already planned visit to 4 April. Genscher said, as subsequently did Schmidt, that the German Government had always maintained that this was a decision to be taken by the US President.

5. Schmidt made a good deal more of the extent to which he had had to prepare German opinion for the opposite decision. Some Germans would welcome the new decision. But he thought the majority would not. But on the whole Schmidt had given Christopher a slightly easier ride than he had expected. He had warmly endorsed Genscher's desire to visit Washington before the decision was announced: and had asked that nothing should be said by the Americans before then to the rest of the Alliance.

6. I said that we too regarded this as a decision for the US President to take. We would do all we could to support his decision. (At this point I asked Sir Michael Palliser to join us.) During the rest of the conversation a certain amount of the foregoing was repeated by Christopher but we concentrated mainly on the crucial importance of the public presentation of President Carter's decision. We suggested that the President should explain quite frankly that this had been a finely balanced decision and that he had indeed come close to deciding to go ahead with ERW; and that he had examined it against the whole background of the military and political situation within the Alliance and of its broad defence posture.

7. I emphasised the importance of opinion in both Europe and the US being convinced that the President was on top of his relationship with the USSR. People must see that there was hope of real progress in the super-power relationship; and that the decision fitted into this pattern.

8. In this context we discussed whether it would be helpful presentationally for the announcement of the decision to coincide with that of a Carter/Brezhnev summit meeting. But Christopher concluded that, in the eyes of American opinion, this would look too much like a trade off. Clearly the Carter/Brezhnev summit, when announced, would encourage hopes of success in SALT. The impending Vance/Gromyko meeting (of which we were given details separately) would however suffice at this stage to sustain those hopes without giving unnecessary ammunition to the hawks.

9. We also agreed that there could be advantage in the President indicating that a negative decision now need not permanently foreclose the ERW option. There were at present three main aspects to arms control – SALT, CTB, and MBFR. We wanted to see progress in all three. In particular we wanted progress in MBFR (where we would soon be tabling our

new initiative) and over the Soviet preponderance e.g. in tank strength, including the deployment of even more powerful tanks. If there was not satisfactory progress in these three areas the ERW decision might have to be reconsidered.

10. I said that while I thought that at the political level the balance of the argument was well understood and people accepted that it could go one way or the other, there had come to be general agreement amongst the military within the Alliance that a favourable decision was desirable. It was therefore important that the decision should be carefully explained to them (and especially to General Haig, who had publicly supported ERW). We must try to avoid any impression of major disagreement with the military leadership. In reply to my question Christopher said that the US Chiefs of Staff did not regard ERWs as essential; but saw their value as largely marginal.

11. I agreed that we would treat the decision with the strictest secrecy until we heard further from the Americans about it. But I pointed out that Christopher's visit here and the fact that ERW was probably the main subject was already under discussion in the press. Both in the Alliance and in the Community we and the Germans could expect questioning from our partners: and you and I would be meeting our Community opposite numbers in Copenhagen at the end of next week – though it looked as if the President's decision would by then have been announced.

12. We then discussed briefly what line to take with the press. Christopher emphasised the secrecy of his communication. We agreed that we would take the same broad line as he had done in Germany ie that we had discussed a wide range of subjects including the Middle East, East Mediterranean, Africa and Alliance questions. If asked specifically whether we had discussed ERW we would decline to disclose what individual questions within these broad headings had been discussed. (This is not too plausible: but I think the only way we can in this situation deal with the press is to belt up tight.)

13. In view of the American emphasis on total secrecy I am for the time being only sending a copy of this minute for his personal information to the Secretary of State for Defence.

DAVID OWEN

1 April 1978
Foreign and Commonwealth Office

DOCUMENT 47

To: Prime Minister James Callaghan, London   6 April 1978

Dear Jim,

I have reached a decision concerning enhanced radiation weapons which is set forth below. It will be released subject to formal consultation in the North Atlantic Council on Friday 7 April. In my judgement, it represents the best solution for the present of the various factors and forces that impinge on this sensitive issue. I would hope that it meets with your approval and that you will find suitable opportunity to express your support.

I have decided to defer production of weapons with enhanced radiation effects. The ultimate decision regarding the incorporation of enhanced radiation features into our modernized battlefield weapons will be made later, and will be influenced by the degree to which the Soviet Union show restraint in its conventional and nuclear arms programs and force deployments affecting the security of the United States and Western Europe.

Accordingly, I have ordered the Defense Department to proceed with the modernization of the Lance missile nuclear warhead and the 8-inch weapon system, leaving open the option of installing the enhanced radiation elements.

The United States has consulted with its allies in the North Atlantic Council on this decision, and will continue to discuss with them appropriate arms control measures to be pursued with the Soviet Union.

We will continue to move ahead with our allies to modernize and strengthen our military capabilities, both conventional and nuclear. We are determined to do whatever is necessary to assure our collective security and the forward defense of Europe.

Sincerely,

Jimmy Carter

5

The Future

The decision of President Obama's new administration in early 2009 to 'press the reset button' on the American relationship with Russia represents a major change in US policy. There are signs that it is being followed by a change in UK policy and in NATO policy as well. The US change was announced in February 2009 by Vice-President Biden at the annual strategic conference in Munich. Two years before, President Putin's speech at the same conference had warned that US plans 'to expand certain elements of the anti-missile defence system to Europe cannot help but disturb us. Who needs the next step of what would be, in this case, an inevitable arms race?' When the President of the Russian Federation, Dmitry Medvedev, met with President Obama in London around the G20 Financial Summit meeting, it was agreed to draft a treaty on reducing both countries' nuclear stockpiles at an accelerated rate in the hope that it could be signed by the two Presidents in the summer of 2009 and ratified by both countries' legislatures before the existing START lapses, after 15 years, in December 2009. That treaty, which was signed by President George H. W. Bush in 1991 before the collapse of the Soviet Union, came into force in 1994 and required both sides to reduce their arsenals to 6,000 warheads. The less binding deal agreed by George W. Bush and Vladimir Putin in Moscow in 2002 will form the basis for any new deal. Both countries then agreed to reduce their deployed nuclear warheads by the year 2012 to between 1,700 and 2,200 each. There is every reason to believe that this will become part of a new SALT deal, and with reduced numbers. It would be wise for the US and Russia to proceed quickly to ratify this limited deal.

The CTBT is a high priority for President Obama, but it is unlikely to receive bipartisan support in Congress. Continuing negotiations on more comprehensive and deeper missile reductions will hopefully follow in the year 2010 or 2011. This is a sound strategy with Russia, consolidating and building on the past.

There are a number of other interesting proposals, including a fissile material cut-off treaty, being pushed by the UK, which could contribute to making reductions in nuclear weapons irreversible; a Russian proposal for a joint missile defence towards the Middle East, including radar sites in Southern Russia; further elimination of theatre nuclear weapons for those countries that still maintain the concept; and an NWS Conference on how to verify nuclear disarmament. All of these and more can contribute in an incremental way. But we need to be seen to be adopting these measures progressively, in a step-by-step approach, carefully and prudently.

One of the lessons I learnt from President Carter's approach to the Soviet Union in 1977 was that it would have been wiser for Carter in his first year as President to pick up in his proposed treaty Kissinger's 1974 protocol, the Vladivostok Accords, with the Soviet Foreign Minister Andrei Gromyko, and have that ratified by Congress, rather than attempting to put on the table new and more far-reaching ideas. When Gromyko rejected this new approach the US Secretary of State, Cyrus Vance, attempted to move back to Kissinger's formulation, but Gromyko angrily rejected this and for some months all strategic negotiations stalled. I visited Moscow in the autumn of 1977, the first visit by a UK Foreign Secretary since 1971, and spent much of my time trying to convince Brezhnev and Gromyko that Carter and Vance were totally genuine in their wish to negotiate larger cuts and that there was no hidden agenda behind their proposals.

The opportunity for bipartisan support in Congress exists, but it is fragile and it can easily disappear as the political fortunes of a new President wax and wane. It was a sound decision by President Obama to cancel the plan of his predecessor, George W. Bush, to place ten ground-based interceptors in Poland and an advanced radar in the Czech Republic. It was, however, unfortunate that the announcement came on 17 September 2009, the seventieth anniversary of the Soviet invasion of Poland. Polish sensitivities towards Russia are important and need to be handled with care. Nevertheless it is a fact that the radar and interceptors planned in central Europe by 2015 had already been delayed by several years because of the Polish and Czech ratification process, so that there would have been no missile defence system in place to protect against possible Iranian intercontinental missiles until at least 2017. Instead Robert M. Gates, the US Secretary of Defense under both Presidents George W. Bush and Barack Obama, who recommended the initial deployment to Bush, also recommended this new plan to Obama. He has publicly and rationally explained why he changed his mind 'in favour of a vastly more suitable approach'.[1]

This new plan, which has the unanimous support of the senior military

---

1 Robert M. Gates, 'A better missile defence', *International Herald Tribune*, Global edition, 21 September 2009, p. 8.

US leadership, in its first sea-based phase will have the SM-3 interceptor missiles deployed in 2011 and its land-based second phase operational by 2015 on the ground in southern and central Europe. Instead of having a mere ten ground-based interceptors targeted on Iranian intercontinental missiles, which have yet to be developed, the new system will have a fully developed missile defence system in place at least four years earlier and be able to shoot down existing short- and medium-range Iranian missiles. In particular it will deal with the Shahab-3 missile which can reach Israel, Saudi Arabia and Egypt and which, according to both American and Israeli intelligence, is the missile most likely to be first equipped with a nuclear warhead – that is, if the present Iranian nuclear warhead development programme continues despite world criticism and potentially tougher sanctions. It was important that President Medvedev conceded in New York on 23 September 2009 in relation to Iran that 'in some cases, sanctions are inevitable'. There is good evidence that Iran did suspend its nuclear weapons work for a while in 2003.

The Russian national interest, which almost always in the end motivates their foreign policy, should be in favour of these deployments. They tend to believe, perhaps realistically, that nothing will now stop some Iranian nuclear enrichment and this is compatible with civil nuclear power, not just the making of nuclear weapons. It will be far easier for President Obama to restrain a pre-emptive Israeli attack and Saudi Arabia and Egypt acquiring nuclear weapons if by 2011 there is in place a credible missile defence system covering these countries. Russia has every interest in containing Iran even if they disagree as to how that containment can be achieved. Perhaps the best we can achieve with the present regime in Iran is that they reach a stage technically that they can produce nuclear warheads but they do not physically manufacture them. That was the position held for some years by both India and Israel; at least the world could not prove that they had nuclear weapons and they preferred not to confirm their possession.

Some Republicans are trying to attack President Obama for his decisions in the nuclear field in the mistaken belief that they represent weakness in the face of Russian protests. I do not believe that this criticism can be sustained on any rational basis. President Obama had made it clear publicly that he does not criticize Bush's original decision in relation to Poland and the Czech Republic, and nor does he believe Russian protests that deployment in central Europe would have provided any credible threat to Russia. Nevertheless it is a fact that the Russian military had persuaded President Medvedev and Prime Minister Putin that this deployment did provide a threat, in that the missiles could be turned around to target Russian missile sites. This fear, whether paranoid or not, was blocking further progress on arms control, and the reality of resetting a relationship is that it does involve changing some of the parameters. Glib talk about Russia and the US going back to a Cold War have even less credibility in 2009 than when it was fashionable a few years ago.

What is now potentially opening up is a return to the sort of confidence-building negotiations on nuclear arms that have long existed between Russia and Republican as well as Democrat administrations in the US. The seeds of an opportunity to move forward on more far-reaching agreements are now in place. Many difficult questions arise as to whether it might be sensible to site interceptors and radars in and around Europe capable of shooting down a potential Iranian intercontinental missile bound for Washington, DC. Much will depend in the next few years on whether President Obama's initiative towards Iran succeeds in enabling both countries to 'unclench the fist'.

Missile defence is an issue on which Moscow and Washington should be able to agree if the political and strategic climate starts to improve. The problem over missile defence is that it has been the subject of political emotion ever since President Reagan's original concept became labelled 'Star Wars'. The truth is that Reagan was right to draw attention to the need to grapple with missile defence and missile elimination if we were ever to move away from the doctrine of Mutually Assured Destruction (MAD). In his somewhat simplistic way, Reagan was drawing attention to the reality that if there are nuclear weapons in the world it is wiser to try and develop a defence system to shoot them down than rely on a fire on warning system. The problem with Reagan's speeches was that they made light of the technical problems of developing such a system in space to shoot down intercontinental missiles. America was then, and still is today, many years away from developing such a system. What has happened is that America has developed a fairly effective way of destroying short-to-medium-range missiles and this reality rather than the dream is what we should be discussing in practical terms and without the emotional overlay of 'Star Wars'.

But missile defence is only a stepping stone towards a far more important long-term goal and that is the elimination of nuclear weapons. This aspiration has many champions today in the US among the realist school of politicians, not least Henry Kissinger and George Schulz. When President Reagan tried, he failed to convince Margaret Thatcher. Now President Obama is already under attack for trying. To take one example, *Newsweek* published an article on 14 September 2009 by Jonathan Tepperman, entitled 'Learning to Love the Bomb; Obama wants to rid the world of nuclear weapons. Why that might be a big mistake.' The author calls for a frank debate but his treatment of what he calls 'that mother of all nuclear stand offs: the Cuban missile crisis' is superficial in the extreme.

We know today a lot more of how close the world came to a nuclear disaster in 1963. Quite apart from Robert Kennedy's famous words soon after the missile crisis that if seven of the distinguished people advising the President around the table in the White House had themselves been President there would have been a nuclear exchange, we also know more from recently published documents. During the night of 26 October 1962, Soviet troops in Cuba moved three FKR cruise missiles, with 14 kt nuclear warheads, to within 25 km of the US naval base at Guantanamo Bay. On the morning of Saturday, 27 October Secretary of Defense, Robert McNamara, asked what the Chiefs of Staff had in mind when they wrote about 'early and timely execution' of the air strike plan against Cuba. The US Air Force chief, General Curtis LeMay gruffly replied: 'Attacking Sunday [next day] or Monday'. Fortunately Khrushchev had already sent an urgent cable to the Soviet commander in Cuba: 'It is categorically confirmed that it is forbidden to use nuclear weapons from the missiles, FKRs and Lunas without approval from Moscow. Confirm receipt.'[2]

I first wrote about the significance of the Cuban missile crisis in 1972[3] and I have never doubted that it represented one of the times when the world came very close to a nuclear exchange. This crisis took place very largely under the public gaze while President Kennedy privately overrode his military advisers with the constant support of Robert McNamara. Kennedy chose a maritime blockade rather than an attack on Cuba and he was ready to give Khrushchev some political leeway to withdraw his missiles. Kennedy promised Khrushchev that the US would never attack Cuba – necessary given Kennedy's earlier involvement in 1961 in the failed invasion of Cuba at the Bay of Pigs. But he also went further and offered secretly that if Khrushchev withdrew the missiles, some months later he would withdraw the US Jupiter missiles in Turkey.

I have also written about Kennedy's health[4] and formed the judgement that he was in far better medical condition to handle the missile crisis in 1962 than ever he would have been in 1961. For example, there is little doubt that when he first met Khrushchev in Vienna in June 1961 he was given by Dr Jacobson an intravenous injection of amphetamine which contributed, along with his Addison's disease and painful back, to a disastrous meeting. This was followed by an underestimation of Kennedy's qualities by

---

2 David Owen, *In Sickness and In Power: Illness in Heads of Government during the Last 100 Years* (London: Methuen, 2008), pp. 181–186.
3 David Owen, *The Politics of Defence* (London: Jonathan Cape, 1972), pp. 35–51.
4 Owen, *In Sickness and In Power*, pp. 164–180.

Khrushchev which led him to deploy missiles and nuclear warheads in Cuba in the spring of 1962.

There have been other occasions when because the nuclear trigger was in reality a 'hair trigger' the world could have been plunged into a nuclear exchange almost by accident. I myself experienced a troubling incident involving the British nuclear deterrent in the late 1960s and I have never forgotten it. More recently, some Russians have revealed how, in 1983, one Soviet, Lieutenant-Colonel Stanislav Petrov, acting on instinct, overrode the warning systems that could have triggered the firing of nuclear weapons while Yuri Andropov, the Soviet leader, was on a kidney dialysis machine in a Moscow sanatorium.[5] Public literature covers a number of other incidents. Anyone who seriously argues that there was stability during the Cold War due to the possession of nuclear missiles by the adversaries is quite simply living in cloud cuckoo land, and it is vital that these bogus arguments are revealed for what they are: an attempt to perpetuate a dangerous myth often by people who did not live their adult life during that period. We had to grapple with the reality of nuclear weapons, but we would have been better off without them. As I argued as Foreign Secretary in a book called *Human Rights*, 'we must keep stressing the appalling magnitude of the problems of the arms race and the imperative need to achieve speedier progress. Complacency in this area of human activity can easily trigger our own destruction. The risks are real, the dangers ever-present.'[6]

For all these reasons I believe it is essential that President Obama's courage in starting to deal with the massive problem of eliminating nuclear weapons in their entirety is fully supported. If progress is made prior to the NPT conference in 2010 between the US and Russia, then a far sharper focus will fall on what the UK intends to do about its minimum deterrent. At the very least a signal has now been sent from the UK government, by postponing the Trident replacement 'initial gate decision' due in September 2009 until May 2010 and saying they are minded to build only three ballistic missile submarines. That means that far from pushing ahead regardless, any newly elected UK government will have the opportunity to look afresh at the 2007 decision to build a third generation of four SSBNs equipped with a US ballistic missile and UK warhead. I discussed some of these issues in a speech in the House of Lords in March 2009 (Annex E).

The cost of the Trident replacement programme is spiralling. By October 2008 around £3 million had already been spent on the Vanguard Life

5 Gordon S, Barrass, *The Great Cold War. A Journey Through the Hall of Mirrors* (Stanford, CA: Stanford University Press, 2009), pp. 1–2.
6 David Owen, *Human Rights* (London: Jonathan Cape, 1978), p. 147.

Optimization Programme (VLOP) designed to provide a five-year life extension to the existing SSBN fleet, and it has 'the potential for rapid cost and risk growth'.[7] The Permanent Under-Secretary to the Ministry of Defence, Sir Bill Jeffrey, in evidence to the Public Accounts Committee on 19 November 2008, referred to the 2006 costings as only 'ball-park estimates'. In July 2008 a senior defence official, David Gould, told the arms industry that the government plans to spend £3 billion replacing the current nuclear warhead arsenal and that it will replace 'the warhead and the missiles'.[8] No longer is it credible to depict these issues as being closed when in fact the minds of politicians are much more open. Current warhead designs are likely to last only into the 2020s and given the experience with Chevaline no grounds for optimism exist as to its costing being controlled, let alone the ability of Aldermaston to ensure it is 'conducted within the UK's commitments under the Comprehensive Test Ban Treaty'. Already it appears that the Atomic Weapons Establishment (AWE) has some doubts regarding how long this can be sustained through its test data and computer modelling techniques. The programme within the US to extend the life of the Trident D5 missile to around 2042[9] to match the life of their Ohio-class submarines is one the UK has already signed up for at a cost of £250 million.[10] We are told that a decision to acquire a successor missile is unlikely until the 2020s, but these costings are going to be in dollars and we have already seen a depreciation of 30 per cent in the value of the pound during the period 2007–2009. Foreign exchange costs may or may not push the sterling estimates substantially higher, making this a bad time to sign contracts for long-lead items. As for a new nuclear reactor to power the new SSBNs, it will either be a variant of the current PWR2 or a new PWR3 reactor. Rolls Royce had an initial contract in 2007 and the design has to be 'completed by the middle of the next decade'.[11] A decision is claimed to be required around 2009 on the development of the reactor core manufacturing plant in Derby. In 2002 the Devonport nuclear facility was reported to be £933 million (33 per cent) over its approved budget,[12] a sign that we are no nearer to developing techniques in the UK to keep cost overruns under control.

I hope that anyone who reads this book, even if they are committed members of CND, feels some sense of relief that while they were legitimately

---

7 National Audit Office Report by the Comptroller and Auditor General, *Ministry of Defence: The UK's Future Nuclear Deterrent Capability*, The Stationery Office, 5 November 2008, p. 13.
8 *Guardian*, 25 July 2008.
9 National Audit Office, *Ministry of Defence*, p. 15.
10 Ibid., p. 25.
11 Ibid., p. 15.
12 Ibid., p. 16.

protesting in the late 1970s their concerns were in large part our concerns within government and the arguments they were putting forward were being taken seriously, even though our response was firmly within the context of multilateral negotiations. I also hope that the public campaign that has been launched by Global Zero[13] to promote the elimination of all nuclear weapons will be supported by everyone of us concerned about nuclear weapons.

FINAL CONCLUSION

It is no longer credible, given all the cost pressures in the pipeline, for the previous estimated acquisition cost of £15–20 billion (in 2006–2007 prices) in the Government's White Paper to be upheld. The UK's nuclear deterrent programme is destined, if it is maintained, to push out from an already overstretched defence budget many other much needed programmes. The nuclear deterrent has *never* been ring-fenced within overall government expenditure; its extra costs have always come out of the overall defence budget. Moreover, British forces are already committed to Afghanistan and the equipment of our troops there needs substantial upgrading which will inevitably lead to cost escalations beyond those budgeted for. These are issues on which the Chiefs of Staff have to exercise their judgement instead of merely shielding themselves by complaining about the size of the defence budget. No defence expenditure levels can be assumed; cutbacks will affect all budgets in 2010–2012.

It is now imperative that we establish an urgent new costing of the entire 2006 nuclear deterrent capability next-generation project and have it assessed by the National Audit Office. While that continues, FCO and MOD officials should be tasked, as was done over the Duff–Mason Report in 1978, to set in hand for any new government elected by June 2010 an objective examination of the two options that were never considered in 2006, namely (1) the use of three SSBNs with both Trident and cruise missiles, discussed briefly on p. 17, and (2) putting nuclear warheads on cruise missiles to be deployed on the new Astute class of SSNs on a guaranteed fleet size of no less than 7–8 and preferably 10, drawing on US experience of the same option, as discussed in this book in some detail. It would also be necessary for officials to examine afresh the need to have one SSBN at sea at any time. This was called into question by the former Chief of Defence Staff, Lord Guthrie, as recently as March 2009.[14]

Since 2001 the UK has experienced more than eight years of disappointing

13 www.globalzero.org.
14 House of Lords Debate on Nuclear Proliferation, 26 March 2009.

military results in association with the US on the battlefields of Afghanistan and Iraq. Initially the invasion went well for both countries, but the aftermath has been handled poorly, not just in the US, but also by British political and military leaders. Take three examples:

1. It was a great mistake in May 2003 not to respond to the request made by our ambassador to Egypt, John Sawers, for British troops to be sent to Baghdad after he had been sent in to report on the situation by Prime Minister Tony Blair.[15]

2. It was folly for the then Defence Minister, John Reid, to announce in 2005 that more troops would be sent to Afghanistan while giving the impression that they might be there for three years without having to fire a shot.

3. It was close to criminal neglect to deploy UK troops at various stages in both countries without sufficient body armour, to have to rely on poorly protected Land Rovers and to have insufficient helicopters. Much of this was due to chronic over-commitment and under-investment by the MOD.

Military intervention, once decided on, demands from us all financial sacrifice to ensure as best we can that our service personnel do not pay the ultimate price. We have tried to have a UK defence policy on the cheap, with disastrous consequences. Nor have we had the political commitment to defence to ensure continuity of leadership, having had four Defence Ministers in the last four years.

Now in the midst of a major fiscal crisis and facing a poor economic outlook, we must discover the will to match commitments to budgets. The failure to choose over the MOD budget has been a failing, above all, by senior politicians, but also by the senior military. That has to stop. We cannot continue the pretence of being able to afford all that the three services are saying is essential.

The US Secretary for Defense, Robert Gates, demanded in May 2009 a shift on defence spending given the new circumstances of fighting insurgents in messy unconventional wars, focusing spending on mine-resistant vehicles, surveillance drones and medical evacuation helicopters at the expense of high-end weapons such as new tanks, bombers and aircraft carriers.

It behoves those of us outside the UK's political battle to urge, at least, that all these options be examined, and that the traditional independence of the diplomatic and civil service is utilized in the run-up to a general election.

---

15 David Owen, *Hubris Syndrome: Bush, Blair and the Intoxication of Power* (London: Politico's, 2007), pp. 93–94.

This means preparing options and detailed strategic concepts and costings for ministers in any new government for big defence projects such as the nuclear deterrent, the carrier programme and aircraft procurement, which have long periods of preparatory work and high expenditures built into their production timetable. After the election some of these big projects will have to be cancelled and the military chiefs cannot stand aside from that choice. High on that list is whether to build another Trident-like SSBN force. This can no longer be afforded; the money is needed to ensure the operational effectiveness of our services in the field, in the air and at sea. We need to consider instead a multi-purpose SSBN feet of three outlined on page 16 or expanding the SSN fleet to make it multi-purpose, capable of deploying nuclear warheads as well as the existing conventional warheads on their cruise missiles.

ANNEX E

1.44 pm

Lord Owen: My Lords, I apologise to the House for having a rather bad throat. I may have to abandon my attempt to speak, but I want to speak because of the way in which the noble Baroness, Lady Williams, has set out the debate and its immense importance.

The decision of the new American Administration under President Obama to "press the reset button" on relations with the Russian Federation is of immense importance. There is a very real possibility now that we will see, even before the non-proliferation treaty starts next year, two important agreements made between the United States and the Russian Federation. The first relates to the agreement, which George W Bush and Vladimir Putin made in Moscow in 2002 to reduce their deployed nuclear warheads by 2012 to 1,700 to 2,200 each.

In my view, when one Administration make a positive move on nuclear disarmament, it is extremely important for the next Administration to consolidate them. In 1977, when President Carter came in with very good intentions, he asked for a dramatic reduction in nuclear missiles and warheads from the then Soviet Union, going beyond the Vladivostok agreement which had been negotiated by Henry Kissinger. Unfortunately, the then Soviet leaders, Gromyko and Brezhnev, mistook this genuine effort, which I believe it was, from President Carter and blocked all future discussion, even when the Americans went back to the Vladivostok agreement. I see tremendous advantages in President Obama doing what President George W Bush was not prepared to do – to put this agreement in treaty form very quickly, and he should be able to easily get ratification. That would be a very significant gesture and an important decision, and it could be done before the NPT starts.

I think that there are quite good prospects now of getting the American Congress to ratify a comprehensive test ban. A treaty has been signed up to, but Congress has not ratified it. If one reads carefully Senator McCain's speeches, particularly during the presidential election campaign, he is ready to look again at this issue, and there are enough Republicans to be able to get ratification of a comprehensive test ban treaty. Of course, if China would do the same it would be doubly significant. That would make it much easier to hold the non-proliferation conference in a genuine spirit. Agreement on non-fissile material is an interesting measure. I do not think we should exaggerate its importance, but that might be possible too.

We all know that haunting a non-proliferation treaty will be the outcome of discussions and negotiations – call it what one will – between the United States and Iran. Here I think we have to recognise a few basic things. There is little doubt – experience of our failure to stop Pakistan getting nuclear weapons shows this – that we always underestimate the extent to which a country has gone in its objective of achieving sufficient nuclear-enriched material to make a bomb. There is little doubt that Iran has passed that threshold. One cannot realistically discuss this without recognising that reality.

There is an air of unreality about the current negotiating position, I will not go into it in depth while negotiations are at a delicate stage; that would not help. However, the idea that countries have to stop enrichment before serious talks start is not realistic. The nature of enrichment is an important question. There cannot be any escape from far more stringent on-ground IAEA inspections, without warning. That is essential; but putting all your weight behind stopping enrichment prior to getting into detailed dialogue is a mistake.

The other questions relate to the business of ultimately giving up nuclear weapons. The idea is not new. The non-proliferation treaty countries would say, with justification, that it is already in the Nuclear Non-Proliferation Treaty. The difference is that people in nuclear weapon states who have a long record of believing that they had to have nuclear weapons are now ready to talk about "disinventing" the nuclear weapon – giving it up. They are realistic people – certainly those in the United States – and they have given credence to this initiative.

I come to the Government's position. We all know that nothing will be done about nuclear weapons this side of a general election. However, this country has been spending far beyond its means. If you look at the decision in the White Paper of 2006 on Trident replacement, and the subsequent papers that have come out of Select Committees and the National Audit Office, it is abundantly clear, taking into account a 25 per cent trade-weighting reduction in the value of sterling, that the bill will be far higher than first thought. Also, we see day by day our defence budget so obviously squeezed that it is causing actual deaths among our servicemen. No Government who come in after the next election will be able to avoid looking again at the question of Trident replacement; that is not credible.

I pray in aid, first, that the decision announced to Parliament in 2007 in another place is more tentative than many people have understood. It says that there must be a review by 2014, and explains the decision-making framework of 2009 – the first phase of submarine replacement – then 2011 and 2013. I was struck by a recent book by Michael Quinlan, the high priest of nuclear theory and a remarkably able man. Even he was not dismissive of the need to reconsider the 2007 choice by Parliament. He wrote that it should take place,

"not later than about 2013".

He went on to write:

"The central decision of principle might at that stage be significantly influenced by whether the cost estimates remained of the same order as those assessed in 2006–07".

He argued that this revisiting should be approached "seriously".

We should try to get from the Government a decision that was made by James Callaghan in 1978. He set up a study by the Civil Service, not influenced by Ministers, to decide what would replace the existing Polaris deterrent, and have it ready for any Government who took office after the general election of 1979. That study was the Duff Mason report. Sir Anthony Duff was a distinguished diplomat and former submariner. Ronald Mason was a chief scientist at the Ministry of Defence. The document was on the desk when Margaret Thatcher came to office, with an explanation written that day by James Callaghan of the discussions about a successor system that he had had in Guadeloupe with President Carter.

These issues are too serious to be left hanging from 2007 until a new Government comes in, with all the tremendous pressures that they will be put under. We should undertake that study now. One option that should be considered was excluded, for ridiculous reasons, from the 2007 decision. That is for the UK to put nuclear weapons on cruise missiles in our SSN fleet. This is what has happened in the United States, which only deploys its nuclear missiles periodically in its SSN fleet. Of course, it has a very different, hyper-sophisticated ballistic missile deterrent. If you can afford it, that is the best system; but I believe increasingly that this country cannot afford it.

If we are serious about ultimately moving to abolition of nuclear weapons, some countries will have to move faster than others. It seems logical that those of us who have chosen a minimum deterrent must be ready at some appropriate moment to take the first step. I agree that this will not be in the immediate future of the next 10 years. However, I find it very hard to consider spending billions of pounds on a deterrent that will last into the

2050s when it is possible to retain our nuclear option over the next 15 to 20 years at a much cheaper rate, and hold open the option of giving up nuclear weapons.

People tell me that it would mean no longer having a veto power in the Security Council. This is a complete misreading of history, and how the veto power came out of the 1946 negotiations over the United Nations. There was never any doubt that a veto power would have to be there, because the United States Congress would never have agreed to anything else. It must also be recognised that the veto power cannot be taken away from Britain. We can veto any measure to take it away, and France and Britain have made it clear that they would do this. I argued this case while still Foreign Secretary in a minute to the Cabinet in December 1978 [Document 10, pp. 156–57].

I do not believe that France will be first to make a move on nuclear weapons. We might persuade France to move with us. However, some time down the track – it might be in 2020, or a little before or after that – I can see all logic backing a UK decision to give up its nuclear weapons, and to claim it as a virtue to justify our continued presence as a permanent member of the Security Council with veto power. I also wish to extend the number of permanent members, though without veto power, and I hope that this will be done in the next year.

I will not go on any longer. These are troubling times. What worries me about the commitment ultimately to give up nuclear weapons is that it has been made by a lot of people who do not really believe what they are saying. The commitment risks going the same way as the pledge in the non-proliferation treaty, and that would be a tragedy. We have to give substance to that commitment. There is no country better placed than the UK to give that substance, and no Government will face the realities of the defence budget more than the Government that takes office in this country in 2010.

1.58pm